Transforming Practice:
Critical issues in equity, diversity and education

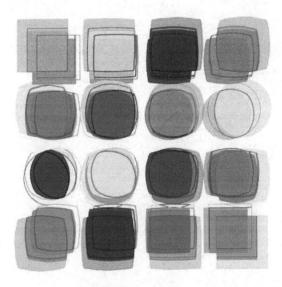

This Reader forms part of *Critical Issues in Equity, Diversity and Education* (E805), a major new 60-credit module in the Masters in Education programme.

The Open University Masters in Education

The Open University Masters in Education is now firmly established as the most popular postgraduate degree for education professionals in Europe, with over 2500 students registered each year. It is designed particularly for those with experience of teaching, the advisory service, educational administration or allied fields. Specialist lines in leadership and management, applied linguistics, equality and diversity are available within the programme. Successful study on the MA entitles students to apply for entry into the Open University Doctorate in Education programme.

Details of this and other Open University modules can be obtained from the Student Registration and Enquiry Service, The Open University, PO Box 197, Milton Keynes MK7 6BJ, United Kingdom: Telephone +44 (0) 845 300 60 90, e-mail general-enquiries@open.ac.uk.

Alternatively, you may wish to visit the Open University website at www.open.ac.uk, where you can learn more about the wide range of modules and qualifications offered at all levels by The Open University.

Transforming Practice: Critical issues in equity, diversity and education

Edited by Janet Soler, Christopher S. Walsh, Anna Craft, Jonathan Rix and Katy Simmons

Trentham Books

Stoke on Trent, UK and Sterling, USA

in association with

Published by Trentham Books Limited
Westview House, 734 London Road, Oakhill, Stoke on Trent,
Staffordshire ST4 5NP United Kingdom
In association with
The Open University
Walton Hall, Milton Keynes MK7 6AA
United Kingdom

First Published in 2012

Edited and designed by Trentham Books Ltd

Printed and bound by 4edge Limited, Hockley

British Library Cataloguing in Publication data
A catalogue record for this book is available from the British Library

ISBN (paperback) 978-1-85856-516-3

Contents

Acknowledgements

We should like to thank the authors who contributed their chapters, as well as colleagues within and outside The Open University who helped with the preparation of the manuscript. Special thanks are due to the following people for their assistance in the production of this book:

Gill Gowans copublishing executive

Jane Hartley course secretary

Fulden Underwood curriculum manager

Grateful acknowledgement is made to the following sources:

Chapter 1	McLaren, Peter *Life in Schools: An introduction to critical pedagogy in the foundations of education*, 5th Edition, (c) 2007. Reprinted by permission of Pearson Education, Inc., Upper Saddle River, NJ;
Chapter 2	*Education, Globalization, and Social Change* by Lauder *et al* (2006) , chp. 53 pp. 766-770, 778. By permission of Oxford University Press;
Chapter 3	Lankshear, C. and Knobel, M. (2004) 'An introduction to teacher research', *A Handbook for Teacher Research: From design to implementation*, Open University Press. Copyright (c) Colin Lankshear and Michele Knobel 2004. Reproduced with the kind permission of Open University Press. All rights reserved.
Chapter 4	Kincheloe, L. J. (2003) 'Introduction: Positivistic standards and the bizarre educational world of the twenty-first Century', *Teachers as Researchers: Qualitative inquiry as a path to empowerment* (2nd ed), RoutledgeFalmer. Copyright (c) 2003 Joe L. Kincheloe. Reproduced by permission of Taylor & Francis Books UK;
Chapter 6	Gainer, S. J., Valdez-Gainer, N., and Kinard, T. (2009) 'The elementary bubble project: Exploring critical media literacy in a fourth-grade classroom', *The Reading Teacher*, vol. 62, no. 8, International Reading Association;
Chapter 7	Jackson, J. (2010) 'How do you spell homosexual?: Naturally queer moments in K-12 classrooms', *International Journal of Critical Pedagogy*, vol. 3, no. 1, pp. 36-51. Reproduced by permission;
Chapter 8	Kincheloe, L.J. and Steinberg, R.S. (2010), 'Why teach against Islamophobia? Striking the empire back', in Kincheloe, L.J., Steinberg, R.S. and Stonebanks, D.C. (eds), *Teaching Against Islamophobia*, Peter Lang. Copyright (c) Peter Lang Publishing, Inc., New York;
Chapter 9	Nilholm, C. and Alm, B. (2010) 'An inclusive classroom? A case study of inclusiveness, teacher strategies, and children's experiences', *European Journal of Special Needs Education*, vol. 25, no. 3, August 2010, pp. 239-252. Copyright (c) 2010 Taylor and Francis;

Chapter 10	Komulainen, S. (2007) 'The ambiguity of the child's 'voice' in social research', *Childhood*, vol. 14, no. 11, SAGE Publications;
Chapter 12	Goodley, D. and Runswick-Cole, K. (2010) 'Len Barton, inclusion and critical disability studies: Theorising disabled childhoods', *International Studies in Sociology* of *Education*, vol. 20, no. 4, pp. 273-290, Taylor & Francis Group;
Chapter 13	Gutierrez, D.K. and Correa-Chavez, M. (2006) 'What to do about culture?', *Lifelong Learning in Europe*, vol. 11, no. 3, pp. 152-159, LLinE;
Chapter 14	Teachers College record by Columbia University, copyright 2012. Reproduced with permission of Teachers College Record in the format textbook and other book via Copyright Clearance Center.
Chapter 15	Ozga, J. (2000) 'Theory, values and policy research in education', *Policy Research in Educational Settings: Contested terrain*, Open University Press. Copyright (c) Jenny Ozga, 2000. Reproduced with the kind permission of Open University Press. All rights reserved.
Chapter 17	Davies, B. (2003) 'Death to critique and dissent? The policies and practices of new managerialism and of 'evidence-based practice'', *Gender and Education*, vol. 15, no. 1, pp. 91-103, reprinted by permission of the publisher, Taylor & Francis Ltd, http://www.tandfonline.com;
Chapter 18	Marilyn Fleer (2003) 'Early childhood education as an evolving 'community of practice' or as Lived 'Social Reproduction': researching the 'taken-for-granted'', *Contemporary Issues in Early Childhood*, 4(1), 64-79. http://dx.doi.org/10.2304/ciec.2003.4.1.7
Chapter 19	Berhanu, G. (2010), 'Even in Sweden? Excluding the included: Some reflections on the consequences of new policies on educational processes and outcomes, and equity in education', *International Journal of Special Education*, vol. 25, no. 3;
Chapter 20	hooks, b. (2000) 'Feminist class struggle', *Feminism is for Everybody: Passionate politics*, South End Press. Copyright (c) 2000 by Gloria Watkins;
Chapter 21	Milbourne, L. (2009) 'Valuing difference or securing compliance? Working to involve young people in community settings', *Children and Society* 2009, vol. 23, no. 5. Copyright (c) 2009 National Children's Bureau;

About the Editors

Janet Soler is a Senior Lecturer and co-convener of the Pedagogy, Learning and Curriculum Group in the Faculty of Education and Language Studies at The Open University, UK.

Christopher S. Walsh is a Senior Lecturer in educational ICT and professional development at The Open University UK.

Anna Craft is Professor of Education in the Department of Education, at The Open University UK, she is also Professor of Education at the University of Exeter.

Jonathan Rix is Senior Lecturer in inclusion, curriculum and learning at The Open University, UK.

Katy Simmons is a Lecturer in inclusive and special education in the Centre for Curriculum and Teaching Studies at The Open University, UK.

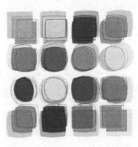

Introduction

This book examines critical educational issues related to equity, diversity and social justice. It explores the ways in which these issues are historically, culturally, economically and socially rooted in educational practice across diverse educational settings. The chapters draw primarily on critical theory to question, understand and investigate current educational practices and pedagogies. The book highlights research, practice and pedagogies that challenge and transform educational experiences to support equity, social justice and inclusivity.

Many books dealing with pedagogy, practice and professional development in education focus on individuals. This often leads to an emphasis on personality, behaviour, learning style and ability, behaviour management, individual achievement and judgements regarding teacher effectiveness. Taking a critical theory perspective stands in stark contrast to this individually-focused viewpoint. Educators engaging with critical theory and critical pedagogy choose, rather, to interrogate and investigate their practice and its relationship to the social world in order to explore inequalities, injustices and uncaring aspects of education.

The emphasis upon the dialectical within critical theory provides a lens for us to review and critique the traditionally accepted techniques, strategies and 'commonsense' notions embedded in professional and other education related discourses. The problems of equity and diversity are no longer seen as the isolated events of individuals or deficiencies in the social structure. Concepts such as behaviour management and inclusion highlight problems associated with an individual. From a critical theory perspective these problems can be critiqued and reflected upon through a foregrounding of the interactive socially constructed contexts children and young people experience as 'education'.

The chapters in this book challenge us as educators and practitioners to reflect critically on, question and research our own positions, discourses and practices. They do this by encouraging us to acknowledge the highly social and participatory nature of society, rather than accepting the commonly accepted discourses. These taken for granted discourses often portray education as neutral and focused on individual and institutional achievement or national economic advancement. It is our hope that the chapters in this book push readers to reflect upon their own practice, critique research and challenge educational practices that continue to exclude and marginalise children and young people. A critical theory perspective opens up possibilities for deconstructing the commonly used pedagogies and practices that continue to fail to make things better for many diverse children and young people, in order to address equity, diversity and social justice. Critical theory helps us view these injustices as socially constructed; arising from social interactions and therefore ripe for transformation within and beyond educational settings.

The first section of this Reader contains five chapters that explore and unpack key theoretical concepts and perspectives underpinning critical theory and related research methodologies. These chapters also reflect upon and critique the potential of critical theory to investigate equity and diversity in relation to pedagogy and transforming educational practice. Chapter 1 is an edited excerpt from Peter McLaren's important book *Life in schools: an introduction to critical pedagogy in the foundations of education* (McLaren, 2007). In this chapter he defines, explores and investigates critical theory and critical pedagogy and the associated notions of socially constructed knowledge, class, culture, hegemony, ideology and prejudice.

Madeleine Arnot and Diane Reay in Chapter 2 further develop and explore pedagogy and learning in relation to social relationships and the structuring of knowledge highlighted by McLaren. They draw upon Basil Bernstein's still relevant theory of pedagogic transmission in schooling. They remind us of the enduring consequences Bernstein associated with current trends towards a strong 'external framing' of performance pedagogy arising from neo-liberal educational reforms in England. Using Bernstein's concept of external framing, they explore how the introduction of performance pedagogies, the National Curriculum and standardized assessments have increased the depth of social stratification and inequity in two English secondary schools.

Chapters 3 and 4 explore the conceptualisation and undertaking of teacher research. Their authors are educationally based critical theorists who have been visibly active in promoting critical pedagogy and teacher research. Chapter 3 by Colin Lankshear and Michele Knobel, and Chapter 4 by Joe L. Kincheloe provide a concise understanding of teacher research that emphasises critical theory and critical pedagogy. Their discussions of the way teacher research is conceptualised and enacted assists readers in understanding the impact of wider educational initiatives on equity and diversity at the classroom level. Both chapters challenge and critique concepts and pedagogical framings arising from the neo-liberal initiatives in education explored in the first section of the book. In the final chapter in this section Janet Soler explores the use of personal narrative inquiry to investigate personal and individual experiences within a critical theory paradigm. Soler argues for the use of narrative as a method of analysis to reflexively explore complexity and diversity through inserting the self and our own voices into the insider research we might undertake as teachers, practitioners and work based researchers.

The second section of this Reader provides contemporary and innovative examples of transformative practice from a critical theoretical perspective. Jesse Gainer and colleagues offer examples in Chapter 6 of how practitioners might use critical and dialogical approaches outlined in the readings in the first section of this reader to raise children's awareness of ideology, power and the relationship between text and readers in an elementary classroom. Janna Jackson in Chapter 7 argues for the need to unmask students' notions of identities related to sexual behaviour as 'natural' or 'unnatural'. Jackson explores the subtle ways queerness can become a seamless part of the curriculum. She describes what she terms 'naturally queer moments' in the classroom and highlights the transformative power these moments can have.

Chapters 8, 9, 10 and 11 emphasise the complexity and diversity surrounding the development of inclusive pedagogies. Each provides specific examples of how critical pedagogy can be developed to foster inclusion in response to the diversity and complexity we face when working with individuals and groups today. In Chapter 8, Joe L. Kincheloe and Shirley R. Steinberg counter the miseducation that continues to shape American views of the world and argue for anti-Islamophobic education. They argue powerfully that there is a need to teach against Islamaphobia by striking the Empire (America) back.

Claes Nilholm and Barbro Alm's classroom study in Chapter 9 suggests that while classrooms can appear to be inclusive, pupils' lived experiences are often more complex and can lead to their exclusion. Nilholm and Alm argue that teachers should therefore aim to create a learning community where differences are valued. Sirkka Komulainen presents case studies in Chapter 10 that explore the notion of child's 'voice' in two 'special educational needs' settings. She recommends reflexivity as a strategy for ensuring ethical research conduct, stressing the importance of recognising the adult mediation and construction of children's 'voices' that operate on local and also wider discursive levels. Chapter 11 by Christopher S. Walsh presents four counternarratives that work to decentre discourses that render individuals 'docile citizens' (Foucault, 1978/1995). The counternarratives presented expose and contest common assumptions around disability, the family and gay, lesbian, bisexual and transgender (LGBT) youth. He views counternarratives as critical stories that work particularly well with the increasing ubiquity of networking and the scope individuals have to design and write resistant texts that can be read and viewed online.

Critical theory often pushes people to take a political stance in relation to ideologies, positioning and values they find at odds to their own beliefs and ideas. Research informed by critical theory, by its very nature, promotes reflexivity and warrants actions that challenge the status quo. Part Three explores these ideas in relation to specific issues, contexts and research activities. Dan Goodley and Katherine Runswick-Cole in Chapter 12 explore the ways in which disabled childhoods overlap with other forms of exclusion. They argue that a political analysis of the struggles of disability politics is imperative to promote resistance and transformation for disabled children. In Chapter 13 Kris Gutierrez and Maricela Correa-Chavez challenge the labeling and categorization of pupils in the use of 'learning styles'. They argue that the assumption of cultural regularity negates and unfairly perpetuates a vision of culture as static and that this leads to highly challengeable essentialist views that the traits of individuals reside in their ethnic or racial group membership.

In Chapter 14 Gloria Ladson-Billings and William Tate argue that immense inequalities persist between the school experiences of middle-class white students and poor African-American and Latino students in the United States. Their groundbreaking work outlines the development of a critical race theory to analyse how these inequalities arise within a racialised society which continues to marginalize and silence discussions of race and racism. In Chapter 15 Jenny Ozga takes a close look at the politics that underpin and define educational policy across a number of western nations. She warns researchers against uncritically accepting the argument that state control of education is diminishing. She points out how the cumulative effect of recent educational policies instead strengthens the regulation of the market and managerialism in a way which adversely influences educational institutions, community settings and the people in them.

In Chapter 16, which concludes this section, Anna Craft provides insights at institutional, community and individual level into how the strengthening of state control, regulation and managerialism, explored by Ozga in the previous chapter, might be resisted. Craft presents three 'creative learning conversations' developed with Chappell and others through three distinctive initiatives. Drawing on their analysis, which is informed by ideas from Lefebvre (on space) and Bakhtin (on dialogue), Craft reflects upon the potential of such creative learning conversations as methodological devices for participatory, creative and emancipatory change.

The final section of the book revisits themes raised in the previous sections to explore issues and possible responses readers might consider for their own practice in the 21st Century. Brownyn Davies, in Chapter 17, focuses upon the issues of managerialism raised by Ozga and other authors in this volume to argue for a need to develop a collective story to challenge the hegemony of new managerialism. Her pivotal work enables practitioners to engage in transformative practices and initiatives towards a different future.

Marilyn Fleer in Chapter 18, Girma Berhanu in Chapter 19 and bell hooks in Chapter 20 discuss issues of best practice in relation to educational reform towards more inclusive and equitable educational experiences for children and young people. These authors examine and problematize how educators might become active agents of change within their educational settings in an increasingly unstable political and social climate. In Chapter 21 Linda Milbourne explores how recent transitions and policies have impacted negatively upon community organisations working with young people. She argues that the research to date suggests significant gaps between the rhetoric of policy makers and the perceptions of what is being implemented at local level.

In the concluding chapter of the Reader, Jonathan Rix takes an historical overview to critically examine how concepts of advancement – which seem fundamentally linked to the betterment of the human condition – are themselves a consequence and cause of inequitable policies and practices. Drawing upon ideas from Gee, Hull, Lankshear, Illich, and Slee, he argues that the current construction of the educational marketplace and its relationship to the professions and workplace undermines our supposed goal of equality through learning and schooling.

Janet Soler
Christopher S. Walsh
Anna Craft
Jonathan Rix
Katy Simmons

Part 1

Investigating educational issues in practice

Chapter 1

Critical pedagogy

Peter McLaren

The importance of theory

[...] Critical theorists begin with the premise that *men and women are essentially unfree and inhabit a world rife with contradictions and asymmetries of power and privilege.* The critical educator endorses theories that are, first and foremost, dialectical; that is, theories which recognise the problems of society as more than simply isolated events or deficiencies in the social structure. Rather, these problems are part of the interactive context between individual and society. The individual, a social actor, both creates and is created by the social universe of which he or she is a part. Neither the individual nor society is given priority in analysis: the two are inextricably interwoven, so that reference to one must by implication mean reference to the other. Dialectical theory attempts to tease out the histories and relations of accepted meanings and appearances, tracing interactions from the context to the part, from the system inward to the event. In this way, critical theory helps us focus simultaneously on both sides of a social contradiction.[1]

Wilfred Carr and Stephen Kemmis describe dialectical thinking as follows:

Dialectical thinking involves searching out ... contradictions (like the contradiction of the inadvertent oppression of less able students by a system which aspires to help all students to attain their 'full potential'), but it is not really as wooden or mechanical as the formula of thesis-antithesis-synthesis. On the contrary, it is an open and questioning form of thinking which demands reflection back and forth between elements like *part* and *whole, knowledge* and *action, process* and *product, subject* and *object, being* and *becoming, rhetoric* and *reality*, or *structure* and *function*. In the process, *contradictions* may be discovered (as, for example, in a political *structure* which aspires to give decision-making power to all, but actually *functions* to deprive some access to the information with which they could influence crucial decisions about their lives). As contradictions are revealed, new constructive thinking and new constructive action are required to transcend the contradictory state of affairs. The complementarity of the elements is dynamic: it is a kind of a tension, not a static confrontation between the two poles. In the dialectical approach, the elements are regarded as mutually constitutive, not separate and distinct. Contradiction can thus be distinguished from paradox: to speak of a contradiction is to imply that a new resolution can be achieved, while to speak of a paradox is to suggest that two incompatible ideas remain inertly opposed to one another.[2] [Italics original]

The dialectical nature of critical theory enables the educational researcher to see the school not simply as an arena of indoctrination or socialisation or a site of instruction, but also as a cultural terrain that promotes student empowerment and self-transformation. My own research into parochial education, for instance, showed that the school functions simultaneously as a means of potentially empowering students around issues of social justice and as a means of sustaining, legitimising, and reproducing dominant class interests directed at creating obedient, docile, and low-paid future workers.[3]

A dialectical understanding of schooling permits us to see schools as sites of both domination and liberation; this runs counter to the view of schooling that claims that schools unproblematically reproduce class relations and passively indoctrinate students into becoming greedy young capitalists. They do reproduce class relationships but also can serve as a site where these class relationships can be contested. This dialectical understanding of schooling also brushes against the grain of mainstream educational theory, which conceives of schools as mainly providing students with the skills and attitudes necessary for becoming patriotic, industrious, and responsible citizens. It argues that schools do create patriotic, responsible citizens and that this is precisely the problem. As recent events have revealed, educated US citizens have difficulty distinguishing between leaders who are bent on imperialist wars to secure 'resources' for accumulating capital and those who are truly committed to peace and social justice.

Critical educators argue that any worthwhile theory of schooling must be partisan. That is, it must be fundamentally tied to a struggle for a qualitatively better life for all through the construction of a society based on non-exploitative relations and social justice. The critical educator doesn't believe that there are two sides to every question, with both sides needing equal attention. For the critical educator, there are many sides to a problem, and often these sides are linked to certain class, race, and gender interests.

Let's turn for a moment to an example of critical theorising as it is brought to bear on a fundamental teaching practice: writing classroom objectives. In this example, I will draw on Henry Giroux's important distinction between micro and macro objectives.[4]

The common use of behavioural objectives by teachers reflects a search for certainty and technical control of knowledge and behaviour. Teachers often emphasise classroom management procedures, efficiency, and 'how-to-do' techniques that ultimately ignore an important question: Why is this knowledge being taught in the first place? Giroux recasts classroom objectives into the categories of macro and micro.

Macro objectives are designed to enable students to make connections between the methods, content, and structure of a course and its significance within the larger social reality. This dialectical approach to classroom objectives allows students to acquire a broad frame of reference or worldview; in other words, it helps them acquire a political perspective. Students can then make the hidden curriculum explicit and develop a critical political consciousness.

Micro objectives represent the course content and are characterised by their narrowness of purpose and their content-bound path of inquiry. Giroux tells us that the importance of the relationship between macro and micro objectives arises out of having students uncover the connections between course objectives and the norms, values, and structural relationships of the wider society. For instance, the micro objectives of teaching about the Vietnam war might be to learn the dates of specific battles, the details of specific Congressional debates surrounding the war, and the reasons given by the 'White House for fighting the war. The micro objectives are concerned with the organisation, classification, mastery, and manipulation of data. This is what Giroux calls productive knowledge.

Macro objectives, on the other hand, centre on the relationship between means and ends, between specific events and their wider social and political implications. A lesson on the Vietnam war, the invasion of Grenada, Desert Storm, the recent invasion of Iraq, or the war in Afghanistan, for instance, might raise the following macro questions: What is the relationship between these invasions as rescue missions in the interests of US citizens and the larger logic of imperialism? During the Vietnam era, what was the relationship between the American economy and the arms industry? Whose interests did the war serve best? Who benefited most from the war? What were the class relationships between those who fought and those who stayed home in the universities? Other than replacing the corrupt Taliban regime and destroying terrorist compounds and networks in the war in Afghanistan, did the United States hope to secure vital resources such as oil?

Developing macro objectives fosters a dialectical mode of inquiry; the process constitutes a sociopolitical application of knowledge, what Giroux calls directive knowledge. Critical theorists seek a kind of knowledge that will help students recognise the social function of particular forms of knowledge. The purpose of dialectical educational theory, then, is to provide students with a model that permits them to examine the underlying political, social, and economic foundations of the larger white supremacist capitalist society.

Critical pedagogy and the social construction of knowledge

Critical educational theorists view school knowledge as historically and socially rooted and interest bound. Knowledge acquired in school – or anywhere, for that matter – is never neutral or objective but is ordered and structured in particular ways; its emphases and exclusions partake of a silent logic. Knowledge is a social construction deeply rooted in a nexus of power relations. When critical theorists claim that knowledge is socially constructed, they mean that it is the product of agreement or consent between individuals who live out particular social relations (eg. of class, race, and gender) and who live in particular junctures in time. To claim that knowledge is socially constructed usually means that the world we live in is constructed symbolically by the mind through social interaction with others and is heavily dependent on culture, context, custom, and historical specificity. There is no ideal, autonomous, pristine, or aboriginal world to which our social constructions necessarily correspond; there is always a referential field in which symbols are situated. And this particular referential field (eg. language, culture, place, time) will influence how symbols generate meaning. There is no pure subjective insight. We do not stand before the social world; we live in the midst of it. As we seek the meaning of events we seek the meaning of the social. We can now raise certain questions with respect to the social construction of knowledge, such as: Why do women and minorities often view social issues differently than white males? Why are teachers more likely to value the opinions of a middle-class white male student, for instance, than those of a middle-class black female?

Critical pedagogy asks how and why knowledge gets constructed the way it does, and how and why some constructions of reality are legitimated and celebrated by the dominant culture while others clearly are not. Critical pedagogy asks how our everyday common-sense understandings – our social constructions or 'subjectivities' – get produced and lived out. In other words, what are the social functions of knowledge? The crucial factor here is that some forms of knowledge have more power and legitimacy than others. For instance, in many schools in the United States, Science and Maths curricula are favoured over the liberal arts. This can be explained by the link between the needs of big business to compete in world markets and the imperatives of the new reform movement to bring 'excellence' back to the schools. Certain types of knowledge legitimate certain gender, class, and racial interests. Whose interests does this knowledge serve? Who gets excluded as a result? Who is marginalised?

Let's put this in the form of further questions: What is the relationship between social class and knowledge taught in school? Why do we value scientific knowledge over informal knowledge? Why do we have teachers using 'standard English'? Why is the public still unlikely to vote for a woman or an African American or a Latino/a for president? How does school knowledge reinforce stereotypes about women, minorities, and disadvantaged peoples? What accounts for some knowledge having high status (as in the great works of philosophers or scientists) while the practical knowledge of ordinary people or marginalised or subjugated groups is often discredited and devalued? Why do we learn about the 'great men' in history and spend less time learning about the contributions of women and minorities and the struggles of people in the exploited economic classes? Why don't we learn more about the American labour movement? How and why are certain types of knowledge used to reinforce dominant ideologies, which in turn serve to mask unjust power relations among certain groups in society?

Forms of knowledge

Critical pedagogy follows a distinction regarding forms of knowledge posited by the German social theorist Jürgen Habermas.[5] Lets examine this concept in the context of classroom teaching. Mainstream educators who work primarily within liberal and conservative educational ideologies emphasise technical knowledge (similar to Giroux's productive knowledge): Knowledge is that which can be measured and quantified. Technical knowledge is based on the natural sciences, uses hypothetico-deductive or empirical analytical methods, and is evaluated by, among other things, intelligence quotients, reading scores, and SAT results, all of which are used by educators to sort, regulate, and control students.

A second type, practical knowledge, aims to enlighten individuals so they can shape their daily actions in the world. Practical knowledge is generally acquired through describing and analysing social situations historically or developmentally, and is geared toward helping individuals understand social events that are ongoing and situational. The liberal educational researcher who undertakes fieldwork in a school in order to evaluate student behaviour and interaction acquires practical knowledge. This type of knowledge is not usually generated numerically or by submitting data to some kind of statistical instrument.

The critical educator, however, will be interested in what Habermas calls emancipatory knowledge (similar to Giroux's directive knowledge), which attempts to reconcile and transcend the opposition between technical and practical knowledge. Emancipatory knowledge helps us understand how social relationships are distorted and manipulated by relations of power and privilege. It also aims at creating the conditions under which irrationality, domination, and oppression can be overcome and transformed through deliberative, collective action. It has the potential to contribute to social justice, equality, and empowerment. Only in the name of the general rights of society can any knowledge claim to be emancipatory. Only if such knowledge abolishes bourgeois civil society can it lay claim to serve the working class. Knowledge that does not go beyond contemplating the world and observing it objectively without transcending given social conditions merely affirms what already exists. Revolutionary critical knowledge combines theory and practice and contributes to the transformation of existing social relations in the interest of emancipation from the rule of capital.

Class

Class refers to the economic, social, and political relationships that govern life in a given social order. Class relationships reflect the constraints and limitations individuals and groups experience in the areas of income level, occupation, place of residence, and other indicators of status and social rank. Relations of class are those associated with surplus labour, who produces it, and who is a recipient of it. Surplus labour is that labour undertaken by workers beyond that which is necessary. Class relations also deal with the social distribution of power and its structural allocation. [...]

Under capitalist relations of production, capitalists purchase the labour power of the worker in exchange for a wage in order to create value that accrues to capital on behalf of the capitalist. In other words, the capitalist purchases from the worker a commodity that has 'use value': the labour power of the worker. Labour power (the capacity to labour) is always of greater value than its own exchange value because it produces profits from capitalists. The wage appears on the surface to be equivalent to the use value (labour power) it purchases from the workers. Surplus labour is unpaid labour and serves as the basis of capitalist profit. The greater the unpaid labour of the workers, the more profit for the capitalists. The law of value states that the value of a commodity can be found in the labour time socially necessary for its production. According to Marx, class struggle leads to the dictatorship of the proletariat. The revolution to come will occur under the banner of class struggle.

To approach the concept of class from a dialectical Marxist conception stipulates a grasp of Marx's philosophy of internal relations. As adumbrated in the work of Paula Allman, Glenn Rikowski, and other Marxist educationalists, the philosophy of internal relations underscores the importance of relational thinking. Relational thinking is distinct from categorical thinking. Whereas the former examines entities in interaction with each other, the latter looks at phenomena in isolation from each other. Relational thinking can refer both to external relations or internal relations. Marx was interested in internal relations. External relations are those that produce a synthesis of various phenomena or entities that can exist outside or independent of this relation. Internal relations are those in which opposite entities are historically mediated such that they do not obtain independent results. In fact, once the internal relationship ceases to exist, the results of their interaction also cease to exist.

A dialectical concept of class examines the internal relations between labour and capital in terms of their dialectical contradictions. A dialectical contradiction is an internal relation consisting of opposites in interaction that would not be able to exist in the absence of their internal relationship to each other. When this internal relationship is abolished, so are the entities. All dialectical contradictions are internal relations. However, not all internal relations are dialectical contradictions. Dialectical contradictions, or the 'unity of opposites', are those phenomena that could not exist, continue to exist, or have come into existence in the absence of their internal relation to one another. The very nature (external and internal) of each of the opposites is shaped within its relation to the other opposite. The antagonistic relation between labour and capital, or the relation between production and circulation and exchange, constitutes the essence of capitalism. Workers' labour is utilised within the capital-labour relation. Workers then constitute the dialectical opposite of capital and enter into a value creation process. The basis of the rift or split within capitalist labour is the relation internal to labour: labour as a value producer and labour as a labour-power developer. One of the oppositions always benefits from the antagonistic internal relationship between capital and labour. Capital (the positive relation) structurally benefits from its relation to labour (the negative relation). To free itself from its subordinate position, labour must abolish this internal relation through the negation of the negation.

To understand class society in this way offers a more profound analytical lens than operationalising notions of class that reduce it to skill, occupational status, social inequality, the esurient actions of capitalists, or stratification. This is because what is at stake in understanding class as a dynamic and dialectical social relation is undressing the forces that generate social inequality. This can only be accomplished by analysing the value form of labour within the entire social universe of capital, including the way that capital has commodified our very subjectivities. This mandates that we grasp the complex dialectics of the generation of the capital-labour relation that produces all value. [...]

Culture

The concept of culture, varied though it may be, is essential to any understanding of critical pedagogy. I use the term culture here to signify the particular ways in which a social group lives out and makes sense of its 'given' circumstances and conditions of life. In addition to defining culture as a set of practices, ideologies, and values from which different groups draw to make sense of the world, we need to recognise how cultural questions help us understand who has power and how it is reproduced and manifested in the social relations that link schooling to the wider social order. The ability of individuals to express their culture is related to the power which certain groups are able to wield in the social order. The expression of values and beliefs by individuals who share certain historical experiences is determined by their collective power in society.[6]

The link between culture and power has been extensively analysed in critical social theory over the past fifteen years. It is therefore possible to offer three insights from that literature which particularly illuminate the political logic that underlies various cultural power relations. First, culture is intimately connected with the structure of social relations within class, gender, and age formations that produce forms of oppression and dependency. Second, culture is analysed not simply as a way of life, but as a form of production through which different groups in either their dominant or subordinate social relations define and realise their aspirations through unequal relations of power. Third, culture is viewed as a field of struggle in which the production, legitimation, and circulation of particular forms of knowledge and experience are central areas of conflict linked to class struggle. What is important here is that each of these insights raises fundamental questions about the ways in which inequalities are maintained and challenged in the spheres of school culture and the wider capitalist society.[7]

Dominant culture, subordinate culture, and subculture

Three central categories related to the concept of culture – dominant culture, subordinate culture, subculture – have been much discussed in recent critical scholarship. Culture can be readily broken down into 'dominant' and 'subordinate' parent cultures. Dominant culture refers to social practices and representations that affirm the central values, interests, and concerns of the social class in control of the material and symbolic wealth of society. Groups who live out social relations in subordination to the dominant culture of the ruling class are part of the subordinate culture. Group subcultures may be described as subsets of the two parent cultures (dominant and subordinate). Individuals who form subcultures often use distinct symbols and social practices to help foster an identity outside that of the dominant culture. As an example, we need only refer to punk subculture, with its distinct musical tastes, fetishistic costumery, spiked hair, and its attempt to disconfirm the dominant rules of propriety fostered by the mainstream media, schools, religions, and culture industry. For the most part, working-class subcultures exist in a subordinate structural position in society, and many of their members engage in oppositional acts against dominant ruling-class interests and social practices. It is important to remember, however, that people don't inhabit cultures or social classes but live out class or cultural relations, some of which may be dominant and some of which may be subordinate.[8] [...]

Cultural forms

Cultural forms are those symbols and social practices that express culture, such as those found in music, dress, food, religion, dance, and education, which have developed from the efforts of groups to shape their lives out of their surrounding material and political environment. Television, video, and films are regarded as cultural forms. Schooling is also a cultural form. Baseball is a cultural form. Cultural forms don't exist apart from sets of structural underpinnings which are related to the means of economic production, the mobilisation of desire, the construction of social values, asymmetries of power/knowledge, configurations of ideologies, and relations of class, race, and gender.

Hegemony

The dominant culture is able to exercise domination over subordinate classes or groups through a process known as hegemony.[9] Hegemony refers to the maintenance of domination not by the sheer exercise of force but primarily through consensual social practices, social forms, and social structures produced in specific sites such as the church, the state, the school, the mass media, the political system, and the family. By social practices, I refer to what people say and do. Of course, social practices may be accomplished through words, gestures, personally appropriated signs and rituals, or a combination of these. Social forms refer to the principles that provide and give legitimacy to specific social practices. For example, the state legislature is one social form that gives legitimacy to the social practice of teaching. The term social structures can be defined as those constraints that limit individual life and appear to be beyond the individual's control, having their sources in the power relations that govern society. We can, therefore, talk about the 'class structure' or the 'economic structure' of our society. Social structures are themselves shaped by the social forces and social relations of production and the dialectical contradiction between labour and capital.

Hegemony is a struggle in which the powerful win the consent of those who are oppressed, with the oppressed unknowingly participating in their own oppression. Hegemony was at work in my own practices as an elementary school teacher. Because I did not teach my students to question the prevailing values, attitudes, and social practices of the dominant society in a sustained critical manner, my classroom pre-served the hegemony of the dominant culture. Such hegemony was contested when the students began to question my authority by resisting and disrupting my lessons. The dominant class secures hegemony – the consent of the dominated – by supplying the symbols, representations, and practices of social life in such a way that the basis of social authority and the unequal relations of power and privilege remain hidden. By perpetrating the myth of individual achievement and entrepreneurship in the media, the schools, the church, and the family, for instance, dominant culture ensures that subordinated groups who fail at school or who don't make it into the world of the 'rich and famous' will view such failure in terms of personal inadequacy or the 'luck of the draw'. The oppressed blame themselves for school failure – a failure that can certainly be additionally attributed to the structuring effects of the economy and the class-based division of labour.[10] [...]

Within the hegemonic process, established meanings are often laundered of contradiction, contestation, and ambiguity. Resistance does occur, however, most often in the domain of popular culture. In this case, popular culture becomes an arena of negotiation in which dominant, subordinate, and oppositional groups affirm and struggle over cultural representations and meanings. The dominant culture is rarely successful on all counts. People *do* resist. Alternative groups do manage to find different values and meanings to regulate their lives. Oppositional groups do attempt to challenge the prevailing culture's mode of structuring and codifying representations and meanings. Prevailing social practices are, in fact, resisted. Schools and other social and cultural sites are rarely in the thrall of the hegemonic process since there we will also find struggle and confrontation. This is why schools can be characterised as terrains of transactions, exchange, and struggle between subordinate groups and the dominant ideology. There is a relative autonomy within school sites that allows for forms of resistance to emerge and to break the cohesiveness of hegemony. Teachers battle over what books to use, over what disciplinary practices to use, and over the aims and objectives of particular courses and programs. [...]

Ideology

Hegemony could not do its work without the support of ideology. Ideology permeates all social life and does not simply refer to the political ideologies of communism, socialism, anarchism, rationalism, or existentialism. Ideology refers to the production and representation of ideas, values, and beliefs and the manner in which they are expressed and lived out by both individuals and groups.[11] Simply put, ideology refers to the production of sense and meaning. It can be described as a way of viewing the world, a complex of ideas, various types of social practices, rituals, and representations that we tend to accept as natural and as common sense. It is the result of the intersection of meaning and power in the social world. Customs, rituals, beliefs, and values often produce within individuals distorted conceptions of their place in the sociocultural order and thereby serve to reconcile them to that place and to disguise the inequitable relations of power and privilege; this is sometimes referred to as 'ideological hegemony'.

Stuart Hall and James Donald define ideology as

the frameworks of thought which are used in society to explain, figure out, make sense of or give meaning to the social and political world. ... Without these frameworks, we could not make sense of the world at all. But with them, our perceptions are inevitably structured in a particular direction by the very concepts we are using.[12]

Ideology includes both positive and negative functions at any given moment: The positive function of ideology is to 'provide the concepts, categories, images, and ideas by means of which people make sense of their social and political world, form projects, come to a certain consciousness of their place in the world, and act in it'; the negative function of ideology 'refers to the fact that all such perspectives are inevitably selective. Thus a perspective positively organises the 'facts of the case' in this and makes sense because it inevitably excludes that way of putting things'.[13]

In order to fully understand the negative function of ideology, the concept must be linked to a theory of domination. Domination occurs when relations of power established at the institutional level are systematically asymmetrical; that is, when they are unequal, therefore privileging some groups over others. According to John Thompson, ideology as a negative function works through four different modes: legitimation, dissimulation, fragmentation, and reification. Legitimation occurs when a system of domination is sustained by being represented as legitimate or as eminently just and worthy of respect. For instance, by legitimising the school system as just and meritocratic, as giving everyone the same opportunity for success, the dominant culture hides the truth of the hidden curriculum – the fact that those whom schooling helps most are those who come from the most affluent families. Dissimulation results when relations of domination are concealed, denied, or obscured in various ways. For instance, the practice of institutionalised tracking in schools purports to help meet the needs of groups of students with varying academic ability. However, describing tracking in this way helps to cloak its socially reproductive function: that of sorting students according to their social class location. Fragmentation occurs when relations of domination are sustained by the production of meanings in a way which fragments groups so that they are placed in opposition to one another. For instance, when conservative educational critics explain the declining standards in American education as a result of trying to accommodate low-income minority students, this sometimes results in a backlash against immigrant students by other subordinate groups.

This 'divide and rule' tactic prevents oppressed groups from working together to secure collectively their rights. Reification occurs when transitory historical states of affairs are presented as permanent, natural, and commonsensical – as if they exist outside of time.[14] This has occurred to a certain extent with the current call for a national curriculum based on acquiring information about the 'great books' so as to have a greater access to the dominant culture. These works are revered as high-status knowledge since purportedly the force of history has heralded them as such and placed them on book lists in respected cultural institutions such as universities. Here literacy becomes a weapon that can be used against those groups who are 'culturally illiterate', whose social class, race, or gender renders their own experiences and stories as too unimportant to be worthy of investigation. That is, as a pedagogical tool, a stress on the great books often deflects attention away from the personal experiences of students and the political nature of everyday life. Teaching the great books is also a way of inculcating certain values and sets of behaviours in social groups, thereby solidifying the existing social hierarchy. [...]

The dominant ideology refers to the naturalisation of particular practices, social differences, and subjectivities by capitalist relations of production. The majority of Americans – rich and poor alike – share the belief that capitalism is a better system than democratic socialism, for instance, or that men are generally more capable of holding positions of authority than women, or that women should be more passive and housebound. Here, we must recognise that the economic system requires the ideology of consumer capitalism to naturalise it, rendering it commonsensical. The ideology of patriarchy also is necessary to keep the nature of the economy safe and secured within the prevailing hegemony. We have been fed these dominant ideologies for decades through the mass media, the schools, and family socialisation.

Oppositional ideologies do exist, however, which attempt to challenge the dominant ideologies and shatter existing stereotypes. On some occasions, the dominant culture is able to manipulate alternative and oppositional ideologies in such a way that hegemony can be more effectively secured. For instance, *The Cosby Show* on commercial television carries a message that a social avenue now exists in America for blacks to be successful doctors and lawyers. This positive view of blacks, however, masks the fact that most blacks in the United States exist in a subordinate position to the dominant white culture with respect to power and privilege. The dominant culture secures hegemony by transmitting and legitimating ideologies like that in *The Cosby Show*, which reflect and shape popular resistance to stereotypes, but which in reality do little to challenge the real basis of power of the ruling dominant groups. [...]

The main question for teachers attempting to become aware of the ideologies that inform their own teaching is: How have certain pedagogical practices become so habitual or natural in school settings that teachers accept them as normal, unproblematic, and expected? How often, for instance, do teachers question school practices such as tracking, ability grouping, competitive grading, teacher-centred pedagogical approaches, and the use of rewards and punishments as control devices? The point here is to understand that these practices are not carved in stone, but are socially constructed within material conditions that function to serve capital's drive to augment value and to reproduce abstract labour and the unjust distribution of use-values. How, then, is the distilled wisdom of traditional educational theorising ideologically structured? What constitutes the origins and legitimacy of the pedagogical practices within this tradition? To what extent do such pedagogical practices serve to empower the student, and to what extent do they work as forms of social control that support, stabilise, and legitimate the role of the teacher as a moral gatekeeper of the state? What are the functions and effects of the systematic imposition of ideological perspectives on classroom teaching practices?

In my classroom journal, what characterised the ideological basis of my own teaching practices? How did 'being schooled' both enable and contain the subjectivities of the students? I am using 'subjectivity' here to mean forms of knowledge that are both conscious and unconscious and which express our identity as human agents. Subjectivity relates to everyday knowledge in its socially constructed and historically produced forms linked to the prevailing mode of production. Following this, we can ask: How do the dominant ideological practices of teachers help to structure the subjectivities of students? What are the possible consequences of this, for good and for ill? Can education be more than the social production of labour-power in ways that reproduce the capitalist form of class society? Is education an aerosol term that hides class exploitation in the mist of its ideological rhetoric?

Prejudice

Prejudice is the negative prejudgment of individuals and groups on the basis of unrecognised, unsound, and inadequate evidence. Because these negative attitudes occur so frequently, they take on a common-sense or ideological character that is often used to justify acts of discrimination.

Critical pedagogy and the power/knowledge relation

Critical pedagogy is fundamentally concerned with understanding the relationship between power and knowledge. The dominant curriculum separates knowledge from the issue of power and treats it in an unabashedly technical manner; knowledge is seen in overwhelmingly instrumental terms as something to be mastered. That knowledge is always an ideological construction linked to particular interests and social relations generally receives little consideration in education programmes.

The work of the French philosopher Michel Foucault is crucial in understanding the socially constructed nature of truth and its inscription in knowledge/power relations. Foucault's concept of 'power/knowledge' extends the notion of power beyond its conventional use by philosophers and social theorists who, like American John Dewey, have understood power as 'the sum of conditions available for bringing the desirable end into existence'.[15] For Foucault, power comes from everywhere, from above and from below; it is 'always already there' and is inextricably implicated in the micro relations of domination and resistance. Foucault's work on power is limited in that he does not link power sufficiently to the production of value within global capitalist social relations.

Discourse

Power relations are inscribed in what Foucault refers to as discourse or a family of concepts. Discourses are made up of discursive practices that Foucault describes as:

a body of anonymous, historical rules, always determined in the time and space that have defined a given period, and for a given social, economic, geographical, or linguistic area, the conditions of operation of the enunciative function.[16]

Discursive practices, then, refer to the rules by which discourses are formed, rules that govern what can be said and what must remain unsaid, and who can speak with authority and who must listen. Social and political institutions, such as schools and penal institutions, are governed by discursive practices:

Discursive practices are not purely and simply ways of producing discourse. They are embodied in technical processes, in institutions, in patterns for general behaviour, in forms of transmission and diffusion, and pedagogical forms which, at once, impose and maintain them.[17]

For education, discourse can be defined as a 'regulated system of statements' that establish differences between fields and theories of teacher education; it is 'not simply words but is embodied in the practice of institutions, patterns of behaviour, and in forms of pedagogy'.[17]

From this perspective, we can consider dominant discourses (those produced by the dominant culture) as 'regimes of truth', as general economies of power/knowledge, or as multiple forms of constraint. In a classroom setting, dominant educational discourses determine what books we may use, what classroom approaches we should employ (mastery learning, Socratic method, etc), and what values and beliefs we should transmit to our students.

For instance, neoconservative discourses on language in the classroom would view working-class speech as undersocialised or deprived. Liberal discourse would view such speech as merely different. Similarly, to be culturally literate within a conservative discourse is to acquire basic information on American culture (dates of battles, passages of the Constitution, etc). Conservative discourse focuses mostly on the works of 'great men'. A liberal discourse on cultural literacy includes knowledge generated from the perspective of women and minorities. A critical discourse focuses on the interests and assumptions that inform the generation of knowledge itself. A critical discourse is also self-critical and deconstructs dominant discourses the moment they are ready to achieve hegemony. A critical discourse can, for instance, explain how high-status knowledge (the great works of the Western world) can be used to teach concepts that reinforce the status quo. Discourses and discursive practices influence how we live our lives as conscious thinking subjects. They shape our subjectivities (our ways of understanding in relation to the world) because it is only in language and through discourse that social reality can be given meaning. Not all discourses are given the same weight, as some will account for and justify the appropriateness of the status quo and others will provide a context for resisting social and institutional practices.[19] [...]

Source: McLaren, P. (2007) *Life in schools: an introduction to critical pedagogy in the foundations of education*, 5th Edition, Reprinted by permission of Pearson Education, Inc., Upper Saddle River, NJ

Notes

1   The sources for this section are as follows: Bertell Ollman, The Meaning of Dialectics, *Monthly Review* (1986, November): 42-55; Wilfrid Carr and Stephen Kemmis, *Becoming Critical: Knowing Through Action Research* (Victoria: Deakin University, 1983); Stephen Kemmis and Lindsay Fitzclarence, *Curriculum Theorising: Beyond Reproduction Theory* (Victoria: Deakin University, 1986); Henry A. Giroux, *Ideology, Culture; and the Process of Schooling* (Philadelphia: Temple University Press and London: Falmer Press, Ltd, 1981); Ernst Bloch, The Dialectical Method, *Man and World* 16 (1983):281-313.

2   Carr and Kemmis, Becoming Critical, 36-7.

3   McLaren, *Schooling as a Ritual Performance.*

4   This discussion of micro and macro objectives is taken from Henry A. Giroux, Overcoming Behavioural and Humanistic Objectives, *The Education Forum* (1979, May): 409-19. Also, Henry A. Giroux, *Teachers as Intellectuals: Towards a Critical Pedagogy of Practical Learning* (South Hadley, MA: Bergin and Garvey, 1988).

5   See Jürgen Habermas, *Knowledge and Human Interests*, trans. J. J. Shapiro (London: Heinemann, 1972); see also Jürgen Habermas, *Theory and Practice*, trans. J. Viertel. (London: Heinemann, 1974). As cited in Kemmis and Fitzclarence, Curriculum Theorising, 70-2.

6   For a fuller discussion of culture, see Enid Lee, *Letters to Marcia: A Teacher's Guide to Anti-Racist Teaching* (Toronto: Cross Cultural Communication Centre, 1985).

7   Henry A. Giroux and Peter McLaren, Teacher Education and the Politics of Engagement: The Case for Democratic Schooling, *Harvard Educational Review* 56 (1986): 3, 232-3. Developed from Giroux's previous work.

8   For this discussion of culture, I am indebted to Raymond A. Calluori, The Kids are Alright: New Wave Subcultural Theory, *Social Text* 4, 3 (1985): 43-53; Mike Brake, *The Sociology of Youth Culture and Youth Subculture* (London: Routledge and Kegan Paul, 1980); Graham Murdock, Mass Communication and the Construction of Meaning, in N. Armstead (ed), *Reconstructing Social Psychology* (Harmondsworth: Penguin, 1974); Dick Hebdige, *Subculture: The Meaning of Style* (London and New York: Methuen, 1979); Ian Connell, D. J. Ashenden, S. Kessler, and G. W. Dowsett, *Making the Difference: Schooling, Families, and Social Division* (Sydney, Australia: George Allen and Unwin, 1982). Also, Stuart Hall and Tony Jefferson, *Resistance Through Rituals: Youth Subcultures in Post-War Britain* (London: Hutchinson and the Centre for Contemporary Cultural Studies, University of Birmingham, 1980).

9   The section on hegemony draws on the following sources: Giroux, *Ideology, Culture, and the Process of Schooling*, 22-6; *Popular Culture* (1981), a second level course at The Open University, Milton Keynes, England, published by The Open University Press and distributed in the United States by Taylor and Francis (Philadelphia, PA). Several booklets in this series were instrumental in developing the sections on ideology and hegemony: Geoffrey Bourne, Meaning, Image, and Ideology, *Form and Meaning* 1, The Open University Press, Block 4, Units 13 and 15, 37-65; see also Tony Bennett, Popular Culture: Defining Our Terms, *Popular Culture: Themes and Issues I*, Block 1, Units 1 and 2, 77-87; Tony Bennett, Popular Culture: History and Theory, *Popular Culture: Themes and Issues II*, Block 1, Unit 3, 29-32. Another important source is a booklet for a third level course at The Open University: *The Politics of Cultural Production*, The Open University Press, 1981. Relevant sections include: Geoff Whitty, Ideology, Politics, and Curriculum, 7-52; David Davies, Popular Culture, Class, and Schooling, 53-108. See also P. J. Hills, A Dictionary of Education (London: Routledge and Kegan Paul, 1982), 166-7; Raymond Williams, *Keywords: A Vocabulary of Culture and Society* (London: Fontana, 1983), 144-6.

10 William Ryan, *Blaming the Victim* (New York: Vintage Books, 1976).

11 For this section on ideology, I am indebted to Henry A. Giroux, *Theory and Resistance in Education: Pedagogy for the Opposition* (South Hadley, MA: Bergin and Garvey, 1983), 143. See also Stanley Aronowitz and Henry A. Giroux, Education Under Siege (South Hadley, MA: Bergin and Garvey, 1985); Douglas Kellner, Ideology, Marxism, and Advanced Capitalism, *Socialist Review* 8, 6 (1978): 38; Gibson Winter, *Liberating Creation: Foundations of Religious Social Ethics* (New York: Crossroad, 1981), 97. See also: Geoff Whitty, Ideology, Politics, and Curriculum, 7-52, and David Davies, Popular Culture, Class, and Schooling, 53-108; Williams, *Keywords*, 153-7; Tony Bennett, Popular Culture: Defining Our Terms, 77-87; and Geoffrey Bourne, Meaning, Image, and Ideology, 37-53.

12 James Donald and Stuart Hall, Introduction, in S. Donald and S. Hall (eds), *Politics and Ideology* (Milton Keynes: Philadelphia, The Open University Press, 1986), ix-x.

13 Donald and Hall, *Politics and Ideology*, x.

14 John Thompson, Language and Ideology, *The Sociological Review* 35, 3 (1987, August):516-536.

15 John Dewey, in J. Ratner (ed), *Intelligence in the Modern World: John Dewey's Philosophy* (New York: The Modern Library, 1939), 784. See also Michel Foucault, Power/Knowledge, in C. Gordon (ed) (L. Marshall, J. Mepham, and K. Spoer, trans.), *Selected Interviews and Other Writings 1972-77* (New York: Pantheon, 1980), 187.

16 Michel Foucault, *The Archaeology of Knowledge* (New York: Harper Colophon Books, 1972), 117.

17 Foucault, *Power/Knowledge*, 200.

18 Richard Smith and Anna Zantiotis, Teacher Education, Cultural Politics, and the Avant-Garde' in H. Giroux and P. McLaren (eds), *Critical Pedagogy, the State, and Cultural Struggle* (Albany, NY: SUNY Press, 1989), 123.

19 See Chris Weedon, *Feminist Practice and Post-Structuralist Theory* (Oxford: Basil-Blackwell, 1987).

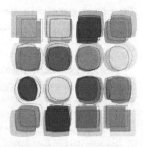

Chapter 2

The framing of performance pedagogies: Pupil perspectives on the control of school knowledge and its acquisition

Madeleine Arnot and Diane Reay

It should be quite clear that the specific application of the concepts [of classification and framing] requires at every point empirical evidence .... We have, for example, little first-hand knowledge which bears upon aspects of framing. (Bernstein, 1977:112, original emphasis and our addition)

There are few developed sociological theories of learning that can successfully combine an analysis of the social relationships of the classroom with the processes of learning acquisition. Bernstein's theory of pedagogy is unique in formulating connections between the organisation and structuring of knowledge, the means by which it is transmitted, and the ways in which acquisition is experienced.

Here we use Bernstein's theoretical concepts to begin to understand the nature of pupils' pedagogic experiences in contemporary English education. We consider the significances for pupil learning of the imposition of a state-regulated national curriculum and a market-oriented pedagogy (Bernstein, 1990). Drawing on findings from research in two differently organised and located state secondary schools, we suggest that the control over classroom learning associated with these educational reforms has privileged those who have already had the advantage of being able to exercise discretion within strongly controlled environments. Even within the strongly framed contexts, such as that now found in English secondary education, there are spaces in which the most successful can gain control of their learning. Yet those pupils who most need to be supported in their learning are likely to find the least opportunities for so doing in this highly structured environment. The consequences of the strong framing of the English version of performance pedagogy becomes the mechanism for sustaining rather than reducing class and gender inequalities.

The restructuring of English secondary education: market-oriented performance pedagogies

Bernstein's analysis of neo-liberal reforms of schooling draws heavily upon his theory of pedagogic transmission that he developed over a period of twenty years. Mainstream sociology of education, in his view, was seriously constrained in its analysis of the depth of social stratification and inequality by the fact that it 'rarely turned its attention to the analysis of the intrinsic features constituting and distinguishing the specialised form of communication realised by the pedagogic discourse of education'. He commented:

Many of the analyses of the sociology of education, especially those carried out by the diverse group of theories of reproduction, assume, take for granted, the very discourse which is subject to their analysis. These theories, in particular, see pedagogic discourse as a medium for other voices: class, gender, and race. The discourses of education are analysed for their power to reproduce dominant/dominated relations external to the discourse but which penetrate the social relations, media of transmission, and evaluation of pedagogic discourse. It is often considered that the voice of the working class is the absent voice of pedagogic discourse, but... what is absent from pedagogic discourse is its own voice. (Bernstein, 1990:165)

If pedagogic discourse is seen as only a relay for patterns of discourse external to itself then its form has no consequences for what is relayed. As a result, 'theories of culture reproduction are essentially theories of communication without a theory of communication' (*ibid*:170).

Bernstein's own analysis of 'the inner structure of the pedagogic' offers such a theory of communication. Drawing on an important Parsonian distinction between the expressive and instrumental orders (Bernstein, 2000:102) he developed an understanding of the ways in which the moral order and the instructional order work in the context of the school, and the relationship between them. He made the important distinction between *what* is transmitted and *how* it is transmitted. Initially he referred to these elements as the classification and framing of knowledge which together make up an educational code (Bernstein, 1977). By the 1990s, Bernstein had developed these concepts further. The classification of knowledge was now referred to as the *instructional discourse* and framing was defined as the *regulative discourse* (the rules of the social order which frame order, conduct, character, manner, relations, and identity (Bernstein, 2000:13). By separating out the rules which govern the instructional from the regulative discourse, the transmission of knowledge from the transmission of the moral order, Bernstein offered researchers the possibility of analysing the complex different social class assumptions built into different aspects of pedagogic practice and the possibility of mapping empirically significant shifts in pedagogy and its 'products'.

Initially the concept of framing only referred to the degrees of control which teachers or pupils had over the mode of transmission (the ways in which knowledge was being taught and learnt) but, in his later writings, Bernstein developed the concept of framing so as to focus on the teacher-pupil relationship and its role in 'creating the pedagogic arena, game ... or specific practice' (Bernstein, 2000:180). In his final volume, Bernstein (2000) moved 'from rules which distinguish the practice to the particular interactional practice and its *specific locational and communicative realisations*'. Framing in his view came to represent the 'inner logic' of a pedagogy (Bernstein, 1990:63), determining how knowledge was to be transmitted. As a result, it plays a critical role in his understanding of how social class inequalities are both shaped, affected, and resisted within the processes of learning (not just within the processes of educational distribution). He therefore explored in great detail the social class assumptions which underlay strong and weak versions of framing (Bernstein 1990, 2000). He favoured the role of the regulative discourse in which instructional discourses were embedded in his theory of social class reproduction within the English educational system.[1]

Bernstein argued that the English education system had previously been distinguished from the mainstream European models by its strong classification but weaker framing (Bernstein, 1977:98). Historically, pupils in the UK had been allowed more discretion and negotiation in relation to their learning than those found in central European systems but, since the 1990s, the English educational system has now shifted far more towards the strong state control of pedagogy found in other European systems (Bernstein, 1990:85). This new form of visible pedagogy is strongly associated with 'selective class-based acquisition' – in this case, with those fractions of the middle classes located within the field of economic production (entrepreneurial professions and those opposed to rises in public expenditure) and with a swing back from the invisible competence-based pedagogies of the 1970s associated with the new middle classes in the field of symbolic control. Although the entrepreneurial/ capital classes are not dependent upon such pedagogies for their privilege, nevertheless such pedagogies, especially with their emphasis on performance in national assessments, provided, whether unintentionally or not, opportunities for the 'reproduction and advancement' of this class fraction.

Whilst the principles of classification are still as strong as those represented by the traditional grammar school curriculum, neo-liberal and neo-conservative reforms of schooling introduced in the Education Reform Act (1988) has led to the strengthening of framing. This can be seen in the explicit principles of selection, sequencing, and criterial/assessment rules found in the state-controlled programmes of study for main subjects, the normative assumptions built into QCA lesson schemes, and the tight sequencing rules (what is learnt in which order) applied through national assessments. The use of national league tables based upon success in GCSE examination performance puts added pressure on schools and teachers to ensure that pupils' learning is in line with government expectations.

The new pedagogic practices that have been put in place are a complex market-oriented visible pedagogy which, Bernstein argues, appears to address left critiques of neo-liberalism and unequal educational systems whilst at the same time meeting the needs of the capitalist formation for a communicative society and a flexibility of learning a veritable 'pedagogic Janus' (Bernstein, 1990:87). The new performance pedagogies offer a confusing, pedagogic regime which introduces extensive, seemingly democratic choices for parents while encouraging individual ownership through student profiles, life-skills courses, etc. Bernstein located the hybrid model of schooling within a range of performance-based pedagogic modes.[2] Key to such performance-based models are strongly classified space, time, and discourse, explicit forms of control, performance as the pedagogic text, different degrees of autonomy, and a low-cost schooling. Evaluation of student's work (the text) is explicit and has to meet certain criteria. The key for pupils was to learn how to recognise or realise what constitutes a legitimate text especially since evaluations are often based on what is missing from the text.[3] These structuring principles which have the effect of differentiating and dividing learners, however, are often hidden in the rhetoric of what is euphemistically called 'independent learning' or what the UK government is now calling 'personalised'. Behind this socially neutral rhetoric is likely to be found the social stratification of learners.

Beck (1999), Bourne (2000) and Moss (2004) have explored various aspects of this regime. Beck, for example, highlighted the shift it represented between knowledge and the knower through a dehumanising and more secular pedagogic approach. Knowledge is thus 'divorced from persons, commitments and personal dedication, separated from inwardness' and the inner self. It becomes competences and skills which are meant to be transferable into different market settings but without personal meaning. Moss (2004) uncovers the elements of the National Literacy strategy which restructure teachers' work, reducing both teachers' and students' control over the selection and pacing of knowledge, while Bourne (2000) outlines the development of a new pedagogic culture in creating new definitions of literacy.

Bernstein speculated about the consequences for marginalised and disadvantaged groups of such strong framing within a performance model of schooling. On the one hand, strong external frames of pedagogy by the state (such as we have seen in England) are likely to aggravate social disadvantage: 'social class may play a crucial role ... where the external frames are strong it often means that images, voices and practices the school reflects make it difficult for children of marginalised classes to recognise themselves in the school' (Bernstein, 2000:5). Similarly, the strengthening of internal framing of performance pedagogy is likely to hinder the academic progress of such children. The key element of strong framing here is the element of pacing (Bernstein, 1990). Greater teacher control over the pacing of learning is encouraged through the pressure which school inspectors (Ofsted) bring to bear. The quality of teachers' practice is judged in part in terms of the pacing of their lessons and the successful acquisition of preordained knowledge. Such is the strength of pacing that new initiatives such as the Literacy hour even provide a diagrammatic clock which teachers are expected to adhere to when teaching the programme (Moss, 2004).

Bernstein's analysis of shifts in educational policy is central to our project on the social conditions of learning. We employ his concept of framing to investigate the social consequences of contemporary performance pedagogies in two educational sites. Using two secondary schools with different political and pedagogic histories, we explore the ways in which different groups of male and female, higher- and lower-achieving pupils from different social and ethnic backgrounds, currently experience learning. Pupils' accounts reveal the 'nature of social relationships' which are associated with these new framings of educational knowledge – the forms by which the curriculum is made public. Of especial concern are the different degrees of control which learners have over the pedagogic 'communication and its social base'.

Research context and design

The two secondary schools in which we conducted our research differ substantially in ideological ethos and in pupil organisation. Nevertheless, both have been affected by the strengthening of the framing of educational knowledge. Each school, although from very different starting points and trajectories, has had to introduce the increasing 'tight framing' of performance pedagogies, geared to nationally assessed performance goals.

The delivery of the National Curriculum and its standardised assessments, while not easy, was always likely to be less problematic for a school we call Greenfield school, located in a predominantly white city. Grammar-school traditions were part of its history and the presence particularly of the professional middle-class students meant that successful educational results could be achieved. The strongly framed instructional discourse in this school which organised its pupils into ability sets (groups) for different subjects provided a relatively strongly framed regulative discourse even though the resulting stratification of learners was masked by the emphasis on individualised and independent learning.

In contrast, the teaching of a strongly segmental curriculum in a predominantly working-class and multiracial urban secondary school which we call Mandela was highly disruptive of its ethos. Since 1988, the school's traditionally weak framing with its egalitarian concerns has had to respond with a stronger discourse of regulation. The pupils here were taught in mixed ability classes, with only limited differentiation of learners. Teachers in this school spoke with anxiety about the consequences of the imposition of state-controlled curriculum and pedagogy, and new testing regimes on social inequalities on working-class pupils who came to the realisation that trying hard was no longer enough to ensure that they did well.

Using Bernstein's framework, we set out to elicit pupil voices, not as independent (client) assessors who might expose underlying social practices, but rather as products of the educational codes operating within the school. Our project involved the creation of discussion groups of male and female, higher- and lower-achieving pupils (aged 12-13 years) from different ethnic and class backgrounds. The aim was to hear collective rather than individual voices, using the categories often relayed through pedagogic discourse itself (see Reay and Arnot, 2004 for a reflexive account of methodology). At a later point we observed and interviewed individual pupils in English and Maths classes and asked the teachers to build in strategies of pupil consultation in their lessons (*ibid*).

In Arnot and Reay (2005) we suggest that the sort of pupil voice we elicited could be called 'code talk'.[4] We asked pupils to tell us about the social conditions of their schooling – the regulative discourse which frames their instruction – by describing the ways in which they experienced their own learning and their confidence in themselves as learners, their sense of social inclusion in the classroom, and the degree to which they felt they could control their learning. Pupils tried therefore to express their understanding of the principles which governed their learning, and the moments of conflict, negotiation, engagement, and disengagement. Put sociologically, their 'code talk' illuminated the tension between transmission of knowledge within contemporary classrooms and the possibilities of their own agency.

As Bernstein (2000) argued, the social/moral order of the school 'is prior to and a condition for, the transmission of competences'. We are interested therefore in the role of social class, ethnic, and gender relations in embedding the contemporary instructional discourse associated with performance pedagogies and how the principles which regulate the selection and transmission of educational knowledge are experienced by these different groups. Below we present a small slice of our findings. We begin our analysis by focusing on the degrees of control different groups of pupils feel they have over the curriculum content and their degrees of freedom to negotiate their own learning. [...]

The successful learner

Integral to the instructional discourse of contemporary performance pedagogy is the notion of the successful learner. In our discussions with pupils we asked them a crude but effective question about whether there was a distinction between the 'good' and 'bad' learner, how they described themselves and how they knew what sort of learner they were. We also asked pupils to discuss what might help them be more successful in the classroom and whether they thought they could be more successful at learning school knowledge.

In both schools most pupils we consulted associated successful learners with features such as listening, hard work, being good at responding, concentrating, giving work in, making an effort, being liked by the teacher, and doing well. The pupils in the top set in Greenfield, however, were more likely to associate the concept of the 'good learner' with enjoyment and 'being challenged', being liked by the teacher, knowing most subjects, and being interested in school work. This particular group of pupils talked about the act of learning rather than just gaining knowledge. In contrast, lower-achieving boys at Greenfield were much more circumspect about the distinction between good and bad learners. They associated good learners with classroom learning behaviour – paying attention, not talking, and doing the homework. Within these definitions they were able to rank themselves in terms of the amount they worked and the amount they talked in class. So long as they made an effort, paid attention, and did the work (even while talking during class) they classified themselves as good learners. In Greenfield, pupils from various sets positioned themselves as independent learners ('I' the learner) as if the school had not already positioned them differentially in a hierarchy of learners.

The language of learning in Mandela, however, was different. Here most pupils appeared ambivalent about this distinction and only the three middle-class boys were prepared to position themselves as good learners. In comparison with Greenfield pupils who could draw information about themselves as learners from their position in various sets, the Mandela pupils were used to mixed ability classrooms and were able to experience 'difference' on a daily basis. They appeared to be less likely to use the classifications of learners and to place more emphasis on social variables such as gender and ethnic group (the visible dominance of regulative discourses).

There were more references to 'we' as a social grouping of learners in this school. The ways in which these pupils constructed differences between learners also had implications for their confidence as learners. If learning was about effort then there is much that can be gained by hard work. The lower-achieving group of boys in Mandela underlined this point: 'It's important to focus', 'Yeah, you need to focus a lot', and persist – 'you need to read over and over to get it done'. Thus the rewards, as Bernstein had argued, of this performance pedagogy still had to be achieved. The mythological discourse operating in this school, that of egalitarianism, masks the reality of differential success in achieving this goal.

Working-class boys appeared to operationalise the principles which underlay the performance pedagogy but in ways that undermined their own position. For example, they used the concept of intelligence to underscore the differences between learners. Working-class boys, in particular, articulated a painful awareness of the readiness of schools to attribute successful learning to 'ability': they catalogued a range of innate factors which combined to exclude themselves. For example: 'You've got to be clever', 'you have to be intelligent to be a good learner', 'you have to be clever to get jobs, important jobs' – although, for Ricky, there seemed to be an element of individual volition 'you've got to be in a good mood to be clever'. The danger for these low-achieving working-class boys was the power such intrinsic qualities played in shaping their confidence as learners. They were the only ones to describe invidious evaluations of their own intelligence:

Ricky: Other people saying you are thick.

Robbie: Yeah, telling you you're stupid.

Dean: People undermine your confidence by putting you down.

Danny: People putting you down makes you feel like you are thick and then you feel like [you] just don't want to try. Your feelings are hurt.

The undermining of their confidence as learners, which all four boys articulated, was further exacerbated by 'being picked on' by teachers because, as Ricky pointed out: 'It makes you think – what's the point of trying?' These boys vividly described how they were made to feel stupid and childlike in classroom encounters with teachers:

Kenny: Some teachers are a bit snobby, sort of. And some teachers act as if the child is stupid. Because they've got a posh accent. Like they talk without 'innits' and 'mans', like they talk proper English. And they say, 'That isn't the way you talk' – like putting you down. Like I think telling you a different way is sort of good, but I think the way they do it isn't good because they correct you and make you look stupid.

Martin: Those teachers look down on you.

Kenny: Yeah, like they think you're dumb ... we don't expect them to treat us like their own children. We're not. But we are still kids. I'd say to them, 'You've got kids. You treat them with love but you don't need to love us. All you need to do is treat us like humans.'

Pupils in the lowest sets at Greenfield had similar experiences. The hierarchical organisation of pupils also had the effect of making some pupils 'feel stupid'. The working-class boys in the lowest English sets also wondered whether there was any point in trying hard at their learning:

Neil: It's too easy, it's like they think you're stupid or something.

Sean: Yeah, like 'How do you write 'the'?'

Rather than using their own assessment of their learning (something which higher-achieving pupils felt confident to do), the lower-achieving groups sought reassurance for the quality of their work from their teachers, other pupils, and their parents. They indicated their reliance on others to motivate them and assess whether they were doing well at school. Lower-achieving working-class boys reported feeling most successful at learning when the teacher or their parents said 'well done'.

As we have argued elsewhere, the experiences of regulation are most acutely felt by those who cannot easily work with the model of the independent learner being promoted as the means by which 'performance' is secured (Arnot and Reay, 2004; Arnot *et al*, 2004). The model of the independent learner is one which involves students having the maturity to engage with teachers and negotiate their own learning progress. As such, the concept of the independent learner represents the mythological aspect of market-oriented performance pedagogies (an attempt to represent such pedagogies as having weak rather than strong frames). However, whilst some pupils were able to work with the notion of being responsible for their own learning, for others these demands were associated with disengagement, confusion, shame, and alienation.

We found that the class gap between pupils was expressed most clearly when we asked them about whether they wished to be consulted by a teacher about their learning. Middle-class girls in both schools appeared to have achieved greater levels of opportunities for consulting teachers in the classroom and therefore did not require new consultation mechanisms (Arnot *et al*, 2004). However, working-class pupils reported far fewer and less successful discussions with teachers. For example, Sean and Neil, both working class, were given discretion about when to finish off their work in the lessons rather than being asked what to learn. They commented:

Neil: It would be good if they said something like 'Oh what do you want to do in the lesson today?' or something.
Sean: Yeah.

The group of lower-achieving boys at Greenfield appeared to know that not only were the teachers in command of their education, even when teachers asked them what they would like to do that day, far more was at stake than just choice of topic. Their experiences of strong framing was reflected in their frustrations with their lack of control over what is transmitted and assessed and the ways in which teachers interpreted their work. The role of discipline and shame, rather than reflection or opportunities to choose activities, played a major part in their understanding of how strong framing works. Control over their learning meant gaining control over what was seen as largely pointless curriculum content. As a result, even if they were consulted, they replied they would respond thus:

Q: If that happened, what would you say?
Neil: Nothing.

The experience and approach of these boys appears to be that teachers rarely listen to them, or respect their views. Similarly, a significant number of working-class boys at Mandela were already switched off from seeing themselves as learners:

Q: If you had a choice what would you choose to learn?
Jason: Nothing.
George: Nothing.
Andy: No idea.
Paul: Definitely nothing!

These working-class boys are positioned in a similar education space to that of Willis's 'lads' in the 1970s even though the form of performance pedagogy was substantially different (the autonomous knowledge-based version). They are clearly alienated from academic learning and see themselves as powerless in relation to the selection of knowledge. More than the other groups in our study, they fit Bernstein's suggestion that:

The stronger the classification and the framing, the more the educational relationship tends to be hierarchical and ritualised, the educand is seen as ignorant, with little status and few rights. These are things which one earns, rather like spurs, and are used for the purpose of encouraging and sustaining the motivation of pupils. (Bernstein, 1977:98)

Performance pedagogies and social inequalities in the classroom

In this chapter we have explored, through the voices of pupils, how performance pedagogies are experienced by different social groups. If strong frames control what can and cannot be said, then the pedagogic relationship between teachers and pupils is always likely to be hierarchical, although often disguised, mystified, or masked. Similarly, knowledge will not be experienced as permeable, nor open. Socialisation will be into an existing order, another form of alienation (Bernstein, 1977:98). In strengthening the frames, the government has strengthened the notion of discipline, or 'accepting a given selection, organisation, pacing and timing of knowledge' (*ibid*).

The teaching of the National Curriculum, with its strong specialist subject discourses, strong boundaries between educational and common-sense knowledge, and its neo-liberal performance pedagogies, transmits messages about the social order. Our data suggest that this 'pedagogical Janus' will, as Bernstein predicted, give special significance to those pupils who possess educational knowledge and who are able to work successfully with its transmission rules. But these differentiations must be seen in context.

In Greenfield, for example, the strong classificatory principles underlying contemporary market-oriented performance pedagogies were supported by the differentiation of learners in Year 8 according to their achievement in particular subjects. The setting structure therefore sent explicit messages to pupils about how their learning was to be controlled and how it reflected, at least in principle, their abilities. Teachers had the power to shape their learning experiences, the content of their learning, and their trajectory through the school structure. In this context pupils' control of their own learning was strongly circumscribed by structures rather than the social dynamics of the classroom.

The instructional discourse had shaped the organisation of pupils, whilst in Mandela the regulative discourse provided the criteria for mixed ability teaching. Here, the competitive performance pedagogies were delivered within a quasi-egalitarian setting in which pupils battled against the lack of control over both their own status and their success in the performance culture. Their success involved relational work in ways that were not found in Greenfield. In Greenfield the instructional discourses appeared dominant whilst in Mandela the regulative discourse was more visible.

In Mandela and Greenfield middle-class children appeared to have gained access to the principle of the discourse. Our data suggests that particularly higher-achieving middle-class girls experience weaker frames in the controls over knowledge and they were able, it seems, to exploit those small opportunities for creativity and the possibilities of their own agency even within a strongly segmented and hierarchised knowledge structure. In both Greenfield and Mandela, Year 8 pupils appeared to accept the principle that the forms of knowledge they are being taught should be in the hands of the school, and mostly in the hands of teachers, although some recognised that teachers themselves are strongly controlled (framed) by government policy. In both sites, there is evidence of an instrumental desire for 'useful knowledge' defined in social-class terms. For working-class boys in particular, this instrumentality, especially for the modern technological world, is tempered by a desire to break down the boundaries between educational and community and cultural knowledge. These class and gender differences in the valuation of school knowledge and its interpretation are noticeable in both schools.

The evidence we have collected also suggests that strong framing of educational knowledge is experienced differentially. As Bernstein argues, what is relayed by strong framing is the notion of difference amongst pupils (Bernstein, 2000). The assumptions about learners underlying the strengthening of pacing in visible pedagogies is more likely to be met by middle-class children who can 'exploit the possibilities of pedagogic practice' (Bernstein, 1990:74). The working-class child is likely to have greater dependency on the teacher and on oral forms of discourse.

There is always the chance that strong framing can be responded to and negotiated. Strong framing creates particular voices but also the strategies for responding to and challenging such controls. In our study, we found only those who have 'shown signs of successful socialisation' (Bernstein, 1977:98) have access to relaxed frames within the strongly structured learning environment. Higher-achieving pupils, for example, found small areas of discretion in what they studied, but for the most part, pupils had little feeling of being in control. In our other reports on the data (Arnot and Reay, 2004) we concluded that higher-attaining middle-class girls were able to employ both strong and weakened frames. They express a desire and are at moments able to gain more control over the pacing and sequencing of their learning (more relaxed frames). They work with notions of individual choice in terms of when to co-operate, when to slow down or speed up (or zoom) through their work. They can work independently, but they can also make considerable demands on the teacher to deal with their needs for extension work. High-achieving middle-class boys speak less about the pace, difficulty, and ease of their work.

In contrast, lower-achieving working-class pupils clearly experience strong controls over the selection and pacing of knowledge in ways that lead to disengagement from learning and a celebration of peer-group bonds (Arnot and Reay, 2004). Their lack of control within the new regulative discourses leads to behaviour responses rather than 'independent learning', a heavy reliance on friendship support, and a desire for teachers to 'get it right'. These pupils experience high levels of surveillance and control and, from their point of view, no discretion over their learning and restricted help or sympathy from teachers. In Mandela, despite an earlier commitment to pupil autonomy and control, the working-class pupils appear to consider their learning as largely the responsibility of others – namely teachers.

The data from these two school settings suggests that we need to examine the extent to which a positive pedagogic identity is achievable for, in particular, working-class boys in the current, strongly framed learning environment. Bernstein writes about how socialisation within schooling can be 'deeply wounding' either for those who wish for but do not achieve a pedagogic identity, or for the majority for whom the pursuit of an identity is early made irrelevant (Bernstein, 1975:250). If, as Bernstein suggests, an increase in the strength of framing often means that the images, voices, and practices that the school authorises makes it even more difficult for working-class children to recognise themselves in schooling, this is likely to be particularly problematic for working-class boys who experience daily the strong regulative culture of the classroom and confrontational relations with teachers. This clearly has profound consequences for the production of positive pedagogic identities so desired by the new goals of lifelong learning.

Bernstein (2000:190) argued that every pedagogy has a voice, one that is never heard. We can hear only its realisations, and its messages. In the context of the curriculum, this pedagogic voice is expressed through the regulative discourse which embeds the teaching of knowledge and skills. Bernstein urges sociologists of education to make the pedagogic voice the 'fundamental theoretical object of sociology of education'. Our research on contemporary performance pedagogies makes a small contribution to that project.

Source: Lauder *et al* (2006) *Education, Globalization, and Social Change*, chp. 53 pp. 766-770, 778. By permission of Oxford University Press

Notes

1 He devoted a chapter in vol. iv to exploring the social class assumptions of strong frames within visible pedagogies.

2 Bernstein calls these singulars, regions, and generic. (1990: vol. ch. 3).

3 In contrast to what he called competence models where only what is present in the text is evaluated.

4 Other forms of pupil talk are classroom talk, subject talk, and identity talk (see Arnot and Reay, 2005).

References

Arnot, M. (2004) 'Freedom's' Children: A Gender Perspective on the Education of the Learner Citizen, Paper to the Plenary Session for the Nordic Educational Research Association, Reykjavik, March

Arnot, M. and Reay, D. (2004) 'The Framing of Pedagogic Encounters: Regulating the Social Order of Classroom Learning', in J. Muller, B. Davies and A. Morais (eds), *Reading Bernstein, Researching Bernstein*, London: RoutledgeFalmer

Arnot, M. (2005) 'Power, Pedagogic Voices and Pedagogic Encounters: The Implications for Pupil Consultation as Transformative Practice', in R. Moore, M. Arnot, J. Beck and H. Daniels (eds), *Knowledge, Power and Social Change*, London: Routledge

Arnot, M., McIntyre, D., Pedder, D. and Reay, D. (2004) *Consultation in the Classroom: Pupil Perspectives on Teaching and Learning*, Cambridge: Pearson

Beck, J. (1999) 'Makeover or Takeover? The Strange Death of Educational Autonomy in Neo-Liberal England', *British Journal of Sociology of Education* 20/2:223-38

Beck, J. (1992) *Risk Society: Towards a New Modernity*, London: Sage

Bernstein, B. (1975) *Class, Codes and Control*, London: Routledge and Kegan Paul

Bernstein, B. (1977) *Class, Codes and Control, Towards a Theory of Educational Transmissions*, 2nd edn. London: Routledge and Kegan Paul

Bernstein, B. (1990) *Class, Codes and Control, The Structuring of Pedagogic Discourse*, London: Routledge

Bernstein, B. (2000) *Pedagogy, Symbolic Control and Identity: Theory, Research, Critique*, 1st edn. Oxford: Rowman and Littlefield

Bernstein, B. (1990) *The Structuring of Pedagogic Discourse: Class, Codes and Control*, London: Routledge

Bernstein, B. (2000) *Pedagogy, Symbolic Control and Identity: Theory, Research, Critique*, 2nd edn. London: Taylor and Francis; Oxford: Rowman and Littlefield

Bourne, J. (2000) 'New Imaginings of Reading for a New Moral Order. A Review of the Production, Transmission and Acquisition of a New Pedagogic Culture in the UK', *Linguistics and Education* 11/1:31-45

Moss, G. (2004) 'Text and Technologies of Regulation: Using Bernstein's Theory to Explore the National Literacy Strategy as a Performance Pedagogy for New Times', Paper presented at the 3rd International Basil Bernstein Conferences, Cambridge.

Reay, D. and Arnot, M. (2004) 'Participation and Control in Learning: A Pedagogic Democratic Right?', in L. Poulson (ed), *Learning to Read Critically in Teaching and Learning*, London: Sage

Chapter 3

An introduction to teacher research

Colin Lankshear and Michele Knobel

Three points of general agreement about teacher research

Three points of broad consensus among those who write about teacher research can be noted here.

Teacher research is non-quantitative (non-psychometric; non-positivist; non-experimental) research

During the past 30 years much teacher research activity has been undertaken to counter the long-standing domination of educational research by quantitative, 'scientistic' research. As an identifiable movement, teacher research has been conceived and 'grown' as intentional oppositional practice to the fact that classroom life and practice is driven by research based on narrow experimental, psychometric ('rats and stats') approaches to social science (see Fishman and McCarthy, 2000: ch.1).

Who teacher researchers are

It is widely agreed that teacher research involves teachers researching their own classrooms – with or without collaborative support from other teachers. As Stephen Fishman and Lucille McCarthy note, it seems that 'there is agreement about the 'who' of [teacher research] ... [T]eacher research means, at the least, teachers researching their own classrooms' (Fishman and McCarthy, 2000: 9). There are two aspects here. First, teacher research is confined to direct or immediate research of classrooms. Second, the chief researcher in any piece of teacher research is the teacher whose classroom is under investigation.

The goals and purposes of teacher research

Several authors (eg. Cochran-Smith and Lytle, 1993; Hopkins, 1993; Fishman and McCarthy, 2000) have clustered a range of widely shared views of the purposes and ideals of teacher research around two key concepts. One is about enhancing teachers' sense of professional role and identity. The other is the idea that engaging in teacher research can contribute to better quality teaching and learning in classrooms.

David Hopkins (1993:34) refers to Lawrence Stenhouse's idea that involvement in research can help contribute to teachers' experiences of dignity and self-worth by supporting their capacity to make informed professional judgements. The main idea here is that teaching should be recognised and lived as a professional engagement. As professionals, teachers do not merely follow prescriptions and formulae laid down for them from on high. Rather, they draw on their expertise and specialist knowledge as educators to pursue educational goals that have been established democratically.

From this perspective, teachers should not be treated like or thought of as 'functionaries' or 'operatives' who carry out closely specified routine tasks. Instead, like doctors, lawyers and architects, they draw on a shared fund of professional knowledge and accumulated experience to take them as far as possible in specific situations. When they need to go beyond that shared 'professional wisdom' they draw on specialist educational knowledge, experience, networks, and their capacity for informed autonomous judgement to make decisions about how best to promote learning objectives. They do this case by case. Doing this successfully, having this success recognised and accorded the respect due to it, and seeing the fruits of their professional expertise and autonomy manifested in objective growth and learning on the part of students, provide the major sources of teacher satisfaction (see Stenhouse, 1975; Hopkins, 1993; Fishman and McCarthy, 2000: ch.1).

Teacher research is seen as an important means by which teachers can develop their capacity for making the kinds of sound autonomous professional judgements and decisions appropriate to their status as professionals. More specific benefits often associated with recognition of professional status include 'increased power for teachers', 'respect for teachers', 'greater justice for teachers', 'greater confidence and motivation on the part of teachers', 'empowerment' and 'greater voice' for teachers (see Fishman and McCarthy, 2000:13-14).

The second generally shared end or purpose of teacher research is that it can contribute demonstrably to improving teaching or instruction. This can happen in different ways. Through their own research teachers may become aware of things they do in their teaching that might result in students learning less than they otherwise could. With this awareness they can make informed changes to try and enhance learning outcomes. Conversely, existing research might identify interventions or approaches that work positively under certain conditions. Teachers in similar contexts to those where research has shown success might then be able to adapt these approaches productively in their own settings. Alternatively, teacher research provides opportunities for teachers to test the effectiveness of interventions they believe could enhance learning outcomes for some or all of their students. Where interventions are successful, the teachers who conducted the original research, and others who become aware of it, may be able to implement and adapt these interventions to obtain improved outcomes beyond the original settings.

Joe Kincheloe (2003:ch.1) advocates a further ideal for teacher research. This is as a means by which teachers can resist the current trend towards the domination of curriculum and pedagogy by 'technical standards' based on 'expert research' and imposed in a top-down manner by educational administrators and policy makers. In the grip of this trend, the curriculum has become highly standardised. The diversity of school communities, school settings, and student needs and backgrounds are dis-regarded. Teachers of the same grades within the same subject areas are required to 'cover the same content, assign the same importance to the content they cover, and evaluate it in the same way' (Marzano and Kendall, 1997; Kincheloe, 2003:4).

According to Kincheloe, this standards-based approach to educational reform subverts democratic education on several levels. It negates the principle of respect for diversity at the level of communities, schools and students alike, pitting likes against unlikes on the myth of a level playing field. It also marginalises teachers in the process of curriculum development and goal-setting based on professional knowledge and interpretation of learning goals for local needs and conditions. Moreover, domination of curriculum and pedagogy by technical standards subverts the proper critical and evaluative purposes of education by confining activity to mastering pre-determined content and subverting the development of analytic and interpretive capacities during the important early and middle years of schooling. Invoking work by Madison (1988) and Capra (1996), Kincheloe argues that the 'reductionist ways of seeing, teaching and learning' inherent in current education reform directions 'pose a direct threat to education as a practice of democracy' (2003:9).

Kincheloe argues that in this context embracing the ideal of teachers as researchers becomes an important facet of challenging the 'oppressive culture created by positivistic standards' (2003:18). He observes that teachers 'do not live in the same professional culture as researchers', and that the knowledge base informing educational directions and emphases is 'still ... produced far away from the school by experts in a rarefied domain' (p18). This, he says, must change 'if democratic reform of education is to take place ... and a new level of educational rigour and quality [is] ever to be achieved'. By joining researcher culture teachers will:

- begin to understand the power implications of technical standards
- appreciate the benefits of research, particularly in relation to 'understanding the forces shaping education that fall outside [teachers'] immediate experience and perception

- begin to understand [in deeper and richer ways] what they know from experience
- become more aware of how they can contribute to educational research
- be seen as learners rather than functionaries who follow top-down orders without question
- be seen as knowledge workers who reflect on their professional needs and current understandings
- become more aware of how complex the schooling process is and how it cannot be understood apart from the social, historical, philosophical, cultural, economic, political, and psychological contexts that shape it
- research their own professional practice
- explore the learning processes occurring in their classrooms and attempt to interpret them
- analyse and contemplate the power of each other's ideas
- constitute a new critical culture of school in the manner of a think tank that teaches students
- reverse the trend toward the deskilling of teachers and stupidification of students (Kincheloe, 2003:18-19; see also Norris, 1998; Kraft, 2001; Bereiter, 2002).

[...]

Against the prevailing view of who teacher researchers are

Our view of teacher research rejects both aspects of teacher researcher identity associated with the mainstream view. First, we do not believe that teacher research must be confined to direct or immediate research of classrooms. Although the ultimate point of impact sought from teacher research is on what occurs in classrooms, it does not follow that this end is best served solely through direct empirical study of classrooms. Teachers may learn much of value for informing and guiding their current practice by investigating historical, anthropological, sociological or psychological studies, and theoretical work conducted in other places and/or at other times. These could be studies of policy, communities, social class, the work world, non-standard language varieties and so on. Teachers with an interest in relating or interpreting documentary data with a view to forming hypotheses or provisional explanations of practice might gain a great deal from purely philosophical and theoretical discussions of educational issues they consider pertinent to their work. Alternatively, they might generate their own analyses of secondary (other people's) data that have been collected in contexts similar in important ways to their own, in order to get perspectives for thinking about their own work prior to researching their own settings. (Such data might reflect patterns of educational attainment associated with variables like ethnic or linguistic background, social class, gender, forms of disability, etc.) To confine teacher research to immediate investigation of classroom settings may cut teachers off from opportunities to gain important insights and knowledge they might miss by simply doing one more classroom study.

Second, we disagree that teacher research should be defined in terms of teachers researching their own classrooms. This is not the same concept as that of conducting research pertinent to one's own professional practice. While the two are related, they are quite distinct. We often get clearer understandings of ourselves and our own practices, beliefs, assumptions, values, opinions, worldviews and the like by encountering ones that are quite different from our own, throwing our own into relief and providing us with a perspective on them. Indeed, obtaining critical and evaluative distance can be extremely difficult if we stay within the bounds of our familiar discursive contexts and experiences.

Jim Gee's (1996) idea that 'bi- (or multi-) discoursal' people are often the most likely agents of innovation and change has important parallels for teacher investigations of teaching and learning in context. Even if we have access to the ideas and perspectives of others – such as where one invites colleagues to assist in investigating one's own classroom – there is no guarantee that variations in available perspectives, attitudes and experiences will be sufficient to help us recognise and question our existing standpoints, or to understand our own practice more fully in ways that can enhance it. On the contrary, confining teacher research to the study of our own classrooms in the company of our peers might actually be a powerful conservative force within what is widely identified as being a very conservative professional domain. As Stephen Hodas (1993:1, citing David Cohen, 1987) observes in relation to the culture of technology refusal in schools, 'the structure of schools and the nature of teaching have remained substantially unchanged for seven hundred years, and there exists in the popular mind a definite, conservative conception of what schools should be like, a template from which schools stray only at their peril'.

Furthermore, we do not think teacher research must be conducted independently of formal academic involvement. We see no reason why teachers might not enrol in formal academic programmes to conduct research relevant to their own teaching needs and interests. The crucial point is that the purposes or objects of teacher research must flow from the authentic (or felt) questions, issues and concerns of teachers themselves (see Berthoff, 1987; Bissex, 1987). This is, perhaps, the key point that demarcates teacher research from academic research, contract research and non-practitioner research in general. In teacher research the ways these issues and concerns are addressed must be answerable and responsive to teachers' own decisions and ideas about what is helpful and relevant.

This is perfectly compatible with formal suggestions, inputs, collaboration and guidance on the part of academic and professional researchers, offered within or outside formal programme settings. Everything depends on the facts of particular cases about how the relations and obligations of teacher researchers and academics running formal programmes are contracted. Under current conditions academic educationists are increasingly expected to be responsive to 'client' demand and to pursue flexibility that is consistent with individual preferences. Hence, the institutional climate is in principle, and very often in practice, perfectly compatible with the ideal of teacher research building on teachers' own questions, wonderings, hypotheses and concerns.

From this standpoint we identify teacher researchers as 'classroom practitioners at any level, from preschool to tertiary, who are involved individually or collaboratively in self-motivated and self-generated systematic and informed inquiry undertaken with a view to enhancing their vocation as professional educators'. The idea of enhancing one's vocation as a professional educator covers internal aspects like achieving greater personal satisfaction and a heightened sense of worth, purpose, direction and fulfilment, as well as external aspects like improving the effectiveness of one's teaching practice in significant areas.

Hence, teacher research can be done in classrooms, libraries, homes, communities and anywhere else where one can obtain, analyse and interpret information pertinent to one's vocation as a teacher. It can be undertaken within formal academic programmes, or as an entirely self-directed individual undertaking, or under any number of semi-formal arrangements that exist between these two extremes. Teacher research may involve empirical observation of classrooms (one's own or other people's), systematic reflection upon one's own documented experiences, or close engagement with theoretical or conceptual texts and issues. It can use people, policy texts, web-based materials, secondary data sets and so on as sources of information. Finally, it can be grounded in data coming from the present or the past, and even in data concerned with the future. Its potential scope and variety are enormous.

Teacher research and professional enhancement

[...] What is it about participating in teacher research that supports the capacity of teachers to make the kinds of informed professional judgements that are conducive to generating improvements in teaching and learning? How does researching contribute to teachers experiencing dignity and self-worth as teachers, and to countering policies and practices that undermine a democratic ideal of education? We think the relationship is best understood as follows.

The process of engaging with well-informed sources through processes of reading relevant literature and talking with people who have thought about and investigated issues and concerns similar to our own is a potent source of obtaining ideas and insights that can produce results and bestow the kind of confidence that comes with being reliably informed. This involves more than just chatting with people and skimming over surfaces of experience. It is about getting in deeply enough to find plausible viewpoints, perspectives and explanations pertaining to our concerns and questions. These are viewpoints and perspectives that require us to make serious evaluative judgements and decisions about which of them are worth trying out, and which it may be best to start with in trying to address our own concerns. It certainly involves looking for approaches that challenge us to question some of our own assumptions and to do more than just go along with the crowd or with what other people we know are doing. There is often a temptation in education to hope for magic bullets and quick fixes, at the level of theory and practice alike. The current fetish for constructivism, which has come to mean all things to all people, is a case in point. The serious professional will take the time to check out what is said by both the supporters and critics of constructivism, and will strive to sort out better and more robust accounts from pop and bandwagon versions, as well as to consider plausible alternative concepts and theories.

The kind of reading and discussion involved here aims at trying to understand and explain the sorts of things with which one is concerned as a teacher. It is not simply a matter of 'looking for something that works' but of aiming to understand why it works and how it works, and to think about where it might not work, and why. This is to have an interest in theory, although not in a highbrow or abstract academic sense. We mean here theory in the sense of seriously looking for patterns, relationships, principles and regularities associated with situations, experiences, and phenomena that help us to understand and explain why something might be the case and how far it might apply beyond our immediate contexts. In this sense a serious teacher researcher is not interested merely in something that works, but in understanding how and why it works and/or how it might need to be adapted in order to work in other circumstances or to apply to other cases. This is about wanting to understand what makes things tick in education. It involves more than just information and ideas *per se*. Moreover, it is about seeing our understandings and explanations as provisional and corrigible so that we are open to understanding issues, problems and challenges more fully and deeply, and from different perspectives.

Of course there is much more to professional enhancement and doing research than reading and reflecting alone. The potential value for professional enhancement of involvement in teacher research has a lot to do with thinking and proceeding in ways that are imaginative and creative and, at the same time, methodical, systematic and logical. This is what we do in research when we 'nut out' how to construct a tool or instrument for collecting data (eg. a survey, an interview schedule or an approach to observing classroom interactions) that is consistent with a concept, belief or theory we want to apply or test out. To develop one's own data collection tools in this manner involves creativity and imagination. At the same time it requires being methodical and rigorous in the sense of trying to translate the original concept or theory into tools that are consistent with it. In other words, our data collection tool must be a faithful practical or applied interpretation of the original concept, belief or theory.

In the first place, this means being very clear about the concept, and understanding what it involves in ways that allow us to ask the kinds of questions or develop the kinds of observation routines that really do tap into what the concept (or theory) is about. This is a demanding form of higher order thinking: it involves careful interpretation and creative appropriation based on clarity and understanding. Even if we decide not to develop our own data collection tool but, rather, to use one that someone has already developed, we need to engage in the same degree of interpretation to know which available option fits best with the concept or theory or, indeed, if one that we are thinking of using actually fits at all.

The same applies to deciding how we will analyse our data – whether this is fresh data we collect in the course of our research, extant (secondary) data collected by others or data we already have available to us through personal and collegial experience (Berthoff, 1987). Knowing how to make sense of one's data – to sort it into appropriate categories, or to identify within it the kinds of patterns or regularities that may help us understand and explain something relevant – is a demanding interpretative and reflective act. We have to devise approaches to analysis that cohere with the concepts and theories that are informing our research and that will throw light on the question or problem we are investigating. Beyond this, we need to know how to interpret our data analysis in ways that are consistent with our problem and our research approach.

These and other qualities and processes add up to being a particular kind of thinker, designer, creator, troubleshooter and practitioner in one's capacity as a teacher. It is this, we believe, that contributes to our professional enhancement. This is what carries a teacher beyond being a routine operative to a person who thinks and acts and reflects in ways that have become associated with being a professional. [...]

Source: Lankshear, C. and Knobel, M. (2004) 'An introduction to teacher research', A Handbook for Teacher Research: *From design to implementation*, Open University Press. Copyright (c) Colin Lankshear and Michele Knobel 2004. Reproduced with the kind permission of Open University Press. All rights reserved

References

Bereiter, C. (2002) *Education and the Mind in the Knowledge Age.* Mahwah, NJ: Lawrence Erlbaum

Berthoff, A. (1987) The Teacher researcher, in D. Goswami and P. Stillman (eds) *Reclaiming the Classroom: Teacher Research as an Agency for Change*, pp28-39. Portsmouth, NH: Boynton/Cook-Heinemann. The original paper was presented in 1979 at the Annual Conference of the Association of English Teachers in San Diego

Bissex, G. (1987) What is teacher research? in G. Bissex and R. Bullock (eds) *Seeing For Ourselves: Case-Study Research by Teachers of Writing*, pp4-5. Portsmouth, NH: Heinemann Educational Books

Capra, F. (1996) *The Web of Life: A New Scientific Understanding of Living Systems.* New York: Anchor Books

Cochran-Smith, M. and Lytle, S. (1993) *Inside/Outside: Teacher Research and Knowledge.* New York: Teachers College Press

Delamont, S. (1992) *Fieldwork in Educational Settings: Methods, Pitfalls and Perspectives.* London: Falmer Press

Fishman, S. and McCarthy, L. (2000) *Unplayed Tapes: A Personal History of Collaborative Teacher Research.* New York: Teachers College Press

Gee, J. (1996) *Social Linguistics and Literacies: Ideology in Discourse*, 2nd edn. London: Falmer Press

Hodas, S. (1993) Technology refusal and the organizational culture of schools, *Education Policy Analysis Archives*, 1(10):1-9

Hopkins, D. (1993) *A Teacher's Guide to Classroom Research*, 2nd edn. Buckingham: Open University Press

Kincheloe, J. (2003) *Teachers as Researchers: Qualitative Inquiry as a Path to Empowerment,* 2nd edn. New York: Falmer

Knobel, M. and Lankshear, C. (1999) *Ways of Knowing: Researching Literacy.* Newtown NSW: Primary English Teaching Association

Kraft, N. (2001) Certification of teachers – a critical analysis of standards in teacher education programs, in J. Kincheloe and D. Weil (eds) *Standards and Schooling in the United States: An Encyclopedia.* Santa Barbara, CA: ABC-Clio

Lincoln, Y. and Guba, E. (1985) *Naturalistic Inquiry.* Beverley Hills, CA: Sage

Madison, G. (1988) *The Hermeneutics of Postmodernity: Figures and Themes.* Bloomington, IN: Indiana University Press

Marshall, C. and Rossman, G. (1999) *Designing Qualitative Research*, 3rd edn. Thousand Oaks, CA: Sage

Marzano, R. and Kendall, J. (1997) *The Fall and Rise of Standards-Based Education: A National Association of School Boards of Education (NASBE) Issues in Brief.* Aurora, CO: Mid-Continent Research for Education and Learning

Norris, N. (1998) Curriculum valuation revisited, *Cambridge Journal of Education*, 28(2):207-19

Stenhouse, L. (1975) *An Introduction to Curriculum Research and Development.* London: Heinemann

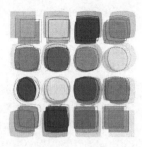

Chapter 4

Positivistic standards and the bizarre educational world of the twenty-first century

Joe L. Kincheloe

[...]

Technicalising and deskilling approaches to education are the direct result of particular Western ways of seeing the world, the nature of human beings, the developmental processes of the young, the composition of the mind, and the production of knowledge. [...]

Technical standards, standardisation, and educational irrationality

The top-down technical standards of the contemporary reform movement are so specific in their prescribed list of 'facts' to be covered that the best teachers are handcuffed in their effort to teach complex concepts and to connect them to the lived experiences of students (Pushkin, 2001). In this irrational context such teachers are victimised by a simplistic and panicky response to social change, youth-in-crisis, or a decline in standardised test scores. Relying on reductionistic measurements of student memorisation of unconnected fragments of information, advocates of top-down, imposed content standards have no basis for evaluating more sophisticated aspects of learning and teaching (Bereiter, 2002). Indeed, they cannot measure even the traditional skills of good scholars, not to mention the innovative and evolving operations of intellects coming from diverse cultures and counter-Cartesian-Newtonian-Baconian locales. Even the work of Albert Einstein in physics – portions of which such as the Special Theory of Relativity are almost a century old – cannot be taught, learned, or evaluated in the intellectual and pedagogical quagmire of top-down standards (Kincheloe, Steinberg and Tippins, 1999).

Technical standards demand that teachers in the same subjects and grade levels cover the same content, assign the same importance to the content they cover, and evaluate it in the same way (Marzano and Kendall, 1999). Such standardisation ignores the profound differences between diverse schools, school settings, student needs, and so on. As teacher-author Susan Ohanian (1999) puts it: 'a one-size-fits-all curriculum ends up fitting nobody' (p43). As it fits nobody, such an educational arrangement subverts the possibility that self-directed teacher professionals might research school atmospheres, the communities surrounding schools, student needs, the disciplinary and counter-disciplinary knowledges constituting the curriculum, and the administrative *modus operandi* of both their districts and their schools. Informed by these understandings, such teachers as researchers could better develop and implement a curriculum connected to the vicissitudes and exigencies of their unique situations.

Such teachers are threats in the eyes of advocates of top-down, technical, and standardised standards. Such teachers seek out diverse perspectives, confront students with conflicting information and different interpretations of the same data. They raise questions in the minds of their students and colleagues – an unappreciated activity in the technicalised status quo. One thing that right-wing advocates of technical standards don't want is for students to question the 'facts'. In this desire they are similar to the educational agents of totalitarian political regimes throughout human history. Democratic educational leaders, simply put, don't repress questions about curriculum or pedagogy. In the contemporary context of top-down, unquestionable standards, the purpose of education becomes based more on the desire for social regulation than for emancipation and freedom. Teachers and students become objects of management, a mode of discipline that serves particular private interests (Weil, 2001b).

In these politico-educational arrangements students – the poor and racially marginalised ones in particular – face the consequences of this pedagogical irrationality: deskilled and dispirited teachers, over-emphasis on standards test preparation, already inadequate educational monies diverted to test preparation materials, and vacuous and fatuous skill and drill exercises (Linne, 2001). Unsurprisingly, many of the more academically talented teachers leave the profession. Such teachers speak with great emotion of the anti-intellectual culture of such schools and the obstacles they faced in their desire to be challenging and inspirational [...] The Cartesian-Newtonian-Baconian view of the mind is one of the numerous historical concepts at work in the technical standards fiasco described here. In this conceptualisation the mind is not a constructor of reality but merely a filing cabinet into which unproblematised, objective data can be stored.

In this reductionistic modernist perspective not only is the mind a filing cabinet but knowledge is a discrete object that is found in people's brains and reference books.

Good teaching, thus, becomes stuffing as much of this knowledge into students' minds as possible. Unfortunately, the Cartesian story goes, some of the students' filing cabinets are much bigger than others and there is nothing educators can do about that (Howley, Pendarvis and Howley, 1993; Bereiter, 2002). The idea that mind and knowledge are complex entities is lost in this context. The notion that understanding this complexity and using it as an embarkation point for future cognitive development and exploration of the cosmos is central to becoming a great scholar and a brilliant teacher is not understood in contemporary schooling. Here is a conceptual window through which we can escape the age of mediocrity and the dumbed-down schools of technical standards. [...]

Even when leaders make grand pronouncements about setting tough new standards, such declarations are rarely accompanied by tangible resources to implement them. This is justified by free-market references to the failure of the public space and the elevation of the private realm of business as the proper locale for educational endeavour. In this right-wing ideological context one might argue that standards reforms are set up to fail. In the wake of such failure it will be much easier to justify corporate-run, for-profit schools. In this privatised context the need for scholarly teachers who raise questions about the curriculum will be finally erased. In this cleansed context the work of ideological regulation can continue uncontested (Apple, 1993; Ohanian, 1999; Malewski, 2001b).

In the short run, however, technical standards work to destroy intellectually rigorous educational programmes (Fenimore-Smith and Pailliotet, 2001) and undermine concern with the nature and best interests of learners. Studies suggest that once top-down technical standards are imposed, students become progressively disengaged from the process of learning. Curricular standardisation particularly subverts the efforts of poor and minority students, as they quickly lose touch with the curriculum and classroom assignments (Novick, 1996). Indeed, technical content standards violate a key pedagogical principle: educational experience should be tied to the psychological and social investments of the learner. This does not mean advocacy of some simplistic effort to be relevant, but a more complex concern with engaging the libidinal energy of students with the pedagogical process.

Brilliant teachers when free from technical constraints work tirelessly to connect disciplinary and counter-disciplinary information with the fears, joys, questions, dreams, aspirations, and interpersonal relationships of their students. Without such connections education can be a supremely empty process. When the real-life experiences and personal investigations of students are no longer germane to curriculum development, the battle for a rigorous intellectual and motivating education is almost lost (Foote and Goodson, 2001; Schubert and Thomas, 2001). Teachers who are researchers study student backgrounds and needs in order to avoid such a pedagogical tragedy. These concerns encompass the basic themes of this book.

Knowledge in top-down standards

As we dig deeper into the educational effects of top-down technical standards we begin to realise that many problematic assumptions are hidden within them. [...] In many ways the technical standards view of knowledge is philosophically impaired. How advocates of technical standards describe knowing, assess what is worthy of being known, and evaluate knowledge exerts profound impact on the nature of class-room teaching (Mayers, 2001b). Technicist educators, John Dewey (1916) argued decades ago, view knowledge as an entity complete in itself unconnected to other forces.

The technicist, positivist tradition of producing knowledge – from which contemporary top-down standards emerge – seeks to provide a timeless body of truth. This so-called 'formal knowledge' is not only unconnected to the world but separate from issues of commitment, emotion, values, and ethical action. The objectivity inscribed in formal knowledge often becomes a signifier for political passivity and elevation to an elite sociopolitical and economic location. Thus, in its lofty position, positivistic formalism refuses to analyse the relationship between knowledge production and educational practices. In technical standards teachers are presented with formal knowledge and expected forthwith to deliver it to their classrooms.

[...]

Reductionism and technical standards: the jail break to complexity

This obsession with order and tidiness is one aspect of Cartesian reductionism (Lemke, 1995). [...] Implicit in this Cartesian reductionism is the belief that there are limited and correct meanings to be derived from any phenomenon. And the purpose of schooling is to simply pass on such meanings to students.

Thus, in a reductionistic pedagogical context meanings need to be discovered, rediscovered, and copied. Student analysis and interpretation in this context are an attempt to reconstruct what the scientist produced or, again, the meaning the author intended. These epistemological dynamics tacitly shape the purposes of schooling and the nature of classroom life. A reductionistic paradigm discourages the preparation of inquisitive, knowledge-producing, critical students and teachers; a more complex paradigm encourages more sceptical participants who appreciate the hidden dimensions of knowledge production and the complicity of power in all aspects of the pedagogical process. My argument here is direct: reductionist ways of seeing, teaching, and learning pose a direct threat to education as a practice of democracy (Madison, 1988; Capra, 1996).

Educators who support teacher professionalism look at the reductionistic technical standards with fear and trembling. Because teaching is viewed as a neat and tidy act, it can be standardised and monitored. Susan Ohanian (1999) describes a question and answer session at a Reading Summit in Illinois in 1996. After an advocate of technical standards had spoken on the need for 'highly structured, intense [reading] programmes that explicitly teach application of phonological rules to print', an educator in the audience raised questions about the desirability and feasibility of controlling a teacher's methods of teaching and individual style. The speaker replied:

We had careful monitoring of the teachers. First there was thirty hours of training during the summer. Then every teacher was monitored in the classroom every other week – or every day, if necessary. We were breathing down the necks both of raw recruits and veteran teachers. The teacher variable does not contribute significantly above and beyond the curriculum, so what we have here is a powerful mathematical model. My hypothesis is the teacher variable will be less significant within the direct instruction group. (Ohaman:1999:49)

This is the language – 'teacher variable' – and mindset of reductionism. The chilling implication here is that teachers are less important than the standards and techniques employed by the experts. The obvious question that arises in this context is why employ educated teachers if this is the case. Find friendly young people, preferably large for purposes of classroom control, who can read at about the seventh-grade level; provide them with scripted material and a six-week training course in teaching techniques and turn them loose in the school. Much money could be saved – hell, we could pay them minimum wages. As soon as the technology is ready, we can replace these functionaries with computer-teachers. No need for teachers as researchers here.

There is something surreal about such perspectives. Proponents of such reductionist, top-down, dehumanised modes of pedagogy and regulation seem to operate at what Ed O'Sullivan refers to as a 'preconscious, non-reflective state' (1999:34). In this Cartesian trance individuals seem to operate without any consciousness of the contradictions operating in their positions, without an awareness of the anti-democratic strategies they implement, without insight into the way their plans degrade and demoralise the teaching profession. In this reductionistic jailhouse questions involving the educational gaps between the rich and poor are deemed inappropriate. Questions about indoctrination fall on deaf ears. Such problems do not lend themselves to neat reductionistic measurement with handy quantitative results.

Technical standards offer profoundly simplistic answers to difficult socio-educational questions. How is it possible to solve educational problems that are connected to so many social, cultural, historical, political, philosophical, and economic dynamics circulating around them? If the lived world is a complex place, then the lived world of school is a complex place squared. Appreciating the complex and diverse forms of knowing that are needed to deal with the lived world is sobering to even the most brilliant among us. Formal thinking and the formal operations of breaking down phenomena into their smallest parts for analysis fail to raise questions of value to employ the insight of diverse contextualisation. Without these more complex dynamics at work we end up with technical-standards-driven schools that stupify more than they edify (Hinchey, 1998, 2001). [...]

In the ethnocentric view 'true knowledge' can only be produced by a detached, disinterested, external observer who works to ignore background (contextual) information by developing objective research techniques. In human history most of the great wisdom generated has not been constructed in this manner (Shotter, 1993, 1998). It is not surprising that no institution has carried these Cartesian blinders more zealously than education. As we see so clearly in the contemporary standards movement – a movement that in a sociopolitical and cultural context might be labelled as part of a broader Cartesian recovery impulse – any historical analysis of what has motivated this mode of pedagogical reform is irrelevant. [...]

In the cultural context the technical standards movement's call for standardisation takes on even more ideological baggage. Not only a manifestation of hyperrationalisation, the standardisation of curriculum becomes a means of ensuring ethnocentrism in the classroom. Such an ethnocentrism is suspicious of concepts such as diversity, multiple perspectives, criticality, difference, and multiculturalism. Ideologically, it works covertly to promote the interests of the dominant culture over less powerful minority cultures. Such interests involve the power of the privileged to maintain their privilege, as students from economically poorer families, those students whose families possess the least formal education, are transformed into 'test liabilities' (Ohanian, 1999; Vinson and Ross, 2001). In such a category their problems in school can be blamed on their inferiority – 'we tried to teach them the information mandated by the standards but they just didn't have the ability to get it. There's nothing more we can do.'

In this power-centred context dominant European interests and needs are validated while those individuals who fall outside dominant cultural borders are forced to struggle for legitimacy. Technical standards become regulatory forces that limit the professional discretion of teachers while ensuring that the individual needs of students in some way alienated from the culture and discourses of schools are rendered irrelevant (Giroux, 1997). In both a macro- and micro-social context we watch the fragmentary influences of Euromodernism and the ethnocentrism it produces do their 'bad work'. At the macro level Westerners are alienated from other cultures around the world, as Cartesian ways of seeing and producing knowledge fragment the wholeness that connects us to both each other and the planet in general (Capra, 1996). In a micro context this Cartesianism separates classroom knowledge from its embeddedness in the lived world and its meaning in our lives, rendering it abstract data to be learned for an absurd standards text.

Positivism and learning: certifying fragmentation

[...] Positivism is the prevalent view of knowledge (epistemology) in the history of Western science. Coming into general philosophical usage in the nineteenth century, positivism assumes that nature is orderly and knowable via scientific method and that all phenomena have natural causes. In a positivistic educational context human-created knowledge is conceptualised as a physical substance handed from one individual to another through teaching. The receiver in this positivistic context is nothing more than a passive recipient who merely accepts the 'physical entity' that has been passed along to him or her (Lee, 1997).

As receivers uncritically take in information in the decontextualised positivistic framework, they are anaesthetised into believing that meaning resides in the information fragment itself rather in the network of relationships from which it was retrieved. When educational leaders operate with such a tacit belief embedded in their consciousness, it is much easier for them to fall into an obsession with standards test performance. Losing sight of the complexity of knowledge production and the contextualised nature of teaching for understanding, superintendents, supervisors, and principals focus on the mastery of those factoids included in standardised tests. The stories teachers tell about these obsessions are chilling. As one teacher in Brooklyn described it:

Our principal has gone nuts. He checks all classrooms to make sure we display charts he made depicting our place in the rankings of school test performance in the city. One teacher had temporarily taken down the chart to put up some student work. The principal screamed at her in front of the students. She was a mess; we thought she was going to get fired. For over two months before students take the test, we are not allowed to do anything but prep them for it: test-taking skills, rote memorisation, flash cards, and things like that. He has spies checking up on us to make sure we do nothing else. I can't stay there another year. It'll make me as crazy as he is.

[...]

Positivism, standards, and student needs

In the rule-orientation, epistemological *naiveté*, and decontextualisation of positivist standards, many educational and political leaders maintain that the 'conditions of schools, the material well-being of families, and the dynamics of communities are not even worth thinking about' (Books, 2001). Such contextual features have nothing to do with schooling or its improvement in a positivistic cosmos concerned only with providing the correct data to be learned and the correct rules for teachers to follow in inculcating this eviscerated information. As long as the proper curricular information is clearly delineated and teachers follow the script, advocates of top-down standards assure the public that the economic, social, and psychological well-being of children and young people is a relatively minor variable. Such damnable nonsense is the common-sense of the twenty-first-century discourse of school reform.

If these student needs are not meet, young people will not learn well regardless of the brilliance of the pedagogy. Moreover, teachers who don't know their students well, don't know how their needs are or are not being met, or don't know what moves them, will always have trouble creating meaningful classrooms where learning takes place (Ohanian, 1999; Books, 2001). At this conceptual way station in the pedagogical journey teachers have to pause and carefully observe the ideological terrain around them. They have to wear their night-vision goggles to discern those forces that exist outside their immediate perceptions and experiences. Schooling, like the culture in general, is a domain of struggle where knowledge and power are always functions of one another.

Positivism is a philosophical/political force of domination. It deftly blinds observers and analysts to the conflicts and interests that covertly shape educational policy and classroom practice. Any force that has the power to convince individuals that student well-being is not a central factor in improving education must be addressed. The exposure and neutralisation of such a force must become a central objective of anyone who cares about children, teachers, democracy, justice, and the reform of education. Positivism's capacity to hide itself makes such a process as difficult as flushing terrorists out of remote mountain caves. Democratic educators must develop the capacity to persuade numerous groups and individuals that any pedagogy that dismisses student experience is inadequate for a humane democratic society.

Positivism in the guise of technical standards ignores students in the way it distorts understanding of self and world. Grounded on a reductionistic view of knowledge and curriculum, top-down standards consciously delete multiple perspectives on a topic and teach one ideologically inscribed perspective as truth. Such a perspective usually grants legitimacy to given institutional configurations, prevailing ways of seeing and being, and dominant cultural belief structures. The bloodstains left in the historical political struggle over these ideological positions are hidden, as conflict, oppression, and violence are conveniently erased.

Paulo Freire's (1970b) notion of the banking model of education still has the power to describe twenty-first-century standards curricula. The information transmitted is made only for deposit in mental filing cabinets – no interpretation is necessary. Such positivistic teaching does not encourage rigorous academic analysis; rather, it numbs the mind, producing intellectual passivity and blind rule following. Students and teachers are taught to accept and respect the power of dominant elites. Of course, not all of them will accept such teachings. Many will discern the ideological project confronting them and resist, while others will passively accept such attempts at consciousness construction (Giroux, 1997). Teachers as critical researchers expose this process and insist that it be analysed and studied by their colleagues and students.

Studying power: ideological consolidation in the twenty-first century

The type of critical inquiry and analysis I am advocating for empowered teacher researchers pays close attention to these issues of power (Horn, 2001). Critical teachers as researchers understand the centrality of power in understanding everyday life, knowledge production, curriculum development, and teaching. Power is implicated in all educational visions, it is omnipresent in reform proposals, and it is visible in delineations of what constitutes an educated person. It is the charge of teacher researchers to grasp these dynamics, to study them and to act on the basis of what they find. In such a process teacher researchers raise questions of intent and larger purpose in relation to particular practices. As students forge their way through elementary and secondary schooling, for example, are their experiences designed to adjust them to the existing social and economic order? What school experiences engage students in questioning the justice of that order and the desirability of such adjustment?

Studying the standards movement in numerous macro- and micro-contexts (Horn and Kincheloe, 2001; Kincheloe and Weil, 2001), I am struck by the absence of concern with the duties of democratic citizenship, the need for social change, and issues of justice. The notion of critique of counter-democratic forces, of threats to fragile democratic institutions, and of ideological indoctrination in the guise of education are simply not part of top-down, positivistic standards. Critical teacher researchers are alarmed by these omissions, as they watch state after state mandate authoritarian compliance audits to ensure that there is no deviation from the official curriculum, from memorisation of the 'approved knowledge of the Party'. The impositional nature of these reforms is a naked form of power that is so confident in its sovereignty it senses little need to mask itself. If such power is not challenged, the education it decrees is little more than an effort to produce social, political, and academic mind control (Nelson, 1998; Norris, 1998; Vinson and Ross, 2001).

The vision: teachers as researchers

In the existing world of schooling and especially in the new educational order being created by technical standards, teachers do not live in the same professional culture as researchers. Knowledge in contemporary education is still something that is produced far away from the school by experts in a rarefied domain. This must change if democratic reform of education is to take place. Teachers must join the culture of researchers if a new level of educational rigour and quality is ever to be achieved. In such a new democratised culture teacher scholars begin to understand the power implications of technical standards. In this context they appreciate the benefits of research, especially as they relate to understanding the forces shaping education that fall outside their immediate experience and perception. As these insights are constructed, teachers begin to understand what they know from experience. With this in mind they gain heightened awareness of how they can contribute to the research on education. Indeed, they realise that they have access to understandings that go far beyond what the expert researchers have produced.

In the new school culture teachers are viewed as learners – not as functionaries who follow top-down orders without question. Teachers are seen as researchers and knowledge workers who reflect on their professional needs and current understandings. They are aware of the complexity of the educational process and how schooling cannot be understood outside the social, historical, philosophical, cultural, economic, political, and psychological contexts that shape it. Scholar teachers understand that curriculum development responsive to student needs is not possible when it fails to account for these contexts. With this in mind they explore and attempt to interpret the learning processes that take place in their classrooms. What are its psychological, sociological, and ideological effects, they ask. Thus, scholar teachers research their own professional practice (Norris, 1998; Kraft, 2001; Bereiter, 2002).

With empowered scholar teachers prowling the schools, things begin to change. The oppressive culture created by positivistic standards is challenged. In-service staff development no longer takes the form of 'this is what the expert researchers found – now go do it'. Such staff development in the new culture gives way to teachers who analyse and contemplate the power of each other's ideas. Thus, the new critical culture of school takes on the form of a 'think tank that teaches students', a learning community. School administrators are amazed by what can happen when they support learning activities for both students and teachers. Principals and curriculum developers watch as teachers develop projects that encourage collaboration and shared research. There is an alternative to top-down standards with their deskilling of teachers and the stupidification of students (Novick, 1996; Jardine, 1998; Morris, 1998).

Promoting teachers as researchers is a fundamental way of cleaning up the damage of technical standards. Deskilling of teachers and dumbing-down of the curriculum take place when teachers are seen as receivers not producers of knowledge, A vibrant professional culture depends on a group of practitioners who have the freedom to continuously reinvent themselves via their research and knowledge production. Teachers engaged in complex, critical practice find it difficult to allow positivistic standards and their poisonous effects to go unchallenged. Such teachers cannot abide the deskilling and reduction in professional status that accompany these top-down reforms. Indeed, teacher empowerment does not occur just because we wish it to. Instead, it takes place when teachers develop the knowledge work skills and pedagogical abilities befitting the calling of teaching.

Technical standards are both based on and promote a reductionistic, truncated view of educational, social, and psychological research. The profound advances in research produced over the last thirty years are virtually ignored by advocates of positivistic standards. What we know or have developed the capacity to know about the complex world of teaching and learning grants educators a far more compelling and diverse view of schooling and its relationship to social, cultural, historical, economic, and psychological forces (Coben, 1998; Symes and Meadmore, 1999; Willinsky, 2001a). It is frustrating to watch these advances in research and knowledge production (Clough, 1998; Denzin and Lincoln, 2000) relegated to the trash heap, while outmoded and destructive modes of enquiry are recovered and legitimated. With their official status, such practices are rendered unquestionable. Teacher researchers have the difficult task of questioning the unquestionable.

Raising the questions: teacher researchers and educational rigour
[...]

In order to produce smarter teachers and higher-quality education, critical teacher researchers push the conceptual envelope. They understand that in some forms of action research issues of historical, sociological, cultural studies and philosophical influences on schooling are irrelevant. Despite the hard work in which teacher researchers might engage, an understanding of forces outside their immediate experiences was lost. Questions such as the following are not to be found in some action research contexts:

■ what is the social role of schooling in a democratic society?
■ what discourses shape the form that schooling takes?
■ what unseen forces help to construct student performance?
■ what are the ideological inscriptions of the curriculum?
■ how do epistemological assumptions affect the everyday life of the classroom?
■ what is the political impact of particular educational practices?
■ who defines what teacher research takes place? (Goodson, 1997, 1999)

Efficacious teacher research that leads to more rigorous and just forms of education assumes the importance of these questions and enquiries like them. In such research contextual factors are carefully studied and then classroom practices are analysed in relation to them. Connections are made, relational links are discerned, and processes and patterns are exposed. Teachers in such a context not only learn about knowledge production, but also learn how to expand their cognitive abilities in relation to inter-connected concepts. Obviously, positivistic standards preclude the need for such sophisticated teacher activity, as meaningful tasks and meaning making itself are subverted. The possibility of the development of rigorous education is undermined. I employ the term 'rigour' here not in its positivistic usage: the careful following of the fixed and predetermined steps of the scientific method. I appropriate and redefine the term as the democratic expression of the best education possible. [...]

Teaching for understanding and democratic social action is a central aspect of this rigorous 'best education possible'. The research process in these contexts is a central aspect of staff development, curricular policy, solving problems that face the school, and classroom activity (Novick, 1996). As we will explore throughout the book, a rigorous and just education demands that teachers research their students (Cannella, 1997; Soto, 1997, 2000; DuBois-Reymond, Sunker, and Krüger, 2001). We need to understand social and psychological conceptions of children and young people, as well as children's and young people's perceptions of themselves. Teachers as researchers explore their students' relationships to the world, the information climate produced by media and popular culture, and new modes of socialisation and enculturation in the twenty-first century. Teacher researchers monitor students' reactions to and perceptions of the new rigour and educational experiences in general. The point is simple: a sophisticated pedagogy cannot take place if teachers don't know their students (de Oliveira and Montecinos, 1998; Zeno, 1998).

If teachers don't know their students, what they know and don't know, their fears and their dreams, their failures and successes, they cannot help them construct a compelling and in-depth view of the world and their role in it. Without such insight, teachers cannot help students become knowledge workers in a knowledge-driven world. Students will find it difficult to make sense of existing data while learning to produce their own knowledge. When teacher researchers know their students, become experts in subject matter, and are adept knowledge workers, they are beginning to put together the skills that will help them become great teachers who motivate and inspire their students. As such teachers engage students with the world, they simultaneously make schools more rigorously academic and more practical in the world. [...]

Source: Kincheloe, L. J. (2003) 'Introduction: Positivistic standards and the bizarre educational world of the twenty-first Century', *Teachers as Researchers: Qualitative inquiry as a path to empowerment* (2nd ed), RoutledgeFalmer. Copyright (c) 2003 Joe L. Kincheloe. Reproduced by permission of Taylor & Francis Books UK

References

Apple, M. (1993) 'The politics of official knowledge: Does a national curriculum make sense?', *Teachers College Record*, 59, 3, pp.249-70

Bereiter, C. (2002) *Education and the Mind in the Knowledge Age*, Mahwah, NJ, Lawrence Erlbaum

Books, S. (2001) 'Saying poverty doesn't matter doesn't make it so', in J. Kincheloe and D. Weil (eds) *Standards and Schooling in the United States: An Encyclopedia*, Santa Barbara, CA, ABC-Clio

Cannella, G. (1997) *Deconstructing Early Childhood Education: Social Justice and Revolution*, New York, Peter Lang

Capra, F. (1996) *The Web of Life: A New Scientific Understanding of Living Systems*, New York, Teachers College Press

Clough, P. (1998) The Ends of Ethnography: From Realism to Social Criticism, New York, Peter Lang

Coben, D. (1998) *Radical Hereos: Gramsci, Freire and the Politics of Adult Education*, New York, Garland

Denzin, N. and Lincoln, Y. (eds) (2000) *Handbook of Qualitative Research*, Thousand Oaks, CA

De Oliveira, W. and Montecinos, C. (1998) 'Social pedagogy: Presence, commitment, identification and availability', *Teaching Education*, 9, 2

Dewey, J. (1916) *Democracy and Education*, New York, The Free Press

Du Bois-Raymond, M., Sünker, H. and Krüger, H. (2001) (eds) *Childhood in Europe*, New York, Peter Lang

Fenimore-Smith, T.K. and Pailliotet, A. (2001) 'Teacher education – Teaching standards of complexity in preservice education', in J. Kincheloe and D. Weil (eds) *Standards and Schooling in the United States: An Encyclopedia*, 3 vols, Santa Barbara, CA, ABC-Clio

Foote, M. and Goodson, I. (2001) 'Regulating teachers – A sword over their heads: The standards movement as a disciplinary device', in J. Kincheloe and D. Weil (eds) *Standards and Schooling in the United States: An Encyclopedia*, Santa Barbara, CA, ABC-Clio

Freire, P. (1970b) 'Research methods', Paper presented to a seminar entitled Studies in Adult Education, Dar-es-Salaam, Tanzania

Giroux, H. (1997) *Pedagogy and the Politics of Hope: Theory, Culture and Schooling*, Boulder, CO, Westview

Goodson, I. (1997) *The Changing Curriculum: Studies in Social Construction*, New York, Peter Lang

Goodson, I. (1999) 'The educational researcher as public intellectual', *British Educational Research Journal*, 25, 3, pp.277-97

Grof, S. (1993) *The Holotropic Mind*, New York, HarperCollins

Hinchey, P. (1998) *Finding Freedom in the Classroom: A Practical Introduction to Critical Theory*, New York, Peter Lang

Hinchey, P. (2001) 'Purposes of education – Educational standards: For whose purpose? For whose children?', in J. Kincheloe and D. Weil (eds) *Standards and Schooling in the United States: An Encyclopedia*, Santa Barbara, CA, ABC-Clio

Horn, R. (2001) 'Texas – A postformal conversation about standardisation and accountability in Texas', in J. Kincheloe and D. Weil (eds) *Standards and Schooling in the United States: An Encyclopedia*, Santa Barbara, CA, ABC-Clio

Horn, R. and Kincheloe, J. (eds) (2001) *American Standards: Quality Education in a Complex World*, New York, Peter Lang

Howley, A., Pendarvis, E. and Howley, C. (1993) 'Anti-intellectualism in US Schools', *Education Policy Analysis Archives*, 1, 6

Jardine, D. (1998) *To Dwell with a Boundless Heart: Essays in Curriculum Theory, Hermeneutics and the Ecological Imagination*, New York, Peter Lang

Kincheloe, J., Steinberg, S. and Tippins, D. (1999) *The Stigma of Genius: Einstein, Consciousness and Education*, New York, Peter Lang

Kincheloe, J. and Weil, D. (eds) (2001) *Standards and Schooling in the United States: An Encyclopedia*, Santa Barbara, CA, ABC-Clio

Kraft, N. (2001) 'Certification of teachers – A critical analysis of standards in teacher education programs', in J. Kincheloe and D. Weil (eds) *Standards and Schooling in the United States: An Encyclopedia*, Santa Barbara, CA, ABC-Clio

Lee, A. (1997) 'What is MIS?', in R. Galliers and W. Currie (eds) *Rethinking MIS*, London, Oxford University Press

Lemke, J. (1995) *Textual Politics: Discourse and Social Dynamics*, London, Taylor and Francis

Linne, R. (2001) 'Urban education – teacher perspectives on standards and high-states testing: from the urban to the suburban', in J. Kincheloe and D. Weil (eds) *Standards and Schooling in the United States: An Encyclopedia*, Santa Barbara, CA, ABC-Clio

Macedo, D. (1994) *Literacies of Power: What Americans are Not Allowed to Know,* Boulder, CO, Westview Press

Madison, G. (1988) *The Hermeneutics of Postmodernity: Figures and Themes*, Bloomington, Indiana University Press

Malewski, E. (2001b) 'Queer sexuality – The trouble with knowing: Standards of complexity and sexual orientations', in J. Kincheloe and D. Weil (eds) *Standards and Schooling in the United States: An Encyclopedia*, Santa Barbara, CA, ABC-Clio

Marzano, R. and Kendall, J. (1999) 'The fall and rise of standards-based education', <http://www.mcrel.org/standards/articles/fall-and-rise-one.dsp>

Nelson, W. (1998) 'The naked truth about school reform in Minnesota', *Phi Delta Kappan*, 79, 9, pp.679-85

Norris, N. (1998) 'Curriculum evaluation revisited', *Cambridge Journal of Education*, 28, 2

Novick, R. (1996) 'Actual schools, possible practices: New directions in professional development', *Education Policy Analysis Archives*, 4, 14

Ohanian, S. (1999) *One Size Fits Few: The Folly of Educational Standards*, Portsmouth, NH, Heinemann

O'Sullivan, E. (1999) Transformative Learning: Educational Vision for the Twenty-first Century, New York, Zed

Pushkin, D. (2001) 'Science – To standardize, or too standardize? What becomes of our curriculum?', in J. Kincheloe and D. Weil (eds) *Standards and Schooling in the United States: An Encyclopedia*, Santa Barbara, CA, ABC-Clio

Schön, D. (1995) 'The new scholarship requires a new epistemology', *Change*, 27, 6

Schubert, W. and Thomas, T. (2001) 'History – Responding to standards: The professor of education's legacy and responsibility', in J. Kincheloe and D. Weil (eds) *Standards and Schooling in the United States: An Encyclopedia*, Santa Barbara, CA, ABC-Clio

Shotter, J. (1993) *Cultural Politics of Everyday Life*, Toronto, University of Toronto Press

Shotter, J. (1998) 'Action research as history making', *Concepts and Transformations: International Journal of Action Research and Organisational Renewal*, 2, 3, pp.279-86

Soto, L. (1997) 'Bilingual education in America: In search of equity and justice', in J. Kincheloe and S. Steinberg (eds) *Unauthorized Methods: Strategies for Critical Teaching*, New York, Routledge

Soto, L. (ed) (2000) *The Politics of Early Childhood Education*, New York, Peter Lang

Symes, C. and Meadmore, D. (1999) *The Extra-Ordinary School: Parergonality and the Pedagogy*, New York, Peter Lang

Thomas, G. (1998) 'The myth of rational research', *British Educational Research Journal*, 24, 2

Vinson, K. and Ross, E. (2001) 'Social studies – Social education and standards-based reform: A critique', in J. Kincheloe and D. Weil (eds) *Standards and Schooling in the United States: An Encyclopedia*, Santa Barbara, CA, ABC-Clio

Weil, D. (2001a) 'Functionalism – From functionalism to neofunctionalism and neoliberalism: Developing a dialectical understanding of the standards debate through historical awareness', in J. Kincheloe and D. Weil (eds) *Standards and Schooling in the United States: An Encyclopedia*, Santa Barbara, CA, ABC-Clio

Weil, D. (2001b) 'Goals of standards – World class standards: Whose world, which economic classes, and what standards?', in J. Kincheloe and D. Weil (eds) *Standards and Schooling in the United States: An Encyclopedia*, Santa Barbara, CA, ABC-Clio

Weil, D. (2001c) 'Florida's advanced academic standards for the assessment of critical and creative thinking', in J. Kincheloe and D. Weil (eds) *Standards and Schooling in the United States: An Encyclopedia*, Santa Barbara, CA, ABC-Clio

Willinsky, J. (2001a) 'Knowledge – Raising the standards for democratic education: Research and evaluation as public knowledge', in J. Kincheloe and D. Weil (eds) *Standards and Schooling in the United States: An Encyclopedia*, Santa Barbara, CA, ABC-Clio

Zeno, G. (1998) 'A cultural critique of the use of networked electronic discourse in a liberatory composition pedagogy', http://ocbbs.odessa.edu/public/oc/staff_dept/mjorday/index.htm

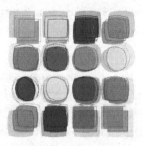

Chapter 5

Multiple lives, disparate voices, different educational experiences: The power of narrative enquiry to investigate diversity and inform pedagogical change

Janet Soler

What is narrative research?

This chapter sets out to explore the possibilities of personal narrative enquiry for providing greater insights into the tensions, contradictions, ambiguities and differences in educational lived experiences. Narrative research and narrative informed pedagogy brings to the fore the stories of our lives and the lives of others. In doing so it enables us to explore the multiplicity, differences and diversity of the lived experiences of education. Personal narrative enquiry can thus provide a vehicle to look at individual and collective stories through a range of approaches, including oral history, life history, life incidents, storytelling, and biography. It also enables us to reveal personal and social histories in order to investigate how we share belief systems and position shared values. Narratives can be extremely powerful in helping researchers understand and represent experience, as they have the potential to explain behaviour and how individuals within cultures develop and share belief systems and position-shared values (Barthes, 1975; Polkinghorne, 1988).

An exploration of narrative and of narrative enquiry is relevant to this reader because of its links to critical theory and in particular to critical pedagogy. The work of critical theorists such as Giroux, McLaren, Ladson Billings and hooks support the view that in order to transform learning, teaching and society for all, critical pedagogy requires reflection on lived experience and culture. Central to this is an understanding of identity, agency and voice so we can take a critical look at the way in which our world and society is linked to dialogues with others. In this chapter I explore the way in which narrative enquiry can provide both paradigmatic and methodological opportunities for us to explore these links within our own and others' teaching and pedagogical practices.

Narrative research is an all-embracing grouping for a range of research interdisciplinary based practices and it implicitly involves 'a particular understanding of the speaker's self' (Casey, 1995:213). Casey lists a number of contemporary research practices which come under the umbrella of narrative research, including:

- autobiographical and biographical accounts
- life writing
- life history
- life stories
- personal accounts
- personal narratives
- narrative interviews
- personal documents
- oral history
- ethnohistory
- ethnobiographies
- autoethnobiographies
- ethnopsychology
- person-centered ethnography
- popular memory (list adapted from Casey, 1995:211–212)

Narrative research involves us as researchers in interacting and dialoguing with individuals so as to construct a narration of their everyday lives within their social environment and society. Narrative is a story about individuals; it is either told in the first person or presented as a story told by another about individuals as characters in a story. It generally follows a logical, sequential, linear style. It also starts at a certain place and moves forward from this beginning to a middle and an end. Narrative analysis is the interpreting of texts that have this common storied form and involves attention to the sequences of action, to interrogate who and why stories are told as well as the content to which the language refers (Riessman, 2008:10).

Narrative research can, therefore, be seen as both a research method and a vehicle used to deliver the telling of a story or stories related to an individual or group of individuals. It can refer to the form of data generation and the method of recording and gathering evidence, such as interview, personal diaries or biography. At its heart lies a conception of a time-based progression within the collected data, which can also relate to themes or aspects of the life of an individual or individuals. The forms or presentation may differ as, for example, biographies and autobiographies or as an oral history, life history or data gathered through narrative practices, such as narrative interviews, and may be integrated into a broader multi-method mode of research.

However, while narrative research can be viewed as both a singular research method and as a number of practices which can be used for data collection, it inevitably gives the individual or a group of individuals the opportunity to present their narratives, stories, and/or versions of their lived experiences including their inspirations and discouragements. It also enables individuals to represent their unique lived experiences and how these have impacted upon the trajectory of their lives. Perhaps most importantly for those of us who want to use narrative enquiry to investigate diversity and inform pedagogical change, narrative research and its practices allows us to take an interest in and work with real people and real life events and to gain insights into how these individuals make sense of and story their own lived experiences and social realities. Insights gained from narrative research in our own work-based research can therefore be utilised to inform how we might shape and change our own and others' pedagogy and educational practice in our own educational contexts.

Recent developments in narrative research

When reading the literature related to narrative and narrative research, it quickly becomes evident that diversity is at the heart of narrative studies and is a key feature of the field. There is diversity and multiplicity in its origins, theory, methods, disciplinary underpinnings and in its subject matter. At the heart of narrative enquiry lies a drive to understand the complex and diverse nature of social reality and our lived experiences (Spector-Mersel, 2010:205).

Roland Barthes, the French literary theorist, philosopher, critic, and semiotician whose work remains a valuable source of insight and tools for the analysis of meaning in any given person made representation, has noted that narrative is part of life itself and extends across national borders, historical and cultural experiences (Barthes, 1985). Narratives and stories provide one solution to the problem of how to translate knowing into telling. They are also used to address the problem of fashioning human experience to form structures of meaning that are generally human rather than culture-specific. They can also cross cultural boundaries without losing meaning in a way in which other literary forms may not (White, 1987:1).

… this suggests that far from being one code among many that a culture may utilize for endowing experience with meaning, narrative is a meta-code, a human universal on the basis of which transcultural messages about the nature of a shared reality can be transmitted. Arising, as Barthes says, between our experience of the world and our efforts to describe that experience in language, narrative ceaselessly substitutes meaning for the straightforward copy of the events recounted. (White, 1987:1)

Recent definitions have emphasised the increasingly interdisciplinary nature and growing appeal of narrative across the social sciences. Riessman (1993), Taylor (1989), Polkinghorne (1988) and Bruner (1986) have stressed the way in which narratives of personal experience and past events are ubiquitous, common in everyday life, and are used to give human life meaning though the way they order experience and construct reality. During the 1970s and into the 1980s the dominance of positivism in social science research was increasingly challenged, producing a narrative turn in the social sciences. This gave increasing legitimacy to personal narrative enquiry. Commentators noted that this happened extraordinarily quickly, and resulted in narrative enquiry becoming legitimised within academia and in education and social work, as well as within other disciplines such as psychotherapy, counselling, mediation, law, medicine, occupational therapy and conflict resolution (Spector-Mersel, 2010).

The increasing use of the language of narrative and storytelling across fields means that narrative enquiry is no longer seen primarily as a tool for seeking 'correspondence' to historical fact (Punday, 2002:1). It has also led to a validation of an interpretative stance in the 1980s and 1990s within the social sciences and the assertion that we must increasingly understand our lives in a narrative form. Jerome Bruner (cited in Casey, 1995:212) argued that by the mid 1970s the social sciences had moved away from their traditional positivist stance towards a more interpretive stance where meaning was central to research enquiry. This stance has come to influence various areas of scholarship research and professional perspectives. It became very evident in the work of, for example, feminist theorists, political philosophers, psychologists, legal theorists, social workers, organisational theorists, anthropologists and medical sociologists. During the 1980s and 1990s it was increasingly felt that the realistic assumptions derived from natural science methods, which had prevailed in the immediate post war years, were 'too limiting for understanding social life' and that, increasingly, 'leading US scholars from various disciplines were turning to narrative as the organising principle for human action' (Riessman, 1993, cited in Casey, 1995:212).

This recent use and development of narrative research has led to new understandings that social life is itself storied and that narrative is a way of being and existing in our social life. As Somers and Gibson (1994:2) note, current narrative has had a long association with the humanities and history. Historians, for example, have traditionally used historical narrative as a way of representing knowledge. However, in recent decades there have been significant changes, as some historians have elected not to rely on narrative explanation. Current narrative research has expanded beyond the humanities and history, and has become embedded in the knowledge base of other disciplines and areas in the social sciences. These include areas related to education and forms of psychology such as cognitive narratology and discursive psychology.

Sommers and Gibson (1994:2) argue that these developments have led to a substantive change in the way in which we think about and use narrative. This in turn has resulted in a move from using narrative to represent knowledge, as in traditional historical narrative, to using it in a way which highlights how narrative underpins our social life. This can also be seen as a move from using narrative as representation to using it in understanding the ontological condition of social life. By taking this ontological stance, academics from areas including psychology and education have been able to show that stories guide action and enable individuals to construct multiple and changing identities. They are able to do so by locating themselves or being located within a selection of stories and sequences of events.

'Experience' can therefore be seen as the construction of multiple changing identities as people assemble and integrate these happenings. This view of narratives has developed new approaches for ways to study meaning, social action, social agency and collective identity.

Investigating 'voices' of difference though narrative enquiry

When individuals provide accounts of their socially constructed stories we can access the lived reality and experiences of education of individuals and groups. They can provide alternative and diverse perspectives, which can counter commonsense and commonly held understandings of individual and collective experiences of equality and justice issues. In doing so they also have the potential to address assumptions that there are normalised, collective and cohesively lived experiences within current and past educational contexts and settings. This in turn can give rise to understandings which enable resistance to the eroding of an individual's and groups' sense of agency.

This raising of consciousness and making the invisible visible can also highlight how, why and where we need to transform pedagogy and support learning for marginalised groups. For example, narrative based approaches such as oral history and life history have made invisible groups visible, as is evident in feminist oral histories and life histories. Studies in this area have given a renewed prominence to recovering women's educational experiences and highlighting the roles women have played in different educational contexts (see for example Gluck and Patai, 1991; Casey, 1993; Middleton, 1993; Middleton and May, 1997).

Peter Clough's narrative based research is an example of the ability of a 'storying' approach to unsettle our commonsense understandings of educational issues and research evidence. For example, Clough utilises a storying methodology in his research in order to 'produce different knowledge, and to produce knowledge differently'. He states that it de-emphasises the 'how to do' and refocuses our attention on 'what it is possible to do?'(Clough, 2002:4). In his book *Narratives and Fictions in Educational Research* (2002) he locates narrative and fictional methods within the traditions of educational research and provides examples of the use of narrative and fictional methods in educational settings. The book is innovative in its use of five 'fictional' stories, which demonstrate how narrative can be used. Clough provides five 'fictional' stories to show the varied role of the author in their creation. This approach enables a consideration of the methodological implications of narrative in reporting research.

Because narrative based work such as Clough's research is often exploratory and seeks to disrupt conventional understandings and assumptions, it also highlights and problematises the ways meaning is created and communicated in the research process. This results in the opening up of exciting and groundbreaking possibilities for new understandings and ways of thinking about difference and diversity for the researcher, participants and for the reader of Clough's book.

The excitement, engagement, lack of constraint and the opening up of new possibilities and the understanding of the world through the eyes of others which can arise through innovative and creative application of narrative enquiry is also evident in the autobiographical approach taken by Maxine Green in her book *Releasing the Imagination: Essays on Education, the Arts, and Social Change* (1995). Green 'envisions classrooms and communities that value multiple perspectives, democratic pluralism, life narratives, and on-going social change' (Slattery and Dees, 1998:46). Green draws upon a narrative of her own life and lived educational experiences and journeys to create a new social and educational vision. Her vision of educational transformational change and new pedagogical possibilities are implicit in movements and the key themes of transformation through literary encounters, pedagogical possibilities and the creation of a community inspired by a passion for multiplicity and change.

Morwenna Griffiths' work is also interesting for the way it demonstrates how it is possible to present diverse voices, experiences and common insights gained through the use of stories. In *Action for Social Justice in Education: Fairly Different* with Sharon Baillon (2003), Griffiths uses narrative enquiry to address the question: how is it possible to understand difference and diversity within a single humanity? In asking this question across the stories in the book she highlights the way in which we are all human and therefore share the agency, creativity and needs associated with being human. These characteristics, however, also ensure that we are also 'all-humanly different' (Griffiths and Baillon, 2003:7).

Griffiths argues that it is important to understand both our shared humanity and the ways in which we are different. We need this understanding in order to work together as members of a community and participate in society. She draws upon the accounts of a diverse group of contributors to explore how understandings of difference can help education to 'best benefit all individuals and also the society in which they live' at both a theoretical and practical level. The accounts also show how the recognition of diversity can be important for educational institutions as society becomes more and more diverse, particularly in areas related to gender, class, disability and sexuality' (Griffiths and Baillon, 2003:10).

However, the growing interest in personal narrative as an acceptable and powerful way to investigate individual and collective experience within the social, political, and cultural worlds of education comes with a cautionary note. Critics, particularly feminists, have been hesitant about asserting the value of narrative in constructing knowledge. As Punday points out:

Although describing conventional knowledge as a narrative can question traditional values that exclude some individuals and groups, the logical and ethical force of any consequent call for social change is weakened when we admit that those calls likewise depend on narratives. Why should we act on knowledge that is 'just a story'? This question haunts contemporary criticism concerned with social change; as Jane Flax remarks, 'if there is no objective basis for distinguishing between true and false beliefs, then it seems that power alone will determine the outcome of competing truth claims. This is a frightening prospect for those who lack (or are oppressed by) the power of others'. (Punday, 2002:4)

The focus on the personal narrative for narrative researchers must be the 'nature of experience', as this is the phenomenon that they are studying (Clandinin and Murphy, 2009). This in turn raises the need to clarify assumptions that may surround the nature of the experience and relate to the relationship between the researcher and the researched.

When utilising personal narrative for educational enquiry we need to be aware that engaging with it can also disrupt and redefine the relationship between the researchers and researched, and the knowing with the known. Researchers reflecting on engaging with the collection of personal narratives have stressed that it is not a straightforward process. They warn that we cannot be complacent about the interviewer/researcher-narrator dynamic it opens up.

As educational researchers have become increasingly engaged in collecting, interviewing and interpreting narratives, they have become even more aware of the interviewer/researcher's responsibilities in relation to how they collect, unfold, analyse, respect and interpret the intensions of the narrator. There has also been an increased awareness of the need to take account of the nuances and subtleties in the interactions, intentions and personal relationships that arise between the interviewer/researcher and the narrator through engagement with personal narrative. Engaging in narrative research reveals the complexities of identity, as it involves the researcher in engagement, identifying, articulating, shaping and enacting the identities of the narrator and ourselves as the researcher (Errante, 2000; Gluck and Patai, 1991). As Punday notes, consciously constructing and naming our writing as a 'narrative', along with styling oneself as a 'narrator', immediately implies particular interests, formal constraints and a 'real world multiplicity' which we are asking our readers to accept (Punday, 2002:3).

Consciously constructing narratives through story making therefore contributes to the construction of identities. This link between narratives and identities is so strong that identities can be seen as narratives people construct about themselves to tell themselves and other people who they are. Embedded in this construction of identity and the sense of belonging and making visible that accompanies it, is the potential for narratives to politicise and mobilise. As Riessman argues, narratives can do political work because of the social role stories can play in connecting us to the 'flow of power in the wider world' (Riessman, 1993:9).

Thinking about the discursive construction of narratives in this way also highlights the political nature of research narrative, which we ourselves construct as researchers. Research narratives are themselves constructed by hidden rules related to what a researcher can and cannot say, and who they can allow to speak or not speak, as well as whose versions and constructions of reality are valid and acknowledged and whose are unimportant. This highlights Foucault's assertion that fields of knowledge take their forms as results of the power relations of discursive practice (Kincheloe, 2005:328).

Narratives of educational practice and investigative directions

If we see narrative as part of the construction of reality rather than as mirroring reality, we can move away from the traditional approach of depicting narrative as merely mirroring the entity we are investigating. From this perspective it is possible to see narratives and narrative research as contributing to the invention of reality rather than merely reflecting an objective reality. This conceptualisation of narratives also implies that narrative research has the power to shape reality. If we narrate ourselves as empowered active educational agents able to shape and change our pedagogy, we will conduct ourselves in the real world very differently than we would if we see our life stories as disempowered trainers and education programme or curriculum deliverers.

Narrative research can give us a clear vision of how we think, feel and conduct ourselves within our educational practice and present us with a worldview that helps us understand the nature of the educational world and our place within it. If we take this path in utilising this view of narrative research in our own teaching and work-based practice, we are moving narrative research beyond a methodology and into a paradigm with a specific philosophical and theoretical framework (see Spector-Mersel, 2010:209; Denzin and Lincoln, 2005:22).

This paradigmatic approach allows us to draw upon the articulation and narration of stories common to the groups of learners we work with, to create and come to understand classroom, institutional, community, organisational and national identities. If we have a distinct vision of our educational practice, our place within it and how we should conduct ourselves, we can engage with narrative enquiry to construct learners' identities and impart meaning to individual and collective experiences. This in turn has the potential to give us the power to shape our pedagogy to meet and promote understandings of diversity within our collective world and the settings we work in.

Source: *newly commissioned for this volume.*

References

Barthes, R. and Duisit, L. (1975) 'An introduction to the structural analysis of narrative', *New Literary History*, vol.6, no.2, p237-272.

Barthes, R. (1985) *The Grain of the Voice: Interviews 1962-1980* (L. Coverdale, Trans.), New York: Hill and Wang.

Bruner, J.S. (1986) *Actual Minds, Possible Worlds,* Cambridge, MA: Harvard University Press.

Carr, D. (1986) 'Narrative and the real world: an argument for continuity', *History & Theory*, vol.25, no.2, p117.

Casey, K. (1993) *I Answer With My Life: Life Histories of Women Teachers Working for Social Change,* London: Routledge.

Casey, K. (1995) 'The new narrative research in education', *Review of Research in Education*, vol.21, p211-253.

Clandinin, D. and Murphy, M. (2009) 'Comments on Coulter and Smith: relational ontological commitments in narrative research', *Educational Researcher*, vol.38, no.8, p598.

Clough, P. (2002) *Narratives and Fictions in Educational Research*, Buckingham and Philidelphia: Open University Press.

Denzin, N.K. (1989) *Interpretive Biography* (vol.17), Newbury Park, CA and London: Sage Publications.

Denzin, N.K. and Lincoln, Y.S. (2005) *The SAGE Handbook of Qualitative Research* (3rd ed.), Thousand Oaks: Sage Publications.

Errante, A. (2000) 'But sometimes you're not part of the story: Oral histories and ways of remembering and telling', *Educational Researcher*, vol.29, no.2, p16.

Gluck, S.B. and Patai, D. (eds.) (1991) *Women's Words: A Feminist Practice of Oral History*, New York and London: Routledge.

Greene, M. (1995) *Releasing the Imagination: Essays on Education, The Arts and Social Change*, San Francisco: Jossey-Bass.

Griffiths, M. and Baillon, S. (2003) *Action for Social Justice in Education: Fairly Different*, Maidenhead: Open University Press.

Kincheloe, J. (2005) 'On to the next level: Continuing the conceptualization of the bricolage', *Qualitative Inquiry*, vol.11, no.3, p323-350.

Middleton, S. (1993) *Educating Feminists: Life Histories and Pedagogy,* New York and London: Teachers College Press.

Middleton, S. and May, H. (1997) *Teachers Talk Teaching 1915-1995: Early Childhood, Schools and Teachers' Colleges*, Palmerston North: Dunmore Press.

Polkinghorne, D.E. (1988) *Narrative Knowing and the Human Sciences*, Albany, N.Y.: State University of New York Press.

Punday, D. (2002) *Narrative After Deconstruction*, Albany, N.Y.: State University of New York Press.

Riessman, C.K. (1993) *Narrative Analysis*, Newbury Park, Calif; London: Sage Publications.

Riessman, C.K. (2008) *Narrative Methods for the Human Sciences*, London: SAGE.

Slattery, P. and Dees, D.M. (1998) 'Releasing the imagination and the 1990s', in Pinar, W. (ed.) *The Passionate Mind of Maxine Greene: 'I am -- not yet'* (p46-57). London: Falmer Press.

Somers, M.R. and Gibson, G.D. (1994) 'Reclaiming the epistemological 'other': narrative and the social constitution of identity', in Calhoun, C. (ed.), *Social Theory and the Politics of Identity*, Oxford: Blackwell.

Spector-Mersel, G. (2010) 'Narrative research: Time for a paradigm', *Narrative Inquiry*, vol.20, no.1, p204-224.

Taylor, C. (1989) *Sources of The Self*, Cambridge, MA: Harvard University Press.

White, H. (1987) *The Content of Form: Narrative Discourse and Historical Representation*, Baltimore; London: Johns Hopkins University Press.

Part 2

Contemporary examples of innovative, transformative practice

Chapter 6

The elementary bubble project: exploring critical media literacy in a fourth-grade classroom

Jesse S. Gainer, Nancy Valdez-Gainer, Timothy Kinard

Cecilia stared at her paper as the seventeen other fourth graders in her class busily wrote at their tables. When I (Jesse, first author) approached to see if I could help, she held up a full-page magazine advertisement for a Dora the Explorer doll that sings in English and Spanish and said, 'There is nothing wrong with this. I think it is a good toy. I'm not sure what to write'.

Cecilia (all student names are pseudonyms) and her classmates were involved in a project focusing on the ways advertising and other mass media communicate messages that can influence the way people think. Their writing assignment, which will be explained later, was to 'talk back' to the ads. When we (the authors) designed the unit, we hoped to guide students to become more critical consumers of mass media. Although we tried to be careful not to crush the pleasure children get from their popular culture (Alvermann, Moon and Hagood, 1999), and we tried not to be too heavy-handed as we guided the students to become critical readers of advertising, Cecilia seemed to have received the message that critical media literacy simply involves finding fault in mass media texts. Cecilia asked me what I thought she should write. I told her that I thought it was fine that she liked the toy, and I encouraged her to respond in a way that reflected her approval of it. She placed a speech bubble coming from the mouth of the Dora doll and wrote, 'My name is Dora. I am a great toy. Someone bought me and said: 'It works. It works'.

A great deal of advertising is directed at young people and is even embedded in their popular culture (Evans, 2005; Tobin, 2004; Vasquez, 2003). Mass media texts, including advertising, reflect certain values even when they appear to be neutral (Giroux, 1999) and such texts can influence people's thinking (King, 2007). Therefore, having students question commercialism in their environment, including popular culture, is a compelling site for a critical dialogic curriculum (Kellner and Share, 2007; Trier, 2006; Alvermann and Hagood, 2000).

The purpose of this chapter is to examine how children in a fourth-grade classroom responded during a media literacy unit that focused on critically reading advertisements. We highlight some of the tensions that arose when we tried to balance social critique with students' pleasure in popular culture. As in the example of Cecilia, we often found ourselves uncertain in our role as teachers when attempting to 'teach' students to engage in critical cultural enquiry. At times we felt we were too leading, and other times we wondered if we were guiding the students to be critical at all. After describing the context of this project, we discuss our efforts to guide a fourth-grade class in critical media literacy activities we call the Elementary Bubble Project.

School context and authors' positionality

Dawson Elementary is located in a city in south-western United States. The ethnic and racial make-up of the student body is 86 per cent Latino, 8 per cent African American, and 6 per cent White. The majority of the students are from low-income families, and 88 per cent have free or reduced-cost lunch.

The first two authors have been or are currently working as teachers at Dawson. Jesse is currently working at a local university but previously taught for eight years at Dawson. Nancy is in her seventh year teaching at the school, and this project took place in her classroom. Tim has over ten years of elementary and pre-school teaching experience. [...]

Like most teachers today, we are familiar with the pressures of 'accountability' and the narrowing of curriculum that often ensues (McNeil, 2000). Too often in schools serving high percentages of children of colour and children of the working poor, test pressure results in low-level, skills-oriented instruction at the sacrifice of higher order critical thinking (Cummins, Brown and Sayers, 2007). We do not wish to fall into this trap and therefore have made conscious political and pedagogical decisions to emphasise critical thinking and to open curricular spaces for dialogic instruction.

Critical media literacy

Although there has been increased attention given to the fact that young people spend significant time engaging with multiple forms of media, this has not translated to wide-scale pedagogical changes in the way we teach literacy in schools (Kellner and Share, 2007). Given the changing face of literacy in the 21st century, it is imperative that educators consider ways to help students develop the skills required to read and write using multiple text forms including but not limited to traditional typographic print (Lankshear and Knobel, 2006). [...]

Critical media literacy within the field of cultural studies offers a way for teachers to scaffold students' learning as they explore and analyse multiple forms of texts. What distinguishes critical media literacy from other forms of media literacy education is the emphasis placed on ideological factors relating to the relationships of texts, readers, and power (Kellner and Share, 2007). Critical media literacy pedagogy scaffolds learners as they begin to question common assumptions embedded in the messages of mainstream media. This style of pedagogy pushes students to explore whose voices are privileged in media texts and whose are not heard at all. Additionally, critical media literacy pedagogy offers students opportunity and space to use media tools to create their own texts and make their own voices heard. Therefore, when students and teachers work together to critically analyse texts including media – a path is opened for transformative pedagogy. Such critical analysis during reading is more urgent now than ever, given the way new technologies have increased our access to so much unfiltered text (Leu and Zawilinski, 2007).

Critical media literacy starts with the assumption that all texts are value laden and privilege some voices while denying others (Semali, 2003). However, this does not mean that audiences – or readers of media texts – passively accept messages found in mass media. Contrary to traditional notions of young people as exceedingly vulnerable to the 'dangers' of media influences, Sefton-Green (2006) argued that consumers of mass media are active meaning makers and sometimes read texts in oppositional ways that counter dominant ideology. Such oppositional readings – or counter narratives – are at the heart of critical media literacy.

The transformational potential of critical media literacy pedagogy is increased when students are given opportunities to use media and information technology tools to tell their own stories and express their own concerns. Thus, a key component of critical media literacy is the opening of space in the curriculum for students to create their own media (Kellner and Share, 2007; Semali, 2003). The process of creating their own media messages can help students 'understand how media acts as a frame and a filter on the world while appearing as a clear window' (Goodman, 2003:6).

Unpacking advertising

Advertisements and other forms of mass media offer great potential for teachers and students to unpack layers of textual meaning and question relations of power and knowledge at work in the texts (Luke, O'Brien and Comber, 2001). Advertisements are particularly useful sites for such work because they are persuasive texts designed to 'add to shaping of identities ... that consumers wish to take on ... as part of their everydayness' (Albers, Harste, Vander Zanden and Felderman, 2008:70). While recognising the agency of students to construct meaning from advertising and other media, teachers interested in fostering critical literacy of students can help develop classroom environments that invite a questioning of rampant consumerist messages found in today's society. [...]

The idea that classrooms should be places where students are encouraged to critically analyse media messages in general – and advertising in particular – is supported by the fact that a great deal of marketing is directed at young people (Goodman, 2003; Tobin, 2004). In a study of fifth-grade children's and pre-service teachers' understandings of critically reading advertisements, Albers *et al* (2008) found that although most of the young people in their study did not respond in oppositional ways to advertising texts, they did possess abilities to critically question the ways in which ads presented consumerist messages. Therefore, critical media literacy pedagogy is not a one-shot deal and it does not start from scratch; it builds on abilities many young people already possess. [...]

Although a great deal of advertising is geared toward adolescent youth, they are not the only young people targeted by mass marketing. People of all ages are targets of advertising and are never too young to begin thinking critically about such texts (Albers *et al*, 2008; Evans, 2005). In the book *Negotiating Critical Literacies With Young Children*, Vasquez (2004) demonstrated how children as young as kindergarten can critically unpack advertising messages geared at them. In this case, 5-year-olds considered McDonald's Happy Meals as text and analysed how the marketers of such products created gendered texts and pushed sales of food products via packaging and other marketing tactics.

The bubble project

The Bubble Project (www.thebubbleproject.com) is an example of anticorporate activism often known as 'culture jamming'. This form of activism takes on a variety of styles but shares a critique of the widespread incursion of corporatism into the daily lives of citizens, especially in areas of health care, education, culture, and government (Lankshear and Knobel, 2006). More examples of such activism can be found online at Adbusters' Culturejammer Headquarters (www.adbusters.org). Lankshear and Knobel (2006) explained how remixing ads, a form of culture jamming, is a literacy practice. 'By turning media images in upon themselves through deft remixing, the Adbusters' culture jamming campaigns show how Photoshop remixes can be socially-aware new literacy practices for everyone' (p132).

Similar to the campaigns of the Adbusters group, guerrilla artist Ji Lee initiated the Bubble Project in New York and online. He has called it a 'counterattack' allowing people to respond to the pervasive advertising of environmental print. The manifesto posted on the project's website explains the purpose: 'Our communal spaces are being overrun with ads .... Once considered 'public', these spaces are increasingly being seized by corporations. ... We the public, [sic] are both target and victim of this media attack' (www.thebubbleproject.com).

By placing blank speech bubbles on ads, Lee encourages others to write responses to the advertising. According to Lee, this process transforms the original advertisement into something more dialogic and inclusive. It should be noted that this form of reader's response is illegal and therefore should not be blindly embraced by teachers as a curricular tool. However, the interactive nature of the 'bubbling' and the space such practice opens for potentially critical dialogue is evident in the examples that are posted on the Bubble Project website. Additionally, 'bubbling' is not a new concept in the area of reading comprehension instruction. Based in research on think-alouds, Wilhelm (2001) used thought bubbles to help students develop metacognition and comprehension strategies while reading. In a similar way, we asked our fourth graders to use speech bubbles in the hope of developing critical thinking when reading media texts.

The elementary bubble project

Interested in ways to incorporate students' popular culture into the curriculum and hoping to find ways to encourage critical dialogue between students, popular culture texts, and ourselves, we devised a plan to adapt the Bubble Project for classroom purposes. We decided that a good way to initiate dialogue would be to have a group discussion about advertising and commercialism in mainstream media. From there, we would guide students as they created their own speech bubbles to 'talk back' to advertising directed at young people.

Getting started

We created a PowerPoint presentation to help stimulate discussion that would lead into the students' critical media literacy work. Our first slide addressed advertising and planted seeds for ideas on why some people are critical of it. One bullet asked students where they find ads. The class brainstormed a list including television, magazines, newspapers, billboards, and the sides of buses. We commented that some people, including us (the teachers), do not like the messages of many advertisements. We asked the students to think about what advertisements and other mainstream media typically tell us about topics like beauty, gender, and products we do not necessarily need.

The purpose of the class discussion around this slideshow was to highlight the fact that we see advertising in many places and that there is often more to such texts than meets the eye. In other words, media texts are value laden and often reflect the ideology of those in power (Giroux, 1999). We hoped students would consider the ways messages are constructed and how the images selected (or omitted) communicate meaning.

Figure 1: A powerpoint slide to help initiate student discussion

---

What is the Bubble Project?

- ■ **Who gets to decide what is advertised and how it is done?**
- ■ **Who does not get to say anything?**
- ■ **Do you have an opinion?**

YOU HAVE SOMETHING TO SAY!!!!!!

Figure 1 posed a question to delve into issues of power and media images. The question, 'Who gets to decide what is advertised and how it is done?' provoked some response from the class. One student said, 'Grown-ups are the ones who make the ads'. Another student added, 'Rich people who own companies make them'. A third student commented, 'Most of the ads you see show mostly white people'. When asked to explain why this is significant, the boy referred to the previous slide and critiqued the underlying message that he interpreted as whites are considered more important. Our students began to analyse issues of class, race, and ethnicity in mainstream media – issues that often remain beneath the surface.

We hoped our short introduction to critical literacy would help springboard the students' critical thinking as we delved deeper into concrete examples. After a brief overview of Lee's Bubble Project, we shared examples of actual 'street bubbles' from New York (www.thebubbleproject.com). As students viewed the examples, the class discussed the meaning behind each one. We selected seven examples from the website that we felt would push students' thinking in terms of social critique and also were appropriate for fourth graders. We chose to introduce this concept using examples from Lee. However, teachers interested in trying a similar lesson could create their own examples by simply downloading photos and inserting speech bubbles using common computer programmes such as Word or PowerPoint. We were careful to stress to the students that these practices are illegal and that we do not condone vandalism.

The first few examples were advertisements for clothing and perfume. The comments written in speech bubbles included a critique about how beauty is represented in mainstream media. One of the ads, for example, features a full shot of a heavily made-up woman wearing a bikini top and miniskirt. Interestingly, it is an ad for shoes, which are barely visible in the picture. The photograph has been digitally distorted so that the woman's head is out of proportion with the rest of her exposed, pencil-thin body. The text of the speech bubble reads, 'I am hideously deformed!' While the vocabulary was difficult for some of the fourth graders, through discussion they were able to understand how this ad and many other media images objectify women and propel unrealistic and unhealthy visions of beauty.

Discussing examples from the Bubble Project helped students deepen their understandings of the ways images in media carry meaning beyond face value. The examples facilitated the students' understandings of ways to critique underlying messages often found in media. Next, we provided students with examples of advertising with blank speech bubbles (from www.thebubbleproject.com) and asked them to offer ideas of what could be written in them. One example, an ad for a pillow, shows a photograph of a woman sleeping. A student raised her hand and in a sarcastic voice offered, 'I always do my hair and put on make-up before I go to sleep'. Through her sarcasm, this fourth grader communicated the absurdity of a media image that depicts a woman completely made up even though she's supposed to be sleeping. This led to further discussion of the ways women are often objectified in media, and students connected this with other examples, including the shoe ad discussed earlier. Another example depicted a sign for a psychic reading service offering a $10 special. A blank speech bubble had been placed on the palm of a hand depicted on the sign. A boy in the class suggested it should say, 'In your future you will waste $10'. This student, who did not believe palm reading to be a good use of money, used humour to critique the message of the advertising text. Again students discussed how this ad and others are trying to convince people to buy a product they felt is of little or no worth. The class continued with ten more examples of advertisements, ranging from breakfast pastry boxes to moving trucks.

By the end of the PowerPoint slideshow, the students were eager to try their hand at 'bubbling'. The discussion and the concrete examples seemed to help raise students' awareness of possible underlying messages in media. Additionally, the discussion helped model potential ways for individuals to resist media messages. Next, we discuss how students engaged in critical media literacy using the Bubble Project as a guiding example.

Students create their own bubbles

After the PowerPoint discussion, we allowed the group to trawl through magazines geared for young people. Popular magazines contain a great deal of advertisements and other forms of text marketing products and style based on television, movies, and music. In these magazines, it is sometimes difficult to distinguish between advertisements for specific products and sleek glossy photographs that purport to be the text of the periodicals. The same pop-star icons are featured prominently in each text type and both work to sell style. In this vein, we considered such texts as part of the students' daily out-of-school reading and a form of virtual environmental print worthy of unpacking.

Each student, equipped with blank speech bubbles, glue sticks, and pencils, began 'talking back'. One of the first things we noticed was the highly interactive way students engaged with the materials. Unlike many reading activities where students work independently, this activity seemed to demand social interaction. While working, students actively sought one another's opinions and eagerly shared their ideas for speech bubbles.

Student responses

The fourth graders read between the lines of the advertising when they created bubbles to 'talk back' to the texts of the magazines. Similarly, we had to read between the lines as we interpreted meanings in the student-made bubbles. Although we do not claim to be experts in the students' popular culture, in order to comprehend the new texts we needed to be somewhat savvy about the popular culture the students were drawing on in their work.

Three categories of responses emerged from the students' work. We found that the fourth graders interacted with the texts of advertising and popular culture mainly through humour, social critique, and a final category we call 'pleasure'. This last category catches the examples that did not fall neatly into one of the first two categories and is defined by evidence of the students' sheer enjoyment of the subject in question.

Out of a total of thirty-five student-made bubbles, seventeen employed humour as a means of interacting with the texts. One such example made use of an advertisement featuring a photograph of the popular singer Shakira with a speech bubble reading, 'I shook it too much in my video and my hips broke'. The joke is a reference to her song 'Hips Don't Lie' and to her famously agile dancing. While the humour may not seem funny to many adult readers, these fourth graders greatly appreciated the joke. [...]

Eleven of the students' work samples contained elements of critical cultural inquiry, and we grouped these in a second category we call 'social critique'. In these examples, students critiqued advertising and other images found in magazines in numerous ways, ranging from the high cost of movie tickets to sugar and fat content in snack foods [...]

Seven examples fell into the final category, 'pleasure', because they include elements of the first two categories but are distinguishable by the way they are situated in the knowledge of the popular culture they reference. It seems that the creators of these bubbles were engaging in acts of pleasure derived from the popular culture texts. We believe it is especially important to highlight this category, because – as teachers promoting critical cultural inquiry in schooling – we recognise that students may find pleasure in popular culture texts we may not appreciate. In these cases students may be hesitant to critique the texts too strongly. [...]

Finally, students displayed their work throughout the room for a 'gallery walk', where they had opportunities to view and discuss the work of their peers. As might be expected, the examples that employed humour or pleasure with popular culture were most popular with the students.

Although students seemed drawn more to the examples using humour, some students critiqued the subtext of the advertising messages. In one example, two boys looked at an ad for a credit card. The ad showed a young couple in a movie theatre, sharing popcorn as they watched the screen. Jason, one of the boys, had placed a bubble over one of the people in the ad: 'Why don't they let us pay less for movies?' Edgar, another boy in the class, looked at the work, and the two boys had the following conversation:

Edgar: We don't really go to the movies.

Jason: I know. It costs too much money.

Edgar: Why do they charge so much?

Jason: They are just trying to make a lot of money even though they know a lot of people can't afford it.

This example, like many of the students' conversations, points to the fact that they were able to think critically about the messages in mainstream advertising. They did not blindly buy into the lifestyle offered in the ad; instead they questioned the motives behind the creators of it. Clearly these fourth-grade students were beginning to read critically, but this does not mean the job is done. In this example, the students made a connection between overspending and the lifestyle promoted in the images of the credit-card advertisement. With more experience and guidance using critical media literacy to question texts, perhaps they might take their critique deeper into the subtext. [...]

Next steps

This project represents only the beginning for our students' and our own explorations into critical media literacy in the classroom. In the process, we enjoyed some feelings of success and also saw areas where we would have liked to dig deeper with the social critique. Based on our classroom experiences, we believe that the inclusion of popular media texts such as advertising has great potential for teachers interested in dialogic instruction focusing on critical media literacy. Like Sefton-Green (2006), we believe that 'understanding media culture is a key element of any kind of child- or learner-centred curriculum' (p294). Media texts are abundant in our lives, and rarely are students equipped with the necessary tools to decode and transform them. As did Albers *et al* (2008), we found that 'critical conversations matter' (p81) and that, when given opportunities to view, discuss, and talk back to media texts, our fourth grade students were quite able and willing to read between the lines of mainstream messages. Students' responses to advertising during our unit of study show initial steps toward becoming 'media literate citizenry that can disrupt, contest, and transform media apparatuses' (Semali, 2003:275). As teachers, we realise that we must continue to provide space in our curriculum for students to proceed on this path to developing critical media literacy.

[...] Any critical media literacy project must allow students opportunities to explore multiple forms of media texts and incorporate technology as much as possible. Should we do this project again, we would adapt it to include more technology and more media sources such as Internet sites, television, radio, and others. In fact, this project lends itself to the usage of technology since digital photos and speech bubbles can be used with simple software readily available on computers found in most schools.

Although we feel our students learned something about reading media texts through this investigation, we plan to expand our endeavours into critical media literacy pedagogy. As we do so, we plan to continue to ask ourselves the important question: How should a teacher determine the line between respect for students' pleasures and pushing for critical narratives from students? Perhaps there is no definitive answer to this question. We have come to believe that the self-reflection on the part of the teacher that is required for this type of question is necessary for the maintenance of student-centred dialogic curriculum. [...]

The road winds on

Thinking back to the opening vignette of Cecilia and her dilemma when 'bubbling' the Dora the Explorer doll ad, perhaps a teachable moment was missed. We were so concerned about not hampering her pleasure with popular culture that we neglected to challenge her to articulate why she liked the doll. Was it because she identifies with Dora, one of the few Latina and bilingual characters in children's media? Or maybe there was a different reason she showed a preference for the doll? Perhaps we could have offered our own analysis of the Dora doll as worthy of praise, critique, or both. The point is, we trod on a delicate area, and even though we consider ourselves to be constructivist teachers attempting to use critical and dialogic approaches to education, we did not fully go there with Cecilia. [...] The reason we veered off the critical road was related to our desire to remain student-centred – and more importantly to avoid a didactic finger-pointing pedagogy that positions students as clueless dupes of mass media. In this vein, we conclude by asserting that we have more questions than answers as we attempt to learn about critical media literacy and its place in our teaching. We have not arrived, but we hope we are going in positive directions as we make the road by walking with our students, reflecting on theory and practice as we go.

Source: Gainer, S. J., Valdez-Gainer, N., and Kinard, T. (2009) 'The elementary bubble project: Exploring critical media literacy in a fourth-grade classroom', *The Reading Teacher*, vol. 62, no. 8, International Reading Association

References

Albers, P., Harste, J.C., Vander Zanden, S., and Felderman, C. (2008) Using popular culture to promote critical literacy practices. In Y. Kim, V. Risko, D. Compton, D. Dickinson, M. Hundley, R. Jiménez, K. Leander, and D. Wells Rowe (eds), 57th Yearbook of the National Reading Conference (pp70-83). Oak Creek, WI: National Reading Conference

Alvermann, D.E., and Hagood, M.C. (2000) Critical media literacy: Research, theory, and practice in 'new times'. *The Journal of Educational Research*, 93(3), 193-205

Alvermann, D.E., Moon, J.S., and Hagood, M.C. (1999) *Popular Culture in the classroom: Teaching and researching critical media literacy*. Newark, DE: International Reading Association and the National Reading Conference

Cummins, J., Brown, K. and Sayers, D. (2007) *Literacy, Technology, and Diversity: Teaching for success in changing times*. Boston, MA: Pearson

Evans, J. (2005) *Literacy Moves On: Popular culture, new technologies, and critical literacy in the elementary classroom*. Portsmouth, NH: Heinemann

Freire, P. (1970) *Pedagogy of the Oppressed*. New York: Continuum

Giroux, H.A. (1999) *The Mouse that Roared: Disney and the end of innocence*. Boulder, CO: Rowman and Littlefield

Goodman, S. (2003) *Teaching Youth Media: A critical guide to literacy, video production, and social change*. New York: Teachers College Press

Kellner, D. and Share, J. (2007) Critical media literacy is not an option. *Learning Inquiry*, 1(1), 59-69. doi:10.1007/s11519-007-0004-2

King, C.R. (2007) Reading race, reading power. In D. Macedo and S. Steinberg (eds), *Media literacy: A reader* (pp197-205). New York: Peter Lang

Lankshear, C. and Knobel, M. (2006) *New literacies: Everyday practices and classroom learning*. New York, NY: Open University Press

Leu, D.J. and Zawilinski, L. (2007) The new literacies of online reading comprehension. *The New England Reading Association Journal*, 43(1), 1-7

Luke, A., O'Brien, J. and Comber, B. (2001) Making community texts objects of study. In H. Fehring and P. Green (eds), *Critical Literacy: A collection of articles from the Australian Literacy Educators Association* (pp112-123). Newark, DE: International Reading Association

McNeil, L.M. (2000) *Contradictions in School Reform: Educational costs of standardized testing*. New York: Routledge

Sefton-Green, J. (2006) Youth, technology, and media cultures. In J. Green and A. Luke (eds), *Review of Research in Education* (Vol. 30, pp279-306). Washington, DC: American Educational Research Association

Semali, L. (2003) Ways with visual languages: Making the case for critical media literacy. *The Clearing House*, 76(6), 271-7

Tobin, J. (2004) *Pikachu's Global Adventure: The rise and fall of Pokémon*. Durham, NC: Duke University Press

Trier, J. (2006) Exemplary introductory critical media literacy documentaries. *Journal of Adolescent and Adult Literacy*, 50(1), 68-71. doi:10.1598/JAAL.50.1.7

Vasquez, V. (2003) What Pokémon can teach us about learning and literacy. *Language Arts*, 81(2), 118-125

Vasquez, V. (2004) *Negotiating Critical Literacies with Young Children*. Mahwah, NJ: Erlbaum.

Wilhelm, J.D. (2001) *Improving comprehension with think-aloud strategies*. New York: Scholastic.

Chapter 7

'How do you spell homosexual?': Naturally queer moments in K-12 classrooms

Janna Jackson

How students, parents, and administrators regard queer topics in the classroom varies widely depending on the climate of the school community. For the most part though, controversy surrounds mixing queerness and K-12 students. In some classrooms, homosexuality is only mentioned in a disparaging way. In others, it is explicitly omitted. In most, the mere mention of the word will grab students' attention because it has been treated as a taboo subject for so long. But in a few instances, queerness has become a natural part of the curriculum. This study, which is a deeper exploration of data from a larger study, examines moments in K-12 classrooms when queerness becomes a part of the fabric of the curriculum instead of a focal point; in other words, moments when students take no particular notice of it. I do not argue that a teacher's experiences of being queer do not shape his or her teaching; in fact, I argue for the opposite stance in my book, *Unmasking Identities: An exploration of the lives of gay and lesbian teachers*. Instead, I point to more subtle ways in which queerness can become a seamless part of the curriculum, what I term 'naturally queer moments' in the classroom, and the transformative power these moments can have.

In 1998, James Collard used the term 'post-gay' to describe a life-stage when being queer no longer defines who you are (Signorile, 1999). [...]

The concept of post-gay generated waves of controversy as people who dealt with discrimination felt it rendered their experiences invisible. Vanasco (2002), however, points out that even though there may be 'pockets of places' that are post-gay, until discrimination ends, post-gayness cannot be realised. [...] This chapter attempts to depict and explore what a specific type of 'queering moments', those I term 'naturally queer', can look like in the hopes of moving toward a world, not where gayness or queerness does not matter as the term 'post-gay' suggests, but where it matters in such a way that it is seen as bringing a playfulness and a way of thinking that turns traditional notions on their heads in productive and useful ways.

Although 'a time where realities other than social hatred exist' (Goldstein, Russell and Daley, 2007:197) has not been achieved on a wide scale, on an individual level some scholars describe a stage in queer identity development when queerness no longer operates as a primary identity. Cass (1979) terms this identity synthesis, and Coleman (1982) calls it integration. Similarly, I described an analogous period in queer teacher development, the authentic teacher phase, when queer teachers 'demonstrate [their] full range of humanity' (Jackson, 2007:75) and no longer tried to hide their queer identities as they did in the closeted stage I describe, nor did they consciously try to act the opposite of stereotypes as I describe in the 'gay poster child' phase. I specify that in using the term 'authentic':

I do not mean to imply that participants were not authentic prior to this phase; indeed, at every moment of their becoming they were authentic by being who they were at that point. Rather, I use the term in the same sense as Cranton (2001), to describe an ongoing self-discovery in teaching that merges the personal and professional. (p73)

I also indicate that by using the term 'authentic' I do not mean to suggest that each person has one true core identity that emerges, rather that in that phase, they are not bifurcating their identity as those I describe as being in the 'closeted' stage did. [...]

Several authors have described specific instances of including queerness in the curriculum such as teaching a book with queer themes in English class (Athanases, 1996; Boutillier, 1994; Hoffman, 1993; Hammett, 1992) and discussing the queer rights movement in a social studies class (Blinick, 1994). Other authors describe the impact of teachers coming out at school and tout the positive ramifications such as becoming what Lipkin (1999) terms 'native informants' (p212) (ie. resources for queer students, straight students, other educators, parents with queer children, and children with queer parents) (Griffin, 1992; Jennings, 1994; Lipkin, 1999; Martinoble, 1999; Sanders and Burke, 1994; Woog, 1995). In his groundbreaking study, Rofes (1999) surveyed and interviewed his students twenty years after taking his class and found that having an openly queer teacher affected all of them in profound ways. Not only did it make them more receptive to their queer friends, but it also 'made them more open ... to the full range of human diversity' (p86). Instead of treating queerness as an add-on to the curriculum, or openly queer teachers as resources or as change agents, this study examines what happens when queerness becomes an unplanned part of the curriculum.

Theoretical Framework

Just as queer theory argues identity is fluid instead of fixed and stable, queer pedagogues make room for 'reinvention' (ie. trying on different identities and ideologies). [...]

Queer theorists promote using education as a tool to challenge binary thinking and explore the complexity of human identity (Luhmann, 1998; Morris, 1998, 2000). Talburt (2000) claims that seeing identity as a process, not as a final destination, places a responsibility on educators 'to disrupt the self-evidence of identities' (p10). By challenging binary thinking, queer theory aligns itself with hooks' (1994) vision of teaching to transgress: 'I celebrate teaching that enables transgressions – a movement against and beyond boundaries. It is that movement which makes education the practice of freedom' (p12). [...]

In addition to exposing identity construction, educators can queer the curriculum in other ways. Morris (1998) describes a 'queer curriculum worker' as someone who: 'digresses from mainstream 'official' discourse'; 'challenges the status quo by queerly reading texts or queering texts'; 'understands that curriculum is gendered, political, historical, racial, classed, and aesthetic'; and 'sees herself or himself as a co-learner with students' (p284). [...] Openly queer teachers engage in queer pedagogy by challenging the 'norm' of teachers as heterosexual.

Just as queer theorists problematise identity and identity formation, they make knowledge and knowledge formation problematic as well. Queer theorists do not see knowledge as stable nor teaching as a transmission of knowledge. Britzman (2000) explains that instead of adults being the ones 'who already know and children people who don't know', education should make sure 'everyone has continuous opportunities to explore different views of the world, to become ethnographers of the imagination, to research how people make meanings, change their minds, use knowledge, pose problems, and create new opportunities for living life' (p49). According to queer theorists, the knowledge and positionalities students bring to the classroom come into play and learning is created in the interactions among teacher, students, and texts. [...]

Methods

In a larger study, I explored the experiences of gay and lesbian educators. I conducted a series of three individual interviews punctuated by a stimulated recall session and document collection with nine K-12 teachers who self-identified as gay or lesbian. I sought a range of outness on the part of participants, allowing me to examine teachers at various stages of the coming-out process. I also sought participants with a range of school experiences and backgrounds. I included teachers with experiences in public and private schools, teachers of different grade levels, teachers of different subject areas, teachers with varying amounts of experience, teachers whose ages ranged from early twenties to mid-sixties, and teachers whose school communities varied in terms of religion, class, and race. I found, not surprisingly, that these contextual factors influenced their comfort levels at school, with teachers at schools with more support and more diversity being more comfortable with their outness and more likely to describe 'naturally queer' moments in their teaching (see Jackson, 2006).

For this study, I used phenomenological approaches to analyse the data generated by the larger study, specifically to examine instances where queerness enters the classroom without dominating it. This focus narrowed the participant pool down to the seven who no longer identified as closeted, as those who were not open about their identities expressed fear about introducing queer topics into the curriculum. As Leonard (1994) recommends, I read the data three ways – by participant, by codes, and by life stages – to identify patterns, salience, and lines of enquiry. [...]

I gave participants copies of their transcripts between each round of interviews – to check that I captured the essence of what they said but also to inspire further reflection by participants. I also used the focus group as a member check. This gave participants the chance to revise my developing findings to more closely resemble their understandings. Fortunately, participants felt comfortable enough to ask for clarification, correct me when I misinterpreted what they said, and shape the findings. [...]

I began the final interview by recounting my understanding of the participant's life history. As I did so, each participant amended, clarified, modified, and expanded upon my rendering. Then, the participant and I discussed how his or her experiences corresponded to the overall findings. This helped to establish credibility – findings that resonate with both the researcher and participants (Ray, 1994).

Because I employed 'co-constructive' techniques advocated by Charmaz (2000), I was able to create a 'validating circle of enquiry' (Van Manen, 1990) by finding shared commonalities from my experiences and the experiences of participants to boil an experience down to its essence. Dreyfuss (1994) states that a researcher knows he or she has expressed the lived experience of participants when they say, 'You have put into words what I have always known, but did not have the words to express' (Benner, 1994:xviii). [...]

Results

Scholarship on queer pedagogy explores ways in which educators can 'queer' the curriculum, or teach in ways that call into question what is often taken for granted. Certainly the teaching practices of participants in this study reflected the queer pedagogy queer theorists advocate by calling into question hegemonies that serve to instantiate inequalities (see Jackson, 2009). But this particular study does not examine those moments of rebellion in the classroom, nor those moments when teachers explicitly challenge students' thinking; instead, it explores those non-moments when queerness was hardly even noticed and argues that this comprises queer pedagogy as well.

Participants discussed instances of queerness entering the natural flow of the curriculum without interrupting it, or, as one participant stated, 'mak[ing] it part of the mainstream conversation'. Several participants described this happening when excluding queerness would create a visible absence, for example, when queerness is pertinent to an author's work; Duncan cited Truman Capote and Willa Cather as two such authors. He also discussed the litmus test he now uses for determining what to include in his curriculum now that he is out:

I'm less likely to hide an issue now about a character who's gay or an author who's gay. Two of the essays I wrote that I read to class were gay related, so I felt freedom to be honest, not a need to control because [of it] so my monitoring is more, 'Why would I not say this thing?'

Health class also provided numerous instances of homosexuality being included in the curriculum – although this became problematic for teachers who were closeted. A teacher's own comfort level set the tone for students' comfort levels with queerness in the classroom.

On the one hand, participants explained that they made sure they did not treat queerness as 'a tack on' to the curriculum. Carolyn used the phrase 'dating relationships' instead of separating out same-sex relationships as she did in the past. Lauren made it clear that, 'There's a lot of stuff in the class that I do that is not, 'Here's the gay unit'. It's simply teaching it as part of the overall curriculum. When I started, I think I actually did do more of that ... it's getting smaller every year as I make the thing more inclusive'. On the other hand, participants made sure they did not bring in queer issues when they were only tangentially related, only when 'relevant'. Participants devised their own measuring devices for determining when and how to integrate queerness instead of forcing it into the curriculum.

In other ways, participants did bring up queer subjects even when not directly related to the curriculum. By making queerness incidental to the object of study, they sent the message that queerness is not a special topic. Duncan explained how he tries to make it 'part of the conversation – not to dispel stereotypes, just making it OK'. He explains that this is 'not intended to make waves, it's just legitimising that aspect [of gayness]'. One way he does this is by incorporating queerness in his worksheets: 'Jane and Martha adopted a child last month' ... 'What's the subject? What's the verb? Is it transitive or intransitive? What's the direct object?' [...]

There are multiple ways in which these participants 'naturalised' homosexuality in their classrooms – both as central to the curriculum and as a tool through which the curriculum was delivered – without 'normalising' it or interpreting 'the notion of equity ... as a state of sameness rather than as a state of fairness' (Goldstein, Russell, and Daley, 2007:186)

Paradoxically, sometimes participants had to force the issue in order to get to the point where queerness does not appear forced. For example, Lauren asked her students 'to imagine they are straight in an all-gay world – what would it be like?' [...]

Summer confronted the controversial nature of discussing homosexuality in class head-on: 'If I taught about gays and lesbians, they're afraid you'll become gays and lesbians' and then asked, 'Ok, how many of you are gay and lesbian today?' [...] By making students' assumptions explicit, these participants were able to create spaces in their classrooms where queerness could naturally flow as part of the classroom conversation instead of being forced.

This intentionality included making sure content, particularly queer content, does not cross the teacher-student boundary and showed a reflection on and respect for the line between pushing the envelope and creating a situation where queerness might prevent learning. [...]

Just as teachers monitored when to introduce queerness into the classroom, they monitored the appropriateness – based on multiple factors – of it as well. The integration of queerness in the classroom was epitomised when students did the work. For Duncan, this occurred when a student asked, 'How do you spell homosexual?' and when students did not react when he mentioned coming out to his Muslim brother even though it was the first time he mentioned his queerness to that class:

Never once did they say, 'Are you gay?' At least one person said in each class, 'Are you close to your brother now?' So they just hear it and run with it. And if they didn't know it, they just took it in because it was just a fact of me that I mentioned in a relevant conversation.

For Carolyn, this occurred when students discussed her partner during a class discussion when she used a personal anecdote as an example of addiction:

'It wasn't just me drinking my coffee. My partner was drinking the coffee, too'. Then this other kid goes, 'Was your partner addicted?' All of a sudden they were having this whole conversation about my partner and it was just totally normal. It was just so wonderful. And it wasn't like people were worried about saying partner or asking me about my partner. It was just like asking Mr. Bridle about his wife. And you have these kinds of experiences and you realise ... there are probably a vast majority that are OK with it, especially at this juncture.

Carolyn described this incident as 'another layer of coming out'. [...]

Although these 'naturally queer' moments in the classroom may appear effortless, particularly when initiated by students, this belies the amount of effort and courage it took for participants to foster an atmosphere where 'natural queerness' can occur, particularly during a time period when queer rights can be so contentious.

Participants did not begin their teaching this way, nor did this just automatically occur after they came out to their students. The participants who were able to create moments of natural queerness in their classrooms were the same participants who described feeling 'authentic' as described earlier in this article. First, though, they had to come out. [...] Coming out to students took different forms for each openly gay participant, but all came out in the context of their curriculum. For example, Carolyn, during a health lesson on homosexuality, asked her students to raise their hands if they knew anyone gay and then told her students 'all of your hands should be up because I'm gay'. Every year, Glen came out in the context of modelling his 'me box', a shoe box decorated with items depicting a person's identities, so as to incorporate coming out naturally into a lesson. [...]

By coming out as part of the classroom context, these teachers set the stage for making queerness part of the curriculum.

Coming out served to bring their queer identities to the forefront, but this led eventually to an integration of their identities. Using terms like 'fullest', 'accurate' and 'authentic', these teachers saw 'humanising' their teaching as a part of being a good teacher and 'integrating all parts of your identity' as part of that. So even though coming out initially may make a teacher's queer identity primary in the classroom in that moment, it paves the way for that identity to recede into the background. [...]

Not only did being out give participants new ways to address homophobia, it prevented anti-gay comments: 'Talking openly about [being gay] diffuses using gay as a weapon. There was no laughter this year'. Because queerness was treated as something natural instead of portrayed as negative or shameful, students no longer viewed it as an insult. Glen cited concrete evidence of the impact of his being openly gay on students' language:

[An eighth-grade English teacher] asked the question to her class about if they hear insults around gays and lesbians. She said she had one student who said, 'We used to all the time until we had Mr Clark last year and now no one uses that language anymore'.

Being themselves and personalising the effects of homophobic language allowed openly gay participants to change the culture of their schools.

By engaging in these potentially risky practices that set the stage for 'naturally queer' moments in their classrooms, participants 'turn[ed] the every day of school life inside out, upside down, and backwards' (Morris, 1998:285), resulting in changing the culture of their school. These particular participants engaged in queer pedagogy by challenging the 'norms' of heterosexuality – by being themselves and by creating classrooms where their controversial selves did not dominate. As Carolyn stated: 'I think [being out] is a lot more meaningful and powerful a message than any lecture or lesson about homophobia or homosexuality could be'.

Conclusion

Even though 'naturally queer' classrooms may currently be an illusion, the impact that 'naturally queer' moments have on students and teachers is very real. A primary means of doing this for our participants was just by being themselves and presenting a real face to what, for some students, was previously a mythical being:

A lot of times people who are prejudiced about anything are prejudiced against a stereotype and not a reality. Then, when you have a reality and maybe you even like that person or respect that person, then it's like, 'OK, well, all the other gay people. Not Ms. Walls She's different'. It makes people start to question, 'Well, maybe the stereotypes aren't so true. Or maybe there's a lot of ways of being gay and the one that I had in my head is an extreme'. (Carolyn) [...]

Although whole schools or even whole classrooms are not free from the prejudices and scorn of society, these 'naturally queer' moments give us a glimpse into a future time when gayness exists without homophobia.

Based on data from these participants, these moments do make a difference. Students' words and actions testified to the impact of Duncan's outness: 'Because you aren't identifiable most of the time and you are gay, you've totally dismantled our conceptions of who would be gay. We have no idea now who's gay' and 'You've just changed my freshman year in college. I can't even wait to go and meet people I don't know. The possibilities are totally endless. If you're gay, who knows what anybody else is'. Duncan also described how 'natural queerness' can be contagious:

I had this group of kids that I think at the start of the year sort of keep a distance, just kind of quiet because they're not sure what it means. I watch them. I can feel that's probably the issue. Then I watch them watch other kids not give a crap. ... In time they come around.

Not only did he do this by being himself, he also did it intentionally: 'I tell them I hunted and I watch them change their minds about what it means to be gay or to be straight, 'How can you be both a hunter and a gay person?' ... So that's a deliberate attempt to push that button'. Duncan concluded, 'I've expanded their definition of what it means to be gay'. It is important to note he expanded their notions of what it means to be heterosexual as well. But perhaps the most powerful testimonial to the impact of 'natural queerness' also comes from Duncan, when he changed a homophobe into an ally:

[My colleague] said, 'I need to tell you that you've changed me. You've totally changed the way that I look at being gay'. He was very serious and very sad. 'I was one of the ones who would have called you faggot. I was one of the ones who would have beat you up with a bat. That would have been me. I was full of that ... I was up until I met you and until I realised, because you're a wonderful teacher, the kids respect you so much, that you were gay'. Then he started crying. He gave me this huge hug, and I was high. I just welled up, even now, thinking about it. And it was very, very sweet. Ever since then, he just loves to ask me questions, [although] he's a little clunky with his gay humour.

Although I term these classroom moments 'naturally queer,' in a world where queers are still discriminated against, a 'naturally queer' classroom still remains an ideal, but the impact of these 'naturally queer' moments hold powerful messages of hope.

Source: Jackson, J. (2010) 'How do you spell homosexual?: Naturally queer moments in K-12 classrooms', *International Journal of Critical Pedagogy*, vol. 3, no. 1, pp. 36-51. Reproduced by permission

Note
Throughout this chapter, the term queer is used as an inclusive term; the terms gay and lesbian are used to indicate how participants in this study identified themselves. All participant names are pseudonyms.

References

Athanases, S. Z. (1996) A gay-themed lesson in an ethnic literature curriculum: Tenth graders' responses to 'Dear Anita'. *Harvard Educational Review*, 66(2), 231-56

Benner, P. (1994) The tradition and skill of interpretive phenomenology in studying health, illness, and caring practices. In P. Benner (ed) *Interpretive Phenomenology* (pp99-128). Thousand Oaks, CA: Sage

Blinick, B. (1994) Out in the curriculum, out in the classroom. In L. Garber (ed), *Tilting the Tower: Lesbians, teaching, queer subjects* (pp142-9). New York: Routledge

Boutillier, N. (1994) Reading, writing, and Rita Mae Brown. In L. Garber (Ed.), *Tilting the Tower: Lesbians, teaching, queer subjects* (pp135-141). New York: Routledge

Britzman, D. (2000) Precocious education. In S. Talburt and S. Steinberg (eds), *Thinking Queer: Sexuality, Culture, and Education* (pp33-60). New York: Peter Lang

Cass, V. (1979) Homosexual identity formation: A theoretical model. *Journal of Homosexuality*, 4(3), 219-36

Charmaz, K. (2000) Grounded theory: Objectivist and constructivist methods. In N. Denzin and Y. Lincoln (eds), *Handbook of qualitative research* (2nd ed, pp509-35). Thousand Oaks, CA: Sage

Coleman, E. (1982) Developmental stages of the coming out process. *Journal of Homosexuality*, 7(2/3), 31-43

Dreyfuss, H. (1994) Preface. In Benner, P. (ed) *Interpretive Phenomenology* (ppvii-xii). Thousand Oaks, CA: Sage

Griffin, P. (1992) From hiding out to coming out: Empowering lesbian and gay educators. In K. Harbeck (Ed.), *Coming out of the Classroom Closet* (pp167-96). New York: Harrington Park Press

Hammett, R. (1992) A rationale and unit plan for introducing gay ad lesbian literature into grade 12 curriculum. In P. Shannon (ed), *Becoming Political: Readings and writings in the politics of literacy education* (pp250-62). Portsmouth, NH: Heinemann

Hoffman, M. (1993) Teaching Torch Song: Gay literature in the classroom. *English Journal*, 83(5), 55-8

hooks, b. (1994) *Teaching to Transgress: Education as the practice of freedom*. New York: Routledge

Huberman, M. (1989) The professional life cycle of teachers. *Teachers College Record*, 91(1), 31-57

Jackson, J. (2006) Removing the masks: Considerations by gay and lesbian teachers when negotiating the closet door. *Journal of Poverty*, 10(2), 27-52

Jackson, J. (2007) *Unmasking Identities: An exploration of the lives of gay and lesbian teachers*. Lanham, MD: Lexington Books

Jackson, J. (2009) Teacher by day; Lesbian by night: Queer(y)ing identities and teaching. *Sexuality Research and Social Policy*, 6(2), 52-70

Jennings, K. (1994) *One teacher in Ten*. Boston: Alyson

Leonard, V. (1994) A Heideggerian phenomenological perspective on the concept of person. In Benner, P. (ed), *Interpretive Phenomenology* (pp43-64). Thousand Oaks, CA: Sage

Lipkin, A. (1999) *Understanding Homosexuality, Changing Schools*. Boulder: Westview Press

Luhmann, S. (1988) Queering/querying pedagogy? Or pedagogy is a pretty queer thing.In. W. Pinaar (Ed.) *Queer theory in education* (p141-156) Mahwah, NJ: Lawrence Earlbaum Associates

Martinoble, R. M. (1999) Lesbian mother and lesbian educator: An integrative view of affirming sexual diversity. In W. Letts and J. T. Sears (eds), *Queering Elementary Education* (pp225-36). Lanham: Rowland and Littlefield Publishers

Morris, M. (1998) Unresting the curriculum: Queer projects, queer imaginings. In W. Pinar (ed), *Queer Theory in Education* (pp275-86). Mahwah, NJ: Lawrence Erlbaum Associates

Morris, M. (2000) Dante's left foot kicks queer theory into gear. In S. Talburt and S. Steinberg (eds), *Thinking Queer: sexuality, culture, and education* (pp15-32). New York: Peter Lang

Palmer, P. (1998) *The courage to teach: Exploring the inner landscape of a teacher's life*. San Francisco: Jossey-Bass

Ray, M.A. (1994) The richness of phenomenology: Philosophic, theoretic, and methodologic concerns. In Morse, J.M. (ed), *Critical Issues in Qualitative Research Methods* (pp117-35). Thousand Oaks, CA: Sage

Rofes, E. (1999) What happens when the kids grow up? The long-term impact of an openly gay teacher on eight students' lives. In Letts, W. and Sears, J. T. (eds), *Queering Elementary Education* (pp83-96). Lanham: Rowman and Littlefield Publishers

Rofes, E. (2000) Transgression and the situated body: Gender, sex, and the gay male teacher. In S. Talburt and S. Steinberg (eds), *Thinking queer: Sexuality, culture, and education* (pp131-150). New York: Peter Lang

Sanlo, R. (1999) *Unheard voices: The effects of silence on lesbian and gay educators*. Wesport, CT: Bergin and Garvey

Sanders, S. and Burke, H. (1994) Are you a lesbian, miss? In Epstein, D. (ed), Challenging Lesbian and Gay Inequalities in Education (pp65-77). Buckingham, England: Open University Press

Signorile, M. (1999, Jan. 19) Ex-gay. Too gay. Postgay. What happened to gay? *The Advocate*, 776/777, 71-5.

Sumara, D. and Davis, B. (1998) Telling tales of surprise. In W. Pinar (ed), Queer theory in education (pp197-220). Mahwah, NJ: Lawrence Erlbaum Associates

Talburt, S. (2000) *Subject to Identity: Knowledge, sexuality, and academic practices in higher education*. Albany: State University of New York Press

Van Manen, M. (1990) *Researching lived experience*. Albany, NY: SUNY Press

Vanasco, J. (2002, March 20) *Future without shock*. [Electronic version]. Chicago Free Press

Woog, D. (1995) *School's Out*. Boston: Alyson Publications

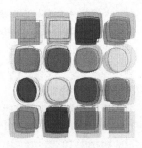

Chapter 8

Why teach against Islamophobia?
Striking the empire back

Joe L. Kincheloe and Shirley R. Steinberg

In the Western tradition of teaching about, writing about, researching, and representing Islam, Europeans have consistently positioned Muslims as the irrational, fanatic, sexually enticing, and despotic others. [...] As educators, we are concerned about these representations in light of the events of the early 21st century, After September 11, 2001, and the wars in Afghanistan and Iraq, the ways images of Islam have been embedded in the Western and especially the American consciousness become extremely important to everyday life. [...] This chapter discusses the role of miseducation within Western and global views of Islam. In order to teach against a traditional paradigm, we contend that we must first historicise how it began.

The empir(ical) creation of Islamophobia

Central to any description, Islamophobia is the West's effort – especially after the Scientific Revolution of the 17th and 18th centuries – to depict its own superiority. In the first decade of the 21st century, it is high time to clean up the historical distortions developed centuries ago and passed down across the generations. [...]

The mature culture/nation is dedicated to learning from difference. In such a nation's schools, for example, citizens come to understand that schools are contested public spaces shaped by diverse forces of power. Learning from difference means that teachers are aware of the histories and struggles of colonised groups and oppressed peoples. Such teachers would understand the complicity of educational institutions themselves in such oppression. Many scholars maintain that the classroom is a central site for the legitimisation of myths and silences about non-Western and often non-Christian peoples. If educators who value the power of difference were to teach about the history of Islam, they would have to rethink the canonical history of the West. Indeed, when school texts distort the history of Islam, they concurrently distort all history. Teachers and educational leaders who act on the power of difference forge such recognition into a politically transformative mode of education. Such pedagogy understands Western societies as collectivities of difference, where the potential exists for everyone to be edified by interaction with the other and the ways of knowing he or she brings to an encounter. [...]

Any description of a rigorous education needs to include an understanding of the power of difference that nurtures a critical sense of empathy. Cornel West (1993) contends that empathy involves the ability to appreciate the anxieties and frustrations of others, never to lose sight of the humanity of the marginalised no matter how wretched their condition – and we would add, no matter how much some of them may express their hatred for us. The point emerging here involves the pedagogical, ethical, and cognitive benefits derived from the confrontation with difference and the diverse vantage points it provides us for viewing the everyday world. Educators who value difference often begin their analysis of a phenomenon by listening to those who have suffered most as a result of its existence. These different ways of seeing allow educators and other individuals access to the new modes of cognition – a cognition of empathy. Such a perspective allows individuals access to tacit modes of racism, cultural bias, and religious intolerance that operate to structure world views.

There is little doubt that this valuing of difference or understanding of the miseducation of the West would not end the terrorist activities of groups such as Al-Qaeda. [...]

A critical education must counter such tendencies and work to conceptualise 9/11 in a variety of contexts (Hesse and Sayyid, 2001). Without this critical challenge, the effort to simply appreciate the perspectives of individuals from other cultures, other social systems, and other religious heritages can be dismissed as irrational, [...] and even anti-Christian. Historically contextualising, the Moors in Europe, for instance, illustrates a specific effort to dismiss the contributions of Islam to Western civilisation. Shirley recounts this incident: 'while touring the Alhambra this year, I asked a guide to describe to me his account of the 'Arab occupation of Spain'. He understood the nuance of my question and admitted that his tour presentation implied that the Moors, and African Muslims who came up the Iberian Peninsula did not *occupy* as he had stated, but instead, *inhabited*.'

[...] In this context, disinformation becomes the rule of the day, as generalisations about the monolithic Islamic world proliferate. The power of difference in this ideological frame is dead. [...]

Tacit ops by the empire

[...] The complexity of the relationship between the West (the United States in particular) and Islam demands that we be very careful in laying out the subtle arguments we are making about the miseducation. The activities of the American Empire have not been the only forces at work creating an Islamist extremism that violently defies the sacred teaching of the religion. American misdeeds have also played an important role in the process. A new critical education, based on an appreciation of difference, can help the United States redress some of its past and present policies toward the diverse Islamic world. While these policies have been invisible to many Americans, they are visible to the rest of the world – the Islamic world in particular. Ignoring the history of the empire, Kenneth Weinstein (2002) writes that the Left 'admits' that differences do exist between cultures –

but paradoxically downplays their violent basis through relativism and multiculturalism. It views cultural diversity and national differences as matters of taste arguing that the greatest crime of all is judgmentalism.

Weinstein concludes this paragraph by arguing that Americans are just too nice and as such are naive to the threats posed by many groups around the world. [...]

With all of their concern for teaching history, right-wing perspectives often ignore the warnings of past American leaders, such as George Washington, against the temptations of empire building. As President John Quincy Adams put it in the 1820s: 'If America were tempted to become the dictatress of the world, she would be no longer the ruler of her own spirit' (Ignatieff, 2003:24). As the American Empire spends massive sums of money on its foreign excursions, it finds it more and more difficult to designate money for democratic essentials at home such as infrastructural needs and education. The costs of the empire consistently undermine the promise of domestic democracy and economic justice.

When teaching and discussing issues involving Iran, it is important to consider the inability of American leaders to understand the impact of empire building in the Persian Gulf on the psyches of those personally affected by such activities. In the case of Iraq in the Second Gulf War, American leaders simply disregarded the views of nations around the world, the Muslim world in particular, as they expressed their opposition to the American invasion. History was erased as Saddam Hussein was viewed in a psychological context as a madman. References to the times when the United States supported the madman were deleted from memory. The empire, thus, could do whatever it wanted, regardless of its impact on the Iraqi people or the perceptions of others (irrational others) around the world. [...]

Understanding the politics of knowledge to teach against Islamophobia

North Americans – as well, of course, as other peoples around the planet – are victimised by the new American Empire's politics of knowledge. In the contemporary electronic world saturated by the information of corporate knowledge producers, many Americans simply are unaware of knowledges constructed by diverse groups and individuals. [...]

The right-wing story about the contemporary world situation conveniently omits the last 500 years of European colonialism, the anti-colonial movements around the world beginning in the post-World War II era and their impact on the US civil rights movement, the women's movement, the anti-war movement in Vietnam, Native American Liberation struggles, the gay rights movement, and other emancipatory movements. In other work, we have labelled the reaction to these anti-colonial movements that have set the tone and content of much of American political, social, and educational experience over the last three decades (Gresson, 1995, 2003; Kincheloe and Steinberg, 1997; Kincheloe, Steinberg, Rodriguez, and Chennault, 1998; Rodriguez and Villaverde, 2000). [...]

How the right wing constructs the barbarian other

[...] One of the lessons scholars around the world learned in the last three decades of the 20th century was that no knowledge is disinterested. All information is produced by individuals operating at a particular place and a specific time – they see the world and employ methods for viewing the world from a particular point in the complex web of reality. Understanding, for example, a speech by an Islamic cleric about his revulsion in relation to American culture's influence in his nation or region involves a different type of contextualised and historcised analysis than a mathematician solving an obstinate mathematical problem. Those from the West who study and examine the words of the Islamic cleric must:

- understand the unique interpretive circumstances of a Western student engaging with an Islamic text
- be sensitive to the power relationships between the interpreter's culture and the culture of the cleric
- be aware of the purposes for which the interpretation will be used.

Thus, a key dimension of the miseducation of the West assumes that Western knowledge of Islam and the Islamic world is objective and disinterested. The West's distorted vie\v of Islam, labelled by Said (1979) as Orientalism, has re-emerged in the last couple of decades of the 20th and the first decade of the 21st centuries in a new and more dangerous version. Post-modern Orientalism is now promoted by TV news, film [...] edutainment CD-ROMs, and video games. A distorted, demonised view of the Islamic world is passed along by a pedagogy much more powerful than traditional academic scholarship. The new cultural pedagogy colonises consciousness via the pleasure of the entertainment media. No matter how horrible the Second Gulf War may have been, it was damn good entertainment for many back home. As a colleague described a conversation between himself and two of his male university students before the outbreak of the war:

Professor: So you understand the reasons many people oppose the war in Iraq?

Student 1:   Yeah, the arguments make a lot of sense but still, you know, uh, uh ...

Student 2:   What we're saying is that it's going to be so much fun to watch on TV. We can hardly wait.

Such a powerful politics of knowledge wins the consent of individuals to dominant American power along an axis of pleasure even when their logical facilities might resist. Despite its new attire and high-tech modes of transmission, postmodern Orientalism still relies on traditional Orientalism's medieval images of Islam as a barbaric and derivative theology of sodomites. [...]

In all of these multimedia works, Islam – and the rest of the world for that matter – is seen through the geo-political interests of the American Empire. America becomes the barometer for all human civilisation with the alumni of the Harvard Business School occupying the highest link of the civilisational food chain. [...] Civilisation and human accomplishment in these contemporary sources are exclusively European phenomena and the contemporary world is viewed through a US Cold War and post-Cold War national interest perspective. In the post-Cold War framework, the icon of the Muslim terrorist represents the general Islamic threat to US global dominance. After the fall of the 'evil empire' of the Communist bloc, the Islamic threat fills the enemy vacuum quite effectively. From these and countless other Western sources on Islam, one would learn that not only did Islam promote ignorance but there was no role for Islam in a grand universal history of mankind. [...]

So when educators with a critical consciousness of the consequences of colonialism and the distortions of the right-wing politics of knowledge began to construct pictures of Islam that considered different ways of seeing the world, right-wing scholars were angered. Although such representations rarely find their way into elementary and secondary curricula, right-wing scholars – especially after 9/11 – asserted that they did and attempted to scare their constituencies with allegations that these perspectives were taking over the field. [...]

Mistrusting the American discourse

One dimension of the story we are telling in this book involves the reasons for the hatred and mistrust of the United States in the Islamic world. It is true that not all Muslims around the world in their cultural, political, social, and theological diversity hate the United States. But why is it that so many do? One answer to this complex question is directly related to the miseducation delineated here: so many people in the Islamic world hate the United States because many Americans have no idea why they should harbour such feelings. Many Muslims around the world express shock at widespread ignorance among Americans about the US role in the world and in Islamic history. When Chester Finn (2002) writes that 9/11 presents a chance for Americans 'to teach our daughters and sons about heroes and villains, about freedom and repression, about hatred and nobility, democracy and theocracy, about civic virtue and vice' the American blindness to colonial and neo-colonial atrocities around the world is revealed. Also, there is a degree of cowardice in Finn's Manichaean binaries for he never simply states that Muslims are the villains, repressers, haters, theocrats, and purveyors of vice – he simply implies it over and over again in order to maintain plausible deniability of racism. [...]

The fundamentalism of the right-wing politics of knowledge is central to our understanding of the hatred and mistrust of the West, the United States in particular. Fundamentalism as used in this context is defined as the belief in the inerrancy of Americana, the American political philosophy in particular as well as the Western scientific creed and its methods for producing objective knowledge. [...]

On one level it is trite to argue that Americans need to know more about the world. But in the context of the right-wing politics of knowledge, progressives must insist on more sophisticated understandings of the perspectives of other cultures, especially the role of the United States in the world. We must demand higher media news standards – TV and radio coverage that provides multiple perspectives and viewpoints from around the world. US media must get beyond representing the United States as victim in international relations and provide insight into America's role in the complex system of world events. In this complex context, understanding and addressing the genesis of terrorism and anti-American sentiments in the world should not constitute a controversial act.

Historicising Islamophobia

When educators struggle to place the events of the late 20th and early 21st centuries in historical context, do they discern historical continuity connecting the intersection of Western (or Christian) cultures and Islam? Is it a misappropriation of history to trace Western-Islamic relations from the rise of Islam in the 7th century through Charles Martel's victory at the Battle of Tours in the 8th century, the Crusades, the Ottoman Empire, and the rise of other Islam societies, European colonialism to the Islamophobia of the present? Obviously, human beings make selective uses of the past to make sense of and rationalise particular dimensions of the present (Runnymede Trust, 1997). To some extent all political positions are historical interpretations. These are important questions that must be kept in mind by educators and policy makers as they attempt to understand contemporary Western and Islamic relations.

Despite the contemporary stereotypes of Muslims as intolerant and prone to terrorism and violence, historical scholarship teaches a very different picture. For example, in Spain from the 8th century to the 14th century, Abukhattala argues, the Muslim empire was one of the most tolerant in history. Jews, Christians, and Muslims lived and worked together in harmony for 800 years. From the First Crusade at the end of the 11th century onward, Muslims in the Middle East experienced European entry into Islamic lands as an assault. As the British and French moved into the Muslim world in the 18th century, the assault from the Islamic perspective continued and intensified (Abukhattala, 2004).

From the Crusades and colonialism the Europeans 'learned' that Muslims were barbaric, ugly, zealous, and ignorant. Such perceptions allowed a moral justification to the European colonial project around the world. With the coming of European modernity in the 17th and 18th centuries, there emerged a new articulation of European superiority that positioned the Muslims and other peoples around the world as profoundly incompetent and inferior. Viewing these 'inferior' peoples played a central role in shaping European self-consciousness. In the medieval period, Europeans had been intimidated by what they knew was the superior learning of the Muslim civilisation. After the Scientific Revolution and the birth of modernity Europe was seen by Europeans as most definitely superior. This notion of European superiority became the foundation for the miseducation of the West.

At the very least, we begin to learn from these historical insights that the Islamophobic depictions of Western-Islamic relations are more complex than the right-wing politics of education would have us believe. While there are no disinterested selections of historical events, we can conclude, at the very least, that there exist many versions of this story. The story told in mainstream media and education cannot be separated from the influence of historical and contemporary Islamophobia. What is interesting here is that these historical and contemporary versions of Islamophobia intersect in what we call the miseducation of the West. The barbaric images of Islam developed during the Crusades and colonialism lay in wait, ready to be deployed when the political climate needed them – as during the oil embargo of 1973 or the First Gulf War of 1991. When most post-Enlightenment Western scholars researched Islam through the conceptual lenses of Western modernity, employing its assumptions about knowledge production, the ways human societies should develop, the nature of civilisation, and the waiting of history, they found – not surprisingly – Islamic culture(s) to be inferior.

Islamic law in these studies was not real jurisprudence and Islamic ways of making meaning not real rationality. Soon a canon of Islamic studies developed and these ethnocentric assumptions became sanctified as the findings of the old masters of the field. Scholars of the tradition maintain that it became quite authoritarian and aggressively resisted criticism, both from within and outside the discipline. Samuel P. Huntington's *The Clash of Civilizations: Remaking of World Order* (1996) is the most popular contemporary articulation of this scholarly tradition. The thesis is by no means original – that violence and barbarism are central traits of Muslims – but in Huntington's hands they are turned into a broader ideology. The ideology that there is an inevitable clash of civilisations between the Western Christian nations and the Eastern Islamic and Confucian societies is injected into the discourse of US foreign policy. If the United States does not act decisively, the ideology asserts, bloody Islam will continue its warring tradition against the West. The idea that Muslims have often been victims of Western violence is conveniently omitted from Huntington's thesis (Hippler, 1995; Lueg, 1995). [...]

The contemporary Islamophobic miseducation of the West is guided by this inevitable cultural conflict model. The notion that the United States exercises new forms of economic and cultural colonialism or that the United States has intervened in the internal affairs of different nations to help install governments favourable to US economic and geo-political interests is forbidden knowledge in these models. The idea that US oil companies might have engaged in corporate practices that were not fair to oil-producing Muslim nations is also erased. The racism toward Muslims sanctioned by such models can be heard in countless media productions. [...]

The miseducation of the West emerges from a long history of distorted Western knowledge about Islam. In the contemporary post-Cold War era we witness a new period of Islamophobia fanned by numerous scholars and the media. What the editors and authors of this book are not arguing is that Islamic nations have no responsibility for intolerance, fundamentalist zealotry, and inhuman terrorism. What we are maintaining is that all of these traits can be found in all cultures and religions, and that Western scholarship and education have often painted a Eurocentric black and white picture of who is 'civilised' and who is not. [...]

Diversity is Islam ... Islam is diverse

A key point that we have already alluded to involves the understanding that there is no essentialised, unified Islamic world about which we can make uncomplicated generalisations. [...] The portraits of Islam delineated by Orientalists both old and new never existed and do not exist in the first decade of the 21st century, The perception of Islam as the 'enemy' is a social construction of Westerners, especially Americans. As argued previously, rejecting this enemy status does not mean that we should affirm all actions of Islamic peoples and societies (Lueg, 1995). When, however, a secondary school textbook such as Petrovich, Roberts, and Roberts's World Cultures chooses a picture of Muslim men praying with their guns beside them, out of the millions of photographs of Muslim men praying, a critical education of Islam 'calls out' such fear-mongering (MESA, 1994).

Obviously, some elements of the Islamic world, specifically some individuals often referred to as Islamic fundamentalists, have made violence a central duty of true believers. These individuals often allude to traditional Western/US colonialism and its new economic and cultural varieties as *al-Salibiyyah* – the Crusade. This new Crusade, while less violent, has exerted a more powerful impact on the Islamic world than did the medieval invasions by Christian warriors. In the new Crusade of economic and cultural colonialism, the Muslim world has been positioned as dependent on the United States, and major cultural displacements have resulted from modernisation and economic development programs. In the Muslim world, as well as in the societies populated by other religions, individuals have been taken aback by the secular dimensions of the new colonialism. In response they have turned to a literal and insular fundamentalist version of their faiths. As they fight back against those they perceive as the infidels, they replace the central values of generosity, love, and justice with more and more strident forms of intolerance and hatred (Armstrong, 2002). The Western/US retaliation for the violent acts that come out of this fundamentalist intolerance increases the cycle of hatred and violence.

Recognition of this complexity and diversity in the Islamic world and the one-dimensional representations of the politics of knowledge which we are referring to here as the miseducation, demands a pedagogical revolution. Such a revolution would involve:

- understanding the United States from the perspectives of diverse groups around the world
- gaining a historical awareness of the relationship between the United States and the rest of the. world
- appreciating the reasons many individuals around the world claim that the US population is historically and politically uninformed.

Without these insights and understanding of the nature of the way US power operates in the world, America is entering into a dangerous period where wars with perceived threats to the American Empire will be the order of the day. We do not believe that the United States, like many militarily overextended empires before it, will survive such a future. As a result of the miseducation, the United States encounters every new international circumstance as if it were a totally new situation, completely unrelated to colonial histories and global political and economic issues. [...]

A complex and rigorous education ignores the right-wing call to dispose of multiculturalism and diversity in our schools (Finn, 2002). A rigorous and critical education analyses the United States and the world as well as the US relationship to the world. Teachers, students, and citizens must understand how knowledge is produced about these subjects, the ways that power shapes the types of knowledge to which we have access. The questions of where do we get our knowledge, how is it produced, and whose interests does it serve grant us access to one of the most important concerns of our time – the politics of knowledge in an age of electronic media. When we are openly discouraged by the advocates of a right-wing politics of knowledge from exploring diverse knowledges and perspectives, our political crap detectors should detonate. Such a policy is not compatible with a democratic society, not to mention a democratic education. A key dimension of a democratic education involves a literacy of power that enables an individual to explore the relation between power and knowledge, to expose the imprint of power on the knowledge that confronts us. 'Inevitable civilisational conflicts' has a Fascist ring to it, as it forces us into direct conflict with Islamic others. If the conflict is inevitable then we might as well go ahead and take their oilfields, because they are just going to use the oil money to attack us anyway. We suggest a pre-emptive strike; we have no choices. We actively teach against Islamophobia, we name it, we historicise it, and we debunk it.

Anti-Islamophobic education

A literacy of power helps us understand that the United States has entered a new phase in its national development. The American Empire in the 2nd decade of the 21st century stands ready to use military action to defend its economic and geo-political interests whenever necessary. Under the rhetorical cover of fighting for democracy and liberation, the United States seeks a new form of global domination. Most of the time it will avoid directly ruling a nation, opting instead for installing friendly governments that allow the US economic and cultural domination. These friendly governments face few restrictions around issues of democracy or human rights as long as they create friendly business climates for American corporations. In these good business climates the nation's land, labour, markets, and natural resources are open to exploitation by transnational corporations (Parenti, 2002).

In the name of democracy, the United States has supported dictators and tyrants in the Islamic world including Saddam Hussein before the First Gulf War and Osama bin Laden in the Afghan fight against the Soviets. Wrapped in the flag of freedom the United States has insisted that Muslim governments silence the voices that criticise American policies in the region (Hesse and Sayyid, 2001). Such contradictions are repressed in the mainstream media and in the right-wing politics of knowledge in general. As William Damon (2002) writes in his chapter in the Fordham report:

To understand that freedom and democracy must he defended, young people need to know three things: 1) What life is like in places that honour these ideals and in places that don't; 2) How these ideals have come to prevail in some places and not in others; and 3) Why some people hate these ideals and what we must do about that.

If it were only that simple and free from contradictions, Damon's first two points reference the simplistic binarism contrasting those (the United States) that support freedom and democracy and those (the despotic Muslims) who don't. His third point deals with the mission of the 21st century empire. Those who hate these ideals must be dealt with so that the empire can function more efficiently.

Despite the power of the US corporate media to produce an information environment that refuses to refer to the American Empire or give credence to alternative views of US. relations with the Islamic world, many Americans still protested the Second Gulf War with Iraq. In speeches Shirley and Joe delivered after 9/11 explaining some of the reasons for the anger many Muslims have felt toward the United States, even politically conservative audiences were interested by the alternative information and perspectives we were providing. Members of the audience wisely asked why they had not heard the information we were providing. We live in an era of depoliticisation, where public discourse around political questions slowly fades away in a world of ideologically charged entertainment. In such a cosmos, a literacy of power becomes more and more important as we struggle to counter the miseducation that continues to shape American views of the world.

Source: Kincheloe, L., J. and Steinberg, R., S. (2010), 'Why teach against Islamophobia? Striking the Empire back', in Kincheloe, L.J., Steinberg, R.S. and Stonebanks, D.C. (eds), *Teaching Against Islamophobia*, Peter Lang. Copyright (c) Peter Lang Publishing, Inc., New York

References

Abukhattala, I. (2004) The new bogeyman under the bed: Image formation of Islam in the Western school curriculum and media. In J. Kincheloe and S. Steinberg (eds), *The Miseducation of the West: How schools and the media distort our understanding of the Islamic world.* Westport, CT: Praeger

Armstrong, K. (2002) *Islam agonistes: The Arrival of the West.* retrieved from http://dhustra.com/book/upd3/2002a/histis.htm

Damon, W. (2002) Teaching students to count their blessings. In Thomas, B. Fordham Foundation. *September 11: What our children need to know.* Retrieved from http://www.edexcellence.net/sept11/september11.pdf

Finn, C. (2002) Introduction. In Thomas, B. Fordham Foundation. *September 11: What our children need to know.* Retrieved from http://www.edexcellence.net/sept11/september11.pdf

Gresson, A. (1995) *The Recovery of Race in America.* Minneapolis, MN: University of Minnesota Press

Gresson, A. (2003) *America's atonement.* New York: Peter Lang

Hesse, B. and Sayyid, S. (2001) *A War Against Politics?* Retrieved from http://opendemocracy.net/forum/document

Hippler, J. (1995) The Islamic threat and Western foreign policy. In J. Hippler and A. Lueg (eds), *The Next Threat: Western Perceptions of Islam.* London: Pluto Press

Huntington, S. (1996) *The Clash of Civilizations: Remaking of World Order.* New York: Touchstone

Ignatieff, M. (2003) The burden. *New York Times Magazine.* (January 5) pp.22-27, 50-54

Kincheloe, J.L. and Steinberg, S.R. (1997) *Changing Multiculturalism.* London: Open University Press

Kincheloe, J.L., Steinberg, S.R., Rodriguez, N. and Chennault, R. (1998) *White Reign: Deploying Whiteness in America.* New York: St Martin's Press

Lueg, A. (1995) The perception of Islam in Western debate. In J. Hippler and A. Lueg (eds), *The Next Threat: Western Perceptions of Islam.* London: Pluto Press

Middle East Studies Association (MESA) (1994) Evaluation of Secondary-level Textbooks for Coverage of Middle East and North Africa. Retrieved from http://www.umich.edu/~iinet/cmenas/textbooks/reviews/summarya.html

Parenti, M. (2002) *The Terrorism Trap: September 11 and Beyond.* San Francisco, CA: City Lights Books

Rodriguez, N. and Villaverde, L. (2000) *Dismantling White Privilege.* New York: Peter Lang

Runnymede Trust (1997) *The Nature of Islamophobia*. Retrieved from http://www.runnymede-trust.org.meb/islamophobia/nature.html

Said, E. (1979) *Orientalism*. London: Vintage

Weinstein, K. (2002) Fighting complacency. In Thomas, B. Fordham Foundation. *September 11: What our children need to know*. Retrieved from http://www.edexcellence.net/sept11/september11.pdf

West, C. (1993) *Race Matters*. Boston: Beacon Press

Chapter 9

An inclusive classroom? A case study of inclusiveness, teacher strategies, and children's experiences

Claes Nilholm and Barbro Alm

This chapter reports on a case study of what appears to be an inclusive classroom in Sweden. Given the long-term focus on inclusion it is rather astonishing that so few in-depth analyses of inclusive processes in the classroom have been attempted. Inclusion is a concept that can mean different things and necessarily involves several dilemmas (Norwich, 1993; Clark, Dyson, and Millward, 1998; Volonino and Zigmond, 2007). The fact that children with disabilities attend ordinary classes is a necessary but insufficient condition for inclusion. In order to talk about inclusion, certain values are central (Booth and Ainscow, 2002; Carrington, 2006); for example, the positive valuation of children's differences (Oliver, 1990) and the importance of children thriving in schools. [...] Several researchers suggest there is a risk that inclusion only involves moving special educational practices into the classroom (McLeskey and Waldron, 2007). Some authors even question whether progress is being achieved towards making education more inclusive (Williamsson *et al*, 2006). [...]

Earlier research

Scruggs, Mastropieri and McDuffie (2007) synthesised the qualitative research of 32 surveys of co-teaching in 'inclusive' classrooms. Interestingly, the dominant co-teaching role was discovered to be 'one teaches, one assists' and the classrooms were characterised by traditional teaching: '...general education teachers typically employ whole class, teacher-led instruction with little individualisation, whereas special education teachers function largely as assistants' (Scruggs, Mastropieri and McDuffie, 2007:411). In an overview of both quantitative and qualitative studies of co-teaching in 'inclusive' classrooms, Weiss and Brigham (2000) reached similar conclusions to Scruggs, Mastropieri and McDuffie (2007). However, there are studies outside of the co-teaching tradition that suggest that other strategies such as cooperative group teaching might be beneficial to inclusive processes (Slavin, 1996; Swanson and Hoskyn, 1998).

Several researchers point out the importance of building a community within the classroom in order to make education inclusive (Han, Ostrovsky and Diamond, 2006; Putney, 2007). Soodak (2003:328) suggests: 'Philosophically and pragmatically, inclusive education is primarily about belonging, membership, and acceptance'. However, Pijl, Frostad and Flem (2008) found that children with special educational needs were often not socially included, in that they were less popular, had fewer relationships, and participated less often as members of a subgroup. Findings of social exclusion are common in articles (Nowicki and Sandieson, 2002; Estell, 2008) which often say that this lack of social inclusion arises because choice of peers is based on similarity (McPherson, Smith-Lovin and Cook, 2001). In addition, social acceptance seems to differ between categories of pupils with different disabilities (Garrison-Harell and Kamps, 1997; Pijl, Frostad and Flem, 2008). It is also well known that children with special educational needs are at risk of being educationally excluded in that they run an increased risk of poor performance at school (Persson, 1998; Emanuelsson and Persson, 2002; Weiss, 2004).

Earlier research thus suggests that what is called inclusion often leaves ordinary teaching unchanged and only involves moving special educational practices into the ordinary classroom. Consequently, it becomes important to analyse in what sense studied classrooms are inclusive. As has been shown, educational and social inclusion seems hard to achieve. If classrooms are found that can be shown to exhibit inclusive features, it becomes very important to study what teachers do in order to accomplish such inclusive features. [...]

The Swedish school system

Sweden has about nine million inhabitants. The school system rests on a rhetoric of 'one school for all', that is, a common school for all children in Grades 1–9 (7–16 years old). Goals for the Swedish school system are set by national authorities. However, the means of achieving these goals are the responsibility of the 290 municipalities and the local schools. As in several other countries, accountability, testing, and training of basic skills have become more significant in recent years (Skolverket, 2009). However, this tendency is not as evident as in the US and the UK. Until recently, grades were not awarded until eighth grade and national tests were not taken until fifth grade. [...] About 10 per cent of children in 'ordinary' school are not eligible for upper secondary education. At any given point in time about 15–20 per cent of the children receive special support. Few children attend special schools, except for the 1.5 per cent of schoolchildren who attend special programmes for pupils with developmental disorders (a minority of these children are integrated in ordinary classrooms). A minority of the children outside the special schools and the special programmes for children with developmental disorders receive additional support in segregated settings. In total, about 3 per cent of children receive their education in segregated settings in the Swedish school system, although there are no exact figures (Nilholm *et al*, 2007).

The case study

The overall framework of the present investigation was a case study approach. [...] Case study analysis is especially suitable for complex phenomena (Yin, 2002; Stark and Torrance, 2007). [...] An important aim of the study was to develop a methodology that makes it possible to study the inclusiveness of classrooms in a transparent way using an explicit definition of inclusion that includes the experience of the pupils. This is a necessary step in order to ask additional research questions concerning what teaching strategies seem to be beneficial to inclusive processes and how these strategies affect the experiences of the children.

Setting and participants

The present case was chosen from eight settings investigated in a pilot study because it seemed more inclusive and involved a very heterogeneous classroom. The eight settings were chosen because they had a reputation of being inclusive in several respects. Around 300 pupils (aged 7–12) attended the school in which the classroom was situated. The buildings were fairly worn. Pupils were recruited from the surrounding area with mixed housing, that is, apartments which are rented or owned, small houses, and some larger houses. The area was of low socio-economic status. The principal displayed a positive attitude towards inclusive education and democratic schooling. The class which was the focus of the present case study was followed over two years (Grades 5 and 6). [...]

There were two teachers in the class. Teacher A had the main responsibility for the class and had taught them since first grade. Normally, she would have been replaced in Grade 4 since she taught Grades 1–3. However, owing to her work with the class she was asked to continue for Grades 4–6. Teacher B was a preschool teacher but was asked to follow the class into Grade 1 and had stayed with the class since then. There were fifteen children in the class, of whom five had been diagnosed by child psychiatrists and one additional child was diagnosed after the study. Teacher A described how she perceived the class when she first met them at the time they were leaving preschool and entering first grade at the age of seven:

That was my first meeting with them and at that time the preschool considered this group to be a disaster. You know they had never seen anything like it and one felt that they would not have a chance at school. (Teacher A)

At that point in time, the group was larger. One child subsequently moved to the special school for children with developmental disabilities, two children moved to a charter school, and some parents moved out of the area. A few new children entered the class; among them a child who was later diagnosed with a neuropsychiatric disorder after the children started secondary schooling. At the time of the study, four of the children had been diagnosed with neuropsychiatric disorders (two with Asperger's syndrome and two with attention deficit hyperactivity disorder [ADHD]) and one additional child had been evaluated as being on the borderline of being developmentally disabled. Three of these children were one year older than the other children in the class. Thus, the class was exceptionally heterogeneous with regard to child characteristics. This is an important point, since inclusion involves teaching children with varying characteristics. Some of these children would, in other circumstances, be educated in more segregated settings. [...]

Data collection

Firstly, the teachers, parents, and pupils were informed about the aim of the study. They signed written agreements to participate, and were notified that they could drop out of the study whenever they wanted to without having to provide a reason for their decision. Furthermore, they were informed that the outcome of the study would be published in a form which would keep the participants anonymous. Everyone agreed to participate in the study.

A prerequisite to data gathering was to develop a methodology which rests on an explicit definition of inclusion and underscores the importance of the experiences of the children. Three criteria were used when analysing the inclusiveness of the class-room. These were the extent of: (1) differences being viewed as ordinary; (2) all students being part of the social community of the classroom; and (3) all students being part of the learning community of the classroom. Interviews with children and teachers were used in order to analyse their views of differences in the classroom. Questionnaires, sociograms, and interviews with children were used in order to evaluate the level of social inclusion. Being part of the learning community was evaluated using results from national testing and using responses to some of the questions in the questionnaire. Thus, these data sources were used as part of the methodology that was developed in order to scrutinise in what sense studied classrooms are inclusive given the aforementioned definition of inclusion. Interviews with teachers were used in order to discern teacher strategies. In-depth analyses of the experiences of the children were based on interviews and poems (see later). Participant observation as well as a member check procedure described later were used in order to validate the data sources mentioned previously. One of the researchers spent a total of 34 days observing class work during a period of about two years.

The interviews were semi-structured and interview guides were used. In the interviews with the teachers, central topics were the history of the class, teacher strategies, and their views of the children. Interviews were conducted in the morning with all the children ($n = 15$) individually in a room adjacent to the classroom. Moreover, some of the children ($n = 9$) voluntarily provided poems that they had written in their 'books of reflections'. The interviews with the children were fairly short (about 10–15 minutes) and centred on similar topics to the ones in the questionnaire, such as how the children felt at school, what their relationships were like, whether they had a best friend, and so on. The observations in the classroom focused on teacher strategies, teacher-child interactions, and class work in general; field notes were taken. The questionnaire to be answered by the children was drawn up for the purposes of the present study and contained eleven statements with yes/no alternatives. The two sociograms were created from the children's responses to the instructions: 'Choose four friends who you would like to work with' and 'Choose four friends who you would like to be with/play with'. Finally, the outcome of national tests taken in Grade 5 was collected.

Data analysis

All interviews were transcribed by the second author. The parts of the interviews that concerned children's and teachers' views of differences were analysed thematically (cf. Braun and Clark, 2006) by the first author of this chapter. Themes were reviewed by the second author and compared to field notes resulting in a few changes. Questionnaires, sociograms, and interviews with children were analysed in order to evaluate the level of social inclusion. Being part of the learning community was evaluated using results from national testing and using responses to some of the questions in the questionnaire as well as to questions in the children's interviews. At the time of the study, grades were not awarded until eighth grade. However, in fifth grade, children take national exams in Swedish, maths, and English, and the results from these exams were used to evaluate whether the children were part of the learning community.

The interviews with the teachers were analysed qualitatively by the first author in order to discern strategies. All the strategies mentioned by the teachers in the interviews were noted and sorted into themes. These themes were reviewed by the second author and compared to field notes resulting in a few changes.

A member check (Creswell, 2000) that applied to all the data involving the teachers was used. Thus, the researcher not involved in collecting data conducted a follow-up two-hour interview with Teacher A after the data had been analysed. In this way, facts as well as observations and interpretations made by the researchers were systematically compared to the teacher's understanding of the same events as reported in the follow-up interview. Open questions were used in order to allow

Teacher A to describe events in her own words. This step led to some changes. The last step involved both Teacher A and Teacher B reading a final draft of the article; this step led to some very minor overall changes.

The final analysis was the in-depth analysis of the children's experiences. Excerpts from the interviews with the children are provided in order to illustrate the general pattern of responses as well as some problematic aspects of some of the children's experiences of the classroom. This analysis was made by the first author and reviewed by the second author. The poems were analysed thematically by the first author and the themes were reviewed by the second author resulting in minor changes. Individual excerpts from the interviews and poems are presented and analysed in order to provide a description of the experiences of the children and to account for the complexities involved.

Results

An inclusive classroom?

View of differences

Two overarching themes were discerned: (1) viewing differences as an asset; and (2) viewing differences as a problem. Almost all participants in the study provided statements in the first category, that is, they expressed a positive view of difference. However, some of them also provided statements belonging to the second theme, viewing differences as problematic. A few of the children pointed out that other children's characteristics could be problematic and a couple of them viewed their own characteristics as problematic. The teachers, on the other hand, alternated between expressing that children's differences were an asset and viewing them as individual shortcomings, for example, as difficulties in thinking theoretically or understanding instructions. However, the children as such were valued by the teachers, although the teachers clearly recognised that some children had shortcomings in specific areas.

Social inclusion

The questionnaire revealed that children felt they were part of the class. All children ($n = 15$) stated that they were content in the class, nearly always had someone to be with during breaks, and that they felt secure. In addition, all children agreed with the statements that their classmates listened to them during group work, that they themselves were good listeners during group work, and fourteen out of the fifteen children agreed with the statement 'I like to work together in a group' (one child wrote 'depends on the subject'). In total, ten out of fifteen children did not agree with the statement 'I like to work by myself best', while five wrote 'at times' or 'depends'. None of the children agreed with the statements that they were afraid of someone in the class and that they often felt alone. Thirteen of the children stated that they had a best friend in the class and one wrote 'kind of best friends'. Eight of the children stated that at times they felt irritated and disturbed by someone else in the class.

The children answered the written questions: 'Choose four friends who you would like to work with' and 'Choose four friends who you would like to be with/play with'. Since there were only minor differences between the responses to these two questions, only the answers to the second question will be presented here. The resulting sociogram indicated that three children were chosen twice, two were chosen three times, five were chosen four times, four were chosen five times, and one pupil was chosen seven times. The children who had a medical diagnosis at the time of the study were on average chosen 2.8 times (range 2–5), in other words, clearly below average. Furthermore, three of the five children with disabilities chose each other. To sum up, the questionnaire and the sociograms indicate that the children on a general level seemed to be content in the classroom, enjoyed working in groups, and no one seemed to be socially isolated. However, the children with disabilities were on average picked less often as someone to be with/play with.

Inclusion in the learning community

As revealed by the answers to the questionnaire, the children seemed to feel involved in the learning community of the class. However, four of the children in the study had problems achieving the goals in fifth grade in one of the subjects, and one child did not achieve the goals in any of the three subjects. As will be elaborated later, two of the children perceived themselves as having problems learning. However, with additional help provided by the special needs teacher, four of the five children passed the exams. Such help is allowed according to exam regulations. The exam results were slightly better than those of other schools in the municipality. Teacher A had been worried about the national exams and expressed some doubts in the interview about the way she had been working. She also expressed sharp criticism towards the national exams which she thought did not take the individuality of children into account and thus might be a hindrance to more inclusive practices (cf. Goodman, 2006; Lloyd, 2008).

So in what sense was the classroom studied inclusive? Perhaps it is wise not to view inclusion as an all-or-nothing phenomenon. Instead, classrooms can be more or less inclusive. Taken in this sense of the word, the classroom studied could be considered as inclusive to a great extent, especially considering the heterogeneous group of children involved. Differences were largely viewed as ordinary and the students were to a large extent part of the social and learning community of the classroom.

What strategies were used by the teachers?

The strategies below emerged from the analysis. For the sake of space, short descriptions are provided:

1 Adapt instruction to the individual needs of children

2 Provide clear frameworks in the form of:

a Ground rules, that is, everyone has the right to voice their opinion and should respectfully listen to others' opinions. This means that you must not laugh at other people's point of view. You do not have to agree on issues, and it is natural and a good thing that people have different points of view and are different

b Clear planning of the school day and of what is expected of the children

c Taking immediate action when problems arise

3 Utilise group activities in order to strengthen social processes and learning, for example, outdoor activities (about 30–40% of the time in Grades 1–6 comprised outdoor activities). Altogether roughly 50 per cent of the activities in the class were conducted in groups, 15 per cent consisted of whole-class instruction, and 30 per cent individual work. The teachers decided on the composition of the groups. The group activities involved play, cooperative problem-solving, and gathering material to be used in class (eg. the children made their own readers in first grade by taking digital photographs and writing about the pictures). The children also went to camps and held group and small-group discussions – often involving controversial social issues, which seem to be rare subjects even among older children in social-science classes (Rossi, 2006). In addition there was a class council run by the pupils in which responsibilities (such as being chairperson and secretary) were rotated [...]

4 Create good relations with the parents, which involved letting them take part in the goals of the schooling, and meeting them often – not only when problems arise [...]

5 Include talking and discussions in academic exercises, even in maths, and encourage joint problem solving

6 Respect the children, be positive and avoid confrontational relations, thus never letting children lose face [...]

The children's experiences of the classroom

As stated previously, two of the children said in the interviews that they felt that their academic achievements were a problem. Both were children who had disabilities. In the middle of the interview, Jeff said the following in response to a question concerning group work:

J: For example [pause] to work in a group? Well it's, I really don't know. I don't think school is fun in any way.

I: You don't think so? Is it hard? Is it difficult?

J: Yes [sounds sad]

I: What is the most difficult thing? Can you name something?

J: What? What is most difficult? Probably maths and then some other things.

Later in the interview, Jeff also suggested that he was not very good at writing. Bob also had similar doubts about his capabilities. In addition, one girl, Anna, who was also a child defined as in need of special support, was mentioned by several of the other children in their interviews, because they felt that she was alone a lot of the time. Most of these children said that they tried to invite her into their activities, but that she often said no. Interestingly, Anna wrote about this topic in one of her poems:

Everyone is different really which I think is good.
Otherwise it would be boring.
You must be allowed to be who you are.
I am never alone, never feel that way,
even though the others seem to think so.
They don't really know what I feel.

Anna did not seem to share the worries of her peers. Furthermore, the notion of how to interpret social inclusion is shown in an interesting light by Anna's poem. Can you be socially excluded if you choose to be alone? [...]

The children's experiences as expressed in the questionnaires, interviews, and poems, and as observed, suggest that the children were content in the class. This observation was corroborated by several different data sources. In general, the children seemed to enjoy the forms of work in the class and liked their peers. Also, the ground rules of the classroom seemed firmly established among the children as they said in the interviews and as seen in participant observations. Interestingly, the interviews, observations, and above all the poems, revealed some complexities that were not visible in the answers to the questionnaire.

Discussion

The critique raised by McLeskey and Waldron (2007) concerning the lack of explicit definitions in the study of 'inclusive' classrooms suggested that such a lack is a threat to the whole research area. The review of co-teaching by Scruggs, Mastropieri and McDuffie (2007) illustrated the fact that too often classrooms are described as inclusive when children with disabilities are placed there. The methodology used in the present study makes it possible to scrutinise levels of social and educational inclusion as well as whether differences are viewed as ordinary. One conclusion of the present study is that in order to label a classroom 'inclusive', it is a necessary prerequisite to use an elaborated methodology (not necessarily identical to the one used in the present investigation). Moreover, classrooms should by no means be labelled 'inclusive' if we do not have firm data regarding how children experience the classroom. [...]

Children with disabilities in the present study were to a larger extent involved in common activities and the co-teacher functioned more as a mediator between the children with disabilities and the activities of the classroom. This illustrates that we have to attend to studied classrooms as communities of practice (Lave and Wenger, 1991; Säljö, 2000) in order to understand what inclusion means in a particular context. This is also interesting since the work methods in the classroom studied deviated to a large extent from what have become dominating forms of work in Swedish classrooms; that is, whole-class teaching mixed with individual work (Skolverket, 2009). [...] It should be taken into account that the general level of social inclusion of the class was high, as is evident from, for example, the answers to the questionnaire. The fact that two of the children displayed doubts about their academic competence is perhaps more problematic. These observations raise the question of whether other teaching strategies could have made the classroom even more inclusive. Of course, any answer to this question would be speculative. However, the educational history of the children would have a bearing on this issue. As stated by one of the teachers, the children seemed ill-prepared for schooling. Thus, earlier intervention might have been beneficial for the academic development of these children.

The teacher strategies discerned in the present study bear resemblance to strategies stated to be favourable to inclusive processes in manuals concerned with how inclusion should be accomplished (Booth and Ainscow, 2002; Eggertsdóttir and Marinósoson, 2005). However, such manuals provide very long lists of strategies (several which did not emerge in the data of the present investigation). The contribution of the present investigation about teacher strategies is to provide a methodologically transparent analysis of the most important strategies that is firmly grounded in an analysis of the inclusiveness level of the classroom studied. One might ask to what extent the high teacher-child ratio is a necessary condition for the enactment of strategies. Both teachers pointed out the importance of the small class size. On the other hand, the class used to be larger and the teachers suggested that they established the ground rules and working methods of the classroom rather early on. It should also be pointed out that children with ADHD and Asperger's syndrome in Sweden increasingly seem to be educated in more segregated settings where the teacher-child ratio is very high.

Finally, the importance of the experiences of the children has been pointed out throughout the chapter. Echoing Soodak (2003), we suggest that feelings of belonging, membership, and acceptance on behalf of the children are necessary prerequisites in order to talk about inclusive classrooms. Thus, studies should report data pertaining to these matters. Interestingly, interviews and poems revealed a more problematic picture than the questionnaire. In future research, we hope that the notion of children's experiences will be further scrutinised. After all, inclusion is supposed to be in the best interest of these very children.

Source: Nilholm, C. and Alm, B. (2010) 'An inclusive classroom? A case study of inclusiveness, teacher strategies, and children's experiences', *European Journal of Special Needs Education*, vol. 25, no. 3, August 2010, pp. 239-252. Copyright (c) 2010 Taylor and Francis

References

Booth, T. and Ainscow, M. (2002) *Index for inclusion. Developing learning and participation in schools.* Bristol, UK: Centre for Studies on Inclusive Education

Braun, V. and Clarke, V. (2006) Using thematic analysis in psychology. *Qualitative Research in Psychology* 3, no. 2: 77-101

Carrington, S. (2006) Inclusive school community: Why is it so complex? *International Journal of Inclusive Education* 10, nos. 4-5: 323-34

Clark, C., Dyson, A. and Millward, A. (eds) (1998) Theorising special education? Time to move on? In *Theorising Special Education*, (ed), C. Clark, A. Dyson and A. Millward, 156-73. London: Routledge

Creswell, J. (2000) *Qualitative Inquiry and Research Design – choosing among five traditions.* London: Sage

Eggertsdóttir, R. and Marinósson, G. (eds) (2005) *Pathways to inclusion – a guide to staff development.* Reykjavík, Iceland: University of Iceland Press

Emanuelsson, I. and Persson, B. (2002) Differentiering, specialpedagogik och likvärdighet. En longitudinell studie av skolkarriärer bland elever i svårigheter [Differentiation, special pedagogics and equality: A study of school careers among pupils with difficulties]. *Pedagogisk Forskning i Sverige* 7, no. 3: 183-99; English summary: 249-50

Estell, D. (2008) Peer groups, popularity, and social preference: Trajectories of social functioning among students with and without disabilities. *Journal of Learning Disabilities* 41, no. 1: 5-14

Garrison-Harell, L. and Kamps, D. (1997) The effects of peer networks on social-communicative behaviors for students with autism. *Focus on autism and other developmental disabilities* 12, no. 4: 241-54

Goodman, G. (2006) Preparing teachers for culturally and cognitively diverse classrooms. What would Dewey say? *Teacher Education and Practice* 19, no. 4: 513-34

Han, J., Ostrovsky, M. and Diamond, K. (2006) Children's attitudes toward peers with disabilities: Supporting positive attitude development. *Young Exceptional Children* 10, no. 1: 2-11

Lave, J. and Wenger, E. (1991) *Situated learning. Legitimate peripheral participation.* Cambridge, UK: University of Cambridge

Lloyd, C. (2008) Removing barriers to achievement: A strategy for inclusion or exclusion? *International Journal of Inclusive Education* 12, no. 2: 221-6

McLeskey, J. and Waldron, N.L. (2007) Making differences ordinary in inclusive classrooms. *Intervention in School and Clinic* 42, no. 3: 162-8

McPherson, M., Smith-Lovin, L. and Cook, J.M. (2001) Birds of a feather: Homophily in social networks. *Annual Review of Sociology* 27: 415-44

Nilholm, C., Persson, B., Hjerm, M. and Runesson, S. (2007) *Kommuners arbete med elever i behov av särskilt stöd – en enkätundersökning* [Municipalities' work with children in need of special support – a questionnaire-based study]. Jönköping, Sweden: Jönköping University Press

Norwich, B. (1993) Ideological dilemmas in special needs education: Practitioners' view. *Oxford Review of Education* 19, no. 4: 527-46

Nowicki, E. and Sandieson, R. (2002) A meta-analysis of school-age children's attitudes towards persons with physical or intellectual disabilities. *International Journal of Disability, Development and Education* 49, no. 3: 243-65

Oliver, M. (1990) *The Politics of Disablement.* London: Macmillan

Persson, B. (1998) Who needs special education? *International Journal of Educational Research* 29: 107-17.

Pijl, J., Frostad, P. and Flem, A. (2008) The social position of pupils with special needs in regular schools. *Scandinavian Journal of Educational Research* 52, no. 4: 387-405

Putney, L. (2007) Discursive practices as cultural resources: Formulating identities for individual and collective in an inclusive classroom setting. *International Journal of Educational Research* 46, nos. 3-4: 129-40

Rossi, J.A. (2006) The dialogue of democracy. *Social Studies* 97, no. 3: 112-20

Säljö, R. (2000) *Lärande i praktiken – ett sociokulturellt perspektiv* [Learning in practice – a sociocultural perspective]. Stockholm, Sweden: Prisma

Scruggs, T.E., Mastropieri, M.A. and McDuffie, K.A. (2007) Co-teaching in inclusive classrooms: a meta-synthesis of qualitative research. *Exceptional Children* 73, no. 4: 392-416

Skolverket (2009) *Vad påverkar resultaten i svensk grundskola?* [What affects the results in the Swedish mandatory school?]. Skolverket report 09:1127. Stockholm, Sweden: Skolverket

Slavin, R.E. (1996) *Education for all: contexts of learning.* Lisse, France: Swets and Keitlinger

Soodak, L.C. (2003) Classroom management in inclusive settings. *Theory into Practice* 42, no. 4: 327-33

Swanson, H.L. and Hoskyn, M. (1998) Experimental intervention research on students with learning disabilities: A meta-analysis of treatment outcomes. *Review of Educational Research* 68, no. 3: 277-321

Stark, S. and Torrance, H. (2007) Case study. In *Research methods in the social sciences*, 33-40. (ed) Somekh, B. and Lewin, C. London: Sage

Volonino, V. and Zigmond, N. (2007) Promoting research-based practices through inclusion? *Theory into Practice* 46, no. 4: 291-300

Weiss, M.P. (2004) Co-teaching as science in the schoolhouse: More questions than answers. *Journal of Learning Disabilities* 37: 218-23

Weiss, M.P. and Brigham, F.J. (2000) Co-teaching and the model of shared responsibility: What does the research support? In *Educational interventions.* Vol. 14 of Advances in learning and behavioral disabilities, ed. T.E. Scruggs and M.A. Mastropieri, 217-45. Oxford, UK: Elsevier.

Yin, R.K. (2002) Case study research. *Design and methods.* Vol. 5 of Applied social science research methods. Thousand Oaks, CA: Sage

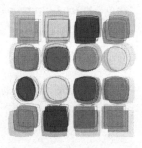

Chapter 10

The ambiguity of the child's 'voice' in social research

Sirkka Komulainen

[...]

The research project

This chapter draws on a research project that was carried out in England between 2000 and 2004. The initial idea of the project was to explore the ways in which children's 'voices' were (if they were at all) taken into account within professional practice, and how the child was positioned as a communicator in multidisciplinary specialist settings. Drawing on social constructionist perspectives, the original research design sought to develop novel sociological understandings of young children's 'communication difficulties' and thereby contribute to child welfare practice (including child protection), childhood sociology and theories of disability. The research began with the working hypothesis that in professional settings, young disabled children's 'voices' may be in danger of remaining marginal. Hence, the project aimed to describe how children's communication and communication difficulties were understood and acted upon in the everyday practices of child welfare specialists.

I conducted ethnographic research in two settings, where I observed interaction among and between young children and adult professionals. The first setting was a day nursery (the 'Children's Centre'), where disabled children were receiving additional support and education in a therapeutic environment. In the second, 'Team Service', setting, a multidisciplinary team of practitioners assessed children's communication and other health, welfare or educational needs. Although entirely different settings, the practices in both were based on clinical and therapeutic knowledge of children with special needs. The two settings operated in the framework of current legal and ethical guidelines for good practice, which aimed to maximise the child's potential through early intervention (eg. Friel, 1997; Dockrell and Messer, 1999).

The fieldwork commenced in the 'Children's Centre', where I spent most of the time observing everyday action (such as meal times and circle times) in the nursery, and occasionally individual therapy sessions. I spent about 9 months observing the 'Children's Centre'. Sometimes I took an opportunity to engage in 'free play' with children, although I mostly remained a 'marginal observer' (Berg, 1995). I also conducted some video recordings, which allowed for detailed data analysis. Prior to video recordings, I had obtained informed consent from the parents of the children.

There were up to 15 children together per day in the centre. All the children were under 6 years old. They had been diagnosed with a disability that involved a range of physical and cognitive impairments. Due to their impairments, most children in the nursery had little or no speech, and they were receiving speech and language therapy.

In the 'Team Service' setting, I conducted 25 observations over 9 months. The assessment team consisted of health, education and welfare professionals, who carried out tests with the children and interviewed their parents. The children who had been referred to the team were under 8. Although 'communication difficulties' were a frequent reason for the referral, not all the children were diagnosed as disabled or as having 'communication difficulties'. My fieldwork involved observing testing sessions with children as well as meetings where the team would plan the assessments and, in the end, come up with a decision about further intervention. In this setting, I always remained behind a one-way screen between an observation room and two assessment rooms. [...]

The ambiguity of interpretations

I first encountered the ambiguity of the child's 'voice' in the nursery practice, where it was a direct object of specialist action, including both verbal and non-verbal communication. The 'good practice' ethos in the setting involved attempts to give children 'voices' through acts of choice-making. However, I found that choice-making crystallised certain understandings of communication and the child. Indeed, both verbal and non-verbal interaction in choice-making situations drew on the idea that children are not only entitled to choices but also willing to make them.

The following two extracts describe verbal choice-making during meal times, where children were served a three course meal, and before each round were given options to choose from, such as apple juice or orange juice, or different kinds of pudding:

Eating goes on as usual. At first, 'Sarah' is the only adult who keeps talking to the children, eg. 'If you don't eat it you will always be as tall as that'. Then two other workers join in – especially

'Tracey' (loudly) and newcomer (quietly): 'Would you like some more? Good boy'. Two workers talk about 'Martin' – they think that he might have chickenpox. 'Robert' is crying – Tracey: 'Enough noise now – you are going to have pudding'. Tracey seems to be in charge of the situation that way. 'Brian' says: 'I would like some custard'. Sarah: 'Well you are allowed to change your mind' (I did not see whether he wanted something else earlier).

Verbal children would sometimes initiate choice-making, like Brian who wanted 'some custard'. However, verbal choice-making was sometimes quite ambiguous. The next extract describes a situation where the child appeared not to be bothered to make a choice:

A worker says to 'Mike': 'You are looking at this one and pointing at other one Mike. Which one do you want?' Mike says: 'Something', and the worker smiles at me. Tracey did a very quick round with the food items; still, quite a lot of speculation is involved in the choice-making. Children are given 'something', anyhow. Martin still cries quite desperately. A worker asks Mike whether he wants to have apple juice; He replies: 'No no no no – yes!' and the workers laugh at this. Then Mike says something but no one hears it. Eventually the worker brings out the actual food items and he points approximately at the apple juice.

In contrast to the previous examples, I now describe a situation where the child actively 'sent a message' – several times – and faced some mixed responses to it:

This appears to be an educational session. The children are sitting at a table and a worker is teaching them numbers through play. 'Jonathan' is complaining about stomach ache. Worker 1: 'It's nearly lunchtime, you must be hungry'. 'Jerry' knows what to do next. The children are banging the table with sticks really loudly. 'Paula' is not with this at all. She keeps banging the table. She repeats 'tick tock'. Jonathan: 'I need to wee'. Worker 1 says no because he has just been to the toilet. Worker 2 then enters the room, hears this and asks Worker 3 to take him to the toilet.

The children sing a pat-a-cake song with playdoh. The worker explains to me how the children anticipate the events, because they remember them from the previous session. Paula is falling asleep. The others are clapping and messing around – they seem to have fun. Some of them shout rather than sing. Jonathan protests: 'I'm tired'.

As in the extract, in daily nursery work different interpretations of the child's verbal intentions would be made. Worker 1 interpreted that Jonathan was complaining because he was hungry, but since lunchtime was approaching it was not a problem for the worker. Worker 1 also dismissed Jonathan's request to go to the toilet, whereas the other two workers took notice of this. These sorts of situational judgements of the child's intentions and needs were typical of the nursery practice. [...]

At its extreme, it appeared that choice-making had become an end in itself so that the adults insisted that the child give an answer. I frequently observed the workers making decisions on behalf of the child when an ambiguous situation arose:

It seems to take quite a long time to feed 'Jemma' (or to teach her to eat by herself) – others have gone through their pudding already. Now she is shown both food items (and a picture card to make the connection). The worker seems to be fed up because Jemma did not look at the 'no' picture card but refused a banana. Another worker says, 'I think Jemma likes custard so let's have that'.

The problem is in that one could never be sure exactly what the children wanted until they either swallowed the food or did not; by then, they might have changed their minds anyway. Thus, there were no exact means to measure whether the task of giving children a choice was successful on each occasion.

I have suggested that verbal communication in the nursery involved ambiguities, but also that non-verbal communication was often even more obscure. This, I stress again, is not simply a matter of a lack of speech on the part of the child. Instead, the ambiguities arose where non-verbal communication – actually or attempted – was treated according to 'ideal' models for verbal communication. This was inevitably a matter of interpretation.

I have drawn attention to the use of picture communication symbols because they featured in daily practice more frequently than other means of augmentative and alternative communication.[1] In this respect, the use of communication aids was part of what I call 'communication as a medium'. They were material objects intended to replace words or enable the child to express a need or choice, and thereby establish shared understandings between the carer and the child.

I observed two main ambiguities in the use of picture communication symbols. First, as I have argued, their use fundamentally involved ambiguous processes of meaning-making: the hoped-for 'shared understandings' between children and adults in the setting had an accomplished and situational character. This meaning-making was based on a certain logic: it imputed rationality to both adults and children. My analysis questions the feasibility of such logic, first and foremost because it was meant to serve moral-pragmatic purposes. I propose that models for good communication that prefer rational, abstract thinking and action discriminate between different groups of people. I observed this taking place between adults and children, although in the guise of meeting the needs and individual rights of the latter. Second, I observed some ambiguities in how routine practice in the nursery constituted the child as an agent; for example, choice-making situations assumed rational thought and action on the part of the child.

Furthermore, adult-child communication in the nursery fundamentally entailed adult interpretations of the children's meanings. The workers expected the children to learn certain 'fixed' meanings that the adults had applied to words, signs or pictures. I argue that this 'literacy training' assumed face-to-face communication to be something rather linear and straightforward. I also suggest that children were typically encouraged to make choices when it was appropriate in terms of adult frameworks, such as daily timetables. It is possible that meal times may have been one of the few opportunities for the children to initiate their preferences. Nevertheless, in this respect, 'communication' in the nursery was tied to adult judgements about the primary task at hand.

There was often a practical reason for addressing children in this way, including, for instance, attempts to manage a number of children in a group. After all, it was the adults who had responsibilities over what happened in the setting. I stress that I am not jumping to the simplistic conclusion that choice-making by adults, for example, was inevitably detrimental to the child. This was clear in terms of the child's daily needs, such as being fed. I am rather noting that the expectation of the child to be an active and purposeful choice-maker has implications for perceptions of the child as a communicator.

These sorts of ambiguities also emerged in the second research setting. The Team Service work involved objects, such as toys, texts or pictures, the use of which had specific meanings and purposes for the practitioners. My analysis suggests that these test 'tools' were structured and that they constituted particular kinds of frames for interaction. The logic of testing overlooked the complexities and ambiguities of meaning-making, and the child's potential for behaving agentically. These points are illustrated in the following extract, which describes speech and language assessment, and suggests how children may interpret the practitioners' questions in various, imaginative and sometimes surprising ways:

The SLT [speech and language therapist] starts a sentence completion test. P: 'What is a dress?' 'Daniel': 'Skirt and a t-shirt'. SLT: 'What is a bed?' D: 'It is for sleeping with a pillow'. SLT: 'What do you need to do when you cross the road?' D: 'Stop, look and listen'. The SLT probes to get a desired answer, by repeating the question if Daniel says something else. SLT: 'It was a lovely day ..'. D: 'And then a ginormous sunflower came' (*excitedly*). SLT: 'What is a hat?' D: 'A hat ... is a sort of planet shape,' does a rim with his hands above his head. Practitioners in the observation room comment that he is probably thinking of Saturn. SLT: 'The bird flies, the fish ..'. D: 'Does not fly'. After that question he seems to give up or gets fed up and replies: 'I don't know'.

The SLT seems to be rushing, looking at the clock and moving forward fast. She then asks Daniel to explain pictures on cards – he does not recognise all of them and the SLT shows the same cards a few times. Daniel starts imitating her: 'We'll go back to that one'. The SLT carries on: 'How are a man and a dog different?' D: 'Because human and a pet are the right answers'.

The speech and language therapist's task was to sort out the 'correct' answers from incorrect ones, based on her interpretation of whether the child had comprehended the question. Interestingly, this time she was allowed to ask the same question more than once; on some other occasions, the professional requirement for standardisation had prevented this.

Thus, meaning-making was a complex activity, both verbally and non-verbally. Sometimes the practitioners expressed their awareness of this to me, as in the following extract:

'Jeremy' is spotting 'mistakes' in practitioner's pictures – he laughs when a person in the picture puts food in the washing machine and not in the oven. Meanwhile, another practitioner in the observation room talks about his enunciation, which seems to be the problem, not comprehension (he starts words with the letter D). This practitioner is convinced that the Team members are 'tuned in to understand' what the child says (when I was wondering whether the parents would understand him). Still they all keep saying, every once in a while, that they don't understand a word that Jeremy is saying during the test. One practitioner says that when she did a test, she just nodded to pretend that she was following him.

It seemed obvious that Jeremy did not have any problems with understanding the intended jokes in the pictures. However, I was having trouble with understanding his speech and I said this to the practitioners who were in the observation room. I then asked whether anyone else could make any sense of it. One practitioner said that as experts they are 'tuned in' to understand the child; another said that she pretended to understand in order to carry on with the assessment.

In sum, the second setting manifested the same themes as the first: specialists' preferences for symbolic communication, expectations of rational thought and action on the part of the child, practical difficulty of interpretation, and the rules and recommendations for 'good' adult practice, which framed adult-child interaction. In light of this, fundamental moral-pragmatic and epistemological questions arose in terms of my research questions. What could I make of the child's 'voice' as an object of enquiry? Could I position the child as a straightforward 'speaking subject' in these circumstances? If not, what kind of approach would be an epistemologically and ethically sound alternative?

The discourse of children's rights emphasises the message that children should be listened to by adults who make decisions concerning their lives, which involves research on/with children. Yet, I repeat: What are children's 'voices' and how should we listen to them (Davis, 1998)? Since fundamental epistemological and moral-pragmatic questions significantly affected every stage of the research process, I now reflect on the uncertainties that arose from the fieldwork experience.

Reflections on the ambiguities in the practices of research

My experiences in these settings led me to recognise the need for 'reflexivity' in research in terms of three different areas. First, in the context of research methods and ethics 'reflexivity' typically refers to the relationship between the knower and the known, with attention to hierarchies, 'good' and 'bad' research, and the normatively constituted speaking positions (Adkins, 2002). Second, reflexivity in my research had to do with the dichotomy between realism and anti-realism in social constructionist research. By this I refer to the problem of using realist methods and then giving reflexive accounts of the data (Coffey, 2002). Third, I link reflexivity to the ambiguity of the researcher's role as an actor in disability/childhood settings. These interrelated three areas constituted an epistemological and moral-pragmatic dilemma for me in terms of the child's 'voice' and its place in ethnographic research practice. [...]

Discussion

[...] I have found that within the so-called 'child-centred' discourse in childhood sociology, children are often granted an individualistic status as subjects/agents and as intentional beings, whose 'voices' may remain unheard because of the 'tyranny' of developmental perspectives over their lives. [...]

At the same time, it has been argued that (disabled) children's needs and rights are also social constructs and that these constructs are interrelated and often contradictory (eg. Doyal and Gough, 1991). For Woodhead (1997), conceptualising 'childhood' in terms of 'needs' reflects the distinctive status accorded to young humanity in contemporary western societies. It is commonplace to regard the needs-led approach as a progressive and enlightened framework for working with children, by contrast with former times and other societies. Nevertheless, the concept of 'need' conceals in practice a complex of latent cultural and personal assumptions and judgements about children, which are not attributable to children's 'innate' nature as such. [...]

I see my research project and the two research settings as being at the heart of this contemporary discourse, which manifests itself in moral-pragmatic justifications and political rhetoric and action. What is important here, as I agree with James *et al* (1998), is that in sociology, we need to consider this urgent focus on children analytically. I argue that the analysis of children's 'voices' must include considerations of the dynamics of human communication and interaction. Young children with little or no speech might make the most striking example of ambiguous communication – yet I suggest all adult-child encounters entail ambiguities. In principle I agree with the call for appreciating children's views on issues that affect their lives; yet I caution against too simplistic and/or sensationalised a usage of the term 'voice'.[2] [...]

Conclusion

In this chapter I have questioned a particular version of a young (disabled or able-bodied) child's 'voice'. This version assumes a rational, autonomous 'agent' as an intentional subject – a notion linked to a wider individualisation process in the western world. Recognising and accounting for children's 'voices' presumes rational action on the part of the speaker. This perspective has the moral goal of giving rights to children; yet, when not clarified, it may dismiss the complexity of communication as a local interactional activity.

I wanted to draw particular attention to the epistemology, ontology and practice of qualitative research. This is particularly important in research that encourages the participation of children in the generation of data. In my research I came to see the multifaceted ambiguity of the idea of 'listening to children'. This recognition undermined the implicit or explicit assumptions in the so-called child-centred research, which takes for granted that children have message-like thoughts that can be exchanged, and intentions that match the situations defined by adults; and that these can be researched in an ethical fashion (Alderson, 1995). My findings in two specialist settings have indicated that ethical and epistemological considerations are more complex than that.

Studying children's lives in the contemporary world is inevitably political. It can be argued, though, that care has to be taken to distinguish rhetoric from practice. For Roberts (2000), listening to children is not necessarily 'good' but may, in fact, be intrusive and the cause of further distress: more listening may not inevitably mean more hearing. In other words, researchers should think about when and how to conduct research with children so that it is as ethical as they claim it to be. [...]

I have offered reflexivity as a strategy for ensuring ethical research conduct. By this I stress the recognition of the adult mediation and construction of children's 'voices', both on local and wider discursive levels. This might involve reflecting on not simply what one 'hears' as a researcher, but on what one expects to hear, and how these expectations may frame the dynamics of adult-child interaction.

Source: Komulainen, S. (2007) 'The Ambiguity of the Child's 'Voice' in Social Research', *Childhood*, vol. 14, no. 11, SAGE Publications

Notes

1 Alternative and augmentative communication (AAC) means any method of communicating that supplements the ordinary methods of speech and handwriting, where these are impaired (Millar and Scott, 2001). Most AAC users use a mixture of unaided (such as signing) and aided communication (physical objects such as symbol charts or books), and a mixture of low tech and high tech aids, depending on the situation.

2 This argument has implications to research on adult voices as well; however, I feel that a fair treatment of this dimension is beyond the scope of this article.

References

Adkins, L. (2002) 'Reflexivity and the Politics of Qualitative Research', in T. May (ed.) *Qualitative Research in Action*, pp.332-48. London: Sage

Alderson, P. (1995) *Listening to Children: Children, ethics and Social Research*. London: Barnardo's

Berg, B.L. (1995) *Qualitative Research Methods for the Social Sciences*. London: Allyn and Bacon

Coffey, A. (2002) 'Ethnography and Self: Reflections and Representations', in T. May (ed.) *Qualitative Research in Action*, pp313-31. London: Sage

Davis, J.M. (1998) 'Understanding the Meanings of Children: A Reflexive Process', *Children and Society* 12: 325-35

Dockrell, J. and Messer, D.J. (1999) *Children's Language and Communication Difficulties: Understanding, Identification and Intervention*. London: Cassell

Doyal, L. and Gough, I. (1991) *A Theory of Human Need*. Basingstoke: Macmillan

Friel, J. (1997) *Children With Special Needs: Assessment, Law and Practice – Caught in the Acts*, 4th edn. London: Jessica Kingsley

James, A., C. Jenks and A. Prout (1998) *Theorizing Childhood*. Cambridge: Polity Press

Mandell, L. (1991) 'The Least-Adult Role in Studying Children', in F.C. Waksler (ed.) Studying the Social Worlds of Children: Sociological Readings, pp38-59. London: Falmer Press

Roberts, H. (2000) 'Listening to Children: And Hearing Them', in P. Christensen and A. James (eds) *Research with Children: Perspectives and Practices*, pp225-40. London: Falmer Press

Woodhead, M. (1997) 'Psychology and the Cultural Construction of Children's Needs', in A. James and A. Prout (eds) *Constructing and Reconstructing Childhood*, pp63-84. London: Falmer Press

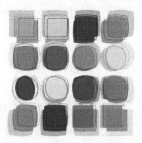

Chapter 11

Docile citizens? Using counternarratives to disrupt normative and dominant discourses

Christopher S. Walsh

Oppressive language does more than represent violence; it is violence; does more than represent the limits of knowledge; it limits knowledge. Whether it is obscuring state language or the faux-language of mindless media; whether it is the proud but calcified language of the academy or the commodity driven language of science; whether it is the malign language of law-without-ethics, or language designed for the estrangement of minorities, hiding its racist plunder in its literary cheek – it must be rejected, altered and exposed. (Toni Morrison, Nobel Lecture December 7, 1993[1])

If there's a book you really want to read, but it hasn't been written yet, then you must write it. (Toni Morrison[2])

Introduction

The nursery rhyme, 'Sticks and bones may break my bones, but names will never hurt me' is widely recognisable. But is it true? I contend that it is not. As Toni Morrison reminds us, words hurt. Words mean something. Consider how you might feel if you were called a *liar* when you told the truth. It does hurt to be called names. It hurts to be bullied and excluded because you have been labelled or set apart and called ugly, fat, stupid, lazy, old, homeless, illiterate, gay, disabled and so on. To be called names, or be labelled, is a form of 'othering' that is disempowering and oppressive. To label another person adversely is careless and insensitive. Negative labels often stay with children and young people for the rest of their lives. Labelling often leads people into believing they are incapable and powerless. Conversely, labelling excuses – even encourages – some individuals to participate in destructive behaviour that upholds certain deficit, racist and homophobic views of the individual. Hurtful labels from careless politicians, parents, relatives, practitioners or teachers are harmful to everyone, especially youth. Name calling and labelling others is a practice that must be rejected and redressed by practitioners working with children and young people. But it is so entrenched in the taken-for-granted and everyday practices of many powerful people, that a formidable strategy is needed to expose the violence oppressive language represents and validates – with the aim of altering it.

This chapter puts forth a rationale for authoring *counternarratives* as a tactic of resistance. It allows those labelled negatively to creatively and critically read and critique the world with the goal of re-writing dominant storylines and discourses. Dominant discourses are generally statements that are institutionally enforced and widely circulated as 'Truths' (Mills, 1997), but which also have the power to alienate and discriminate. Through critical reason and reflection (Barnett, 1997) of their own physical, social, and political 'situationality' (Freire, 1970:90), I encourage practitioners deliberately to create spaces where the children and young people they work with can author counternarratives to reject the often hidden, contextualised and localised (and global) narratives that marginalise them. Historically, counternarratives are recognised for the power they have to challenge and disrupt normative and dominant discourses (Giroux *et al*, 1996).

This chapter presents four counternarratives that work to decentre discourses that render individuals 'docile citizens' (Foucault, 1978/1995). The counternarratives presented do this by exposing and contesting common assumptions around disability, the family and gay, lesbian, bisexual and transgender (LGBT) youth. Authoring counternarratives gives children and young people a voice to overcome the ways they have been labelled so they no longer remain victims of discrimination, inequity and exclusion. When pupils author counternarratives, they re-appropriate, reframe and challenge dominant images and representations by rupturing the chains of signification to create new narratives that dismantle hegemony.

Counternarratives act as a tool to: (1) challenge the perceived wisdom of subscribers of a dominant culture by providing a context to understand and transform an established belief system; and (2) open new windows into the reality of marginalised citizens by showing them the possibilities beyond where they live, and the shared aims of their struggle. (McKay, 2010:26-27)

The counternarratives I present represent diverse practitioners' intentional acts of 'everyday resistance' (Scott 1985; Collins, 1997). They illustrate how counternarratives can be used to contest master narratives or frameworks that lead to labelling and/or name calling across educational and social contexts. Furthermore, counternarratives are oppositional stories that work particularly well in times characterised by new media and the ability of individuals to design and author resistant texts that can be read and viewed widely online.

Counternarratives disrupting normative and dominant discourses

The four counternarratives described here work to disrupt mainstream narratives that perpetuate the separation of people with disabilities from community life (*Passion Works*), victimhood associated with single mother status (*Single Mothers by Choice*) and discourses on sexualities that construct limited representations and understanding of LGBT youth (*Writing themselves in*) and those that promote bullying based on perceived and/or disclosed sexuality (*It Gets Better Project*).

Passion Works

Passion Works (www.passionworks.org) is a remarkable not-for-profit organisation in the US whose purpose is to inspire and liberate the human spirit through the arts by supporting collaborations between artists with and without developmental disabilities. *Passion Works* has developed a successful product line of one-of-a-kind art pieces, jewellry, ornaments, flowers and greeting cards that generates ongoing funding to continue its arts programmes. Harter *et al*'s (2006) ethnographic fieldwork of *Passion Works* reveals how members 'reweave the tattered civic fabric of exclusion as they engage in communal collaboration and integration' (p4). *Passion Works* confronts:

stubbornly persistent dualisms including public/private and autonomy/connection that too often position people with disabilities as 'less than' others. *Passion Works* emerges as a community characterised by 'embodied rhetoricity', communication processes that work out of the mind-body as a merged entity ... Individuals are physically, cognitively, and affectively involved in cooperatively exploring the unique talents of members ... client artists, claim and exercise their rights of citizenship, including the rights of expression and participation in community life, and move away from historical patterns of isolation. We position *Passion Works* as an alternative discourse community ... that challenges prevailing ways in which difference and power intersect. Our own journey demanded entry points for understanding the denaturalisation of disability. (Harter *et al*:5)

Passion Works powerfully disrupts discourses of difference that sustain the exclusion of people with disabilities from community life. To date, the organisation has hosted 20 visiting artist residencies, participated in a host of gallery exhibitions and has its own studio where artists' works are on display and for sale. *Passion Works* successfully organises active engagement with the arts for populations otherwise excluded from the public life and the more established 'art world'. Their work harnesses the power of creativity and community building by providing voice to client artists marginalised not only from community life, but 'the arts' in general.

Passion Works' website hosts a number of inspiring counternarratives that challenge the dominant gaze of disability, where their client artists perform 'disability' and 'art'. Their performances resist and challenge the stereotypical representation of those with a disability as incapable or unable to participate. Take Harry Grimm, a client artist who was inspired to draw a picture of Ronald and Nancy Reagan after hearing of the late president's death. Working with two staff artists, he articulated how he also wanted to draw the White House. The staff artists found him pictures of the White House in publications that had been donated to the organisation. As he was looking at the pictures he kept asking where the ramp was:

'Where is the Ramp?' 'What do you mean Harry,' asked both Deb and Wendy. 'The ramp. The ramp'. He was talking about a wheelchair ramp. There were no wheelchair ramps visible in any of the pictures on the calendar. As someone who experiences the world from the vantage point of a wheelchair, this issue was important to Harry. Wendy told him that he could still draw a ramp. He was reluctant at first, and didn't seem to want to imagine something that wasn't there. 'You are an artist Harry,' Wendy said, 'you can envision whatever you want'. Harry drew a ramp that was wide and deep.[3]

Harry Grimm performs a counternarrative of disability as he collaborates with the artists to create art that goes beyond artistic expression. His painting materialised as a political and social statement where through critical reason and reflection he engaged in critical action (Barnett, 1997) and actively advocated for the rights of people in wheelchairs to access one of the world's most famous government buildings. This represents a collective reconstruction of the world in an attempt to make it more inclusive by rejecting and exposing what appeared to be structures that impede the access and inclusion of people with disabilities from social life.

Single mothers by choice

Single mothers by choice explores the difficulties and possibilities of 25 single mothers attending universities across Southern Ontario. The study disrupts negative discourses usually associated with single mothers by offering a more 'comprehensive picture of the experiences of single mothers using a strengths-based analysis focusing not only on the troubles, but also on the rich possibilities of single motherhood as a legitimate constructive family status' (Ajandi, 2011:45). *Single mothers by choice* does this by focusing on the resistance, strength and agency of single mothers that tends to be absent from research literature and popular media. As a counternarrative, it portrays single mothers not as victims but as champions who were selfless in the face of extreme hardship, poverty and social stigma.

The normative storyline of teenage motherhood is generally seen as a pernicious social problem (Morgan, 1998) and teenage mothers as concerned only with their immediate self-interest. However, in this study, Sally recounts how becoming a teenage mother was truly a worthy experience because it made her committed to her own education:

I often say getting pregnant at 16 saved my life, even though I was in high school. I was involved in a lot of dangerous activities and so I think, yeah, actually it was having a child that made my commitment to it [education] even greater. I remember I hung my high school diploma over his crib when he was young...that brings up a lot of emotions. I remember how proud I was of that stupid high school diploma, before even knowing the benefits of post-secondary education. I didn't even think I would get in. (from Ajandi, 2011:423)

A counternarrative like Sally's disrupts the traditionally heteronormative conceptualisation of the family and provides an alternative story of the family and education. Another single mother, Gemma, expresses how in the absence of having a partner, she found strength in her role as a student attending university. Even though she experienced barriers daily, overcoming them gave her power and raised her self-esteem:

It's freedom, it's an opportunity for me to shine in an area that has nothing to do with family or home. And if you put the work in, you get the rewards back. I mean in my marriage, there was very little self-esteem building, confidence building, there was very little affirmation – well none basically...I walk through these halls and I feel so liberated, in control of myself, on a path, and part of something. (from Ajandi, 2011:419)

Gemma's counternarrative is one of empowerment and independence. It also portrays how being a single mother gave her the strength and the resilience to believe in herself in ways she was often incapable of when she was in a relationship.

The 25 participating single mothers were diverse in terms of race, ethnicity, sexuality, age, immigration status and religious affiliation, but most of them experienced poverty. They saw being a single mother as a positive experience; it empowered them to advocate for themselves and their children when they faced discrimination and exclusion:

The school, it was predominately White and I felt the principal, vice principal, right down to the teachers, had strong racist undertones. The way they even spoke about him, 'sitting like a possum' and taking away marks because he didn't speak loud enough – because he is very soft spoken. There were so many things, even the way that they spoke to me in their condescending manner. I expressed if this is any indication of how they speak to my son, I can see why he was traumatised. And instead of looking at what was going on there, they suggested something must be wrong in my home ... Once I made the decision to remove him, they were like, 'oh, we're sorry to see him leave'. I'm like, 'let's be real, you have traumatised him'; he went from the school that he was at getting high grades to being 'at risk' in a matter of months and then when I moved him to the school that he is currently at, his grades are back up. So I said to them, 'Do you not see that he came here with high grades and dropped in a short time?' Do you not see something going on here? You're just going to automatically assume that it is something within my home as opposed to something within your school system?' (Meena from Ajandi, 2011:420)

These counternarratives challenge dominant discourses and previous research which focuses on single mothers' dependence on financial aid from the state. *Single mothers by choice* presents strong single women who confront oppression, racism, ableism and heterosexism by making their families strong. Their counternarratives stand in stark opposition to deficit models that view them as greedy, a drain on the state, a waste of taxpayers' money and a threat to the nuclear heterosexual family.

Writing themselves in *and the* It Gets Better Project

In the case of LGBT youth, dominant heterosexist discourses fuel discrimination and hatred. In more serious cases they lead youth to commit suicide or experience violence. With LGBT youth or those thought to be from these groups, dominant discourses often lead to situations where they experience bullying and cyberbullying. International media is rife with examples of school-based homophobic bullying and heartbreaking stories of young people suffering extreme harassment, while many teachers, schools and social service providers lack the guidance or training needed to address and reverse this endemic problem (Jones, 2010; Rivers, 2011).

Two innovative projects stand out as powerful counternarratives that work to confront bullying and disrupt the discourses that work to promote discrimination, exclusion and violence directed at LGBT youth. The first, *Writing themselves in,* is an Australian project that describes the experiences of 1739 LGBT people aged 14–21 at home, school and in the community. It aims to prove to schools, teachers and any social service practitioner who works with LGBT youth that they have a responsibility to provide a safe space for the 10 per cent of this population who are LGBT. If they fail to take responsibility to provide services, it is likely that LGBT youth will not receive an equal education or access to social services. *Writing themselves in* encouraged LGBT youth to tell stories about their lives and experiences:

We are interested in reading more about your experiences of growing up knowing that you are sexually attracted to people of your own sex. We want to know about your own story including when you first knew about your sexual feelings, your experiences with friends and family, your good times and your bad, and your hopes for the future. (Hillier, Turner and Mitchell, 2005:18)

The study found that in general, many LGBT youth were eager to tell their stories and articulate their experiences, both positive and negative. In other words, they were eager to 'write themselves in.'

My mom said that I was a disappointment to the family and that I was no longer her son. (Paul, 18 years)

I got smashed by my Dad. I was forced to sleep on the streets. (Jess, 15 years)

My parents have been the most supportive. They have educated themselves about lesbians and helped me too. They have really stood by me even though it has meant changing their politics (they were always Liberal voters but now get so angry with what John Howard says, does and doesn't do, about LGBT's that they won't vote Lib again), and also they have protested to the church they used to belong to; when my mum heard the Pope called gay people 'depraved' she just went off about how these people call themselves 'Christians' etc. Its been hard for them but they know I am the same as I have always been, I just don't have a huge secret from them anymore. It has made our relationship heaps more honest and so heaps better. (Abbey, 20 years) (From Hillier, Turner and Mitchell, 2005:65)

These stories are counternarratives, not only because they name the often brutal realities these youth face simply because of being LGBT, but also because they present a juxtaposition to the dominant discourses of deviance so often attributed to anyone who identifies as LGBT. Discourses of deviance often work to legitimise violence against them. A potent example is this statement by Tony Abbott, the current Leader of the Opposition in the Australian House of Representatives and federal leader of the Liberal Party of Australia:

I probably feel a bit threatened [by them], as so many people do. It's a fact of life.[4]

Writing themselves in is an example of how counternarratives can be used as an effective pedagogical tool. This is because it empowers children and young people with the courage and support to engage in resistant tactics and take critical action to confront stereotypes and name those who perpetuate negative representations of them. Their counternarratives are in opposition to storylines fuelled by Abbott, and others like him, who use fear tactics or words like 'unnatural' or 'sinful' to ensure – often from a political standpoint – that LGBT youth continue to suffer and be persecuted for a 'lifestyle' that is often referred to as 'a choice'.

I first had feelings for a guy [same-sex] in year 10 of high school. I first recognised what these feelings actually were towards the end of year 12. I was in an all boys school, very shy, the atmosphere was very anti-gay and homosexuality was never even mentioned by any of the teachers which I believe kept me from working things out and then not being able to deal with it for a few years after that ... I think society in general is either neutral or positive towards gay relationships and think it's about damn time governments around the world realise this and grow up. I was in high school in 2000, at that time there was no mention of non-straight sexuality anywhere. I think that if it's just mentioned in English classes as an 'issue', or hopefully discussed in sex ed., that first 'hurdle' would be so much easier to cope with. My ultimate hope is that there'll never need to be such a thing as 'coming out'. (Paul, 20 years) (Hillier, Turner and Mitchell, 2005:67-68)

The second example is the US based *It Gets Better Project* (http://www.itgetsbetter. org/) launched in 2010 by Dan Savage, a popular syndicated columnist and author. Savage created a YouTube video with his partner Terry Miller to inspire hope for young LGBT youth who face bullying in school. The project was a direct response to a number of pupils taking their own lives after experiencing homophobic bullying in schools across the US. Savage and Miller's aim was to get 100, maybe 200 videos uploaded to YouTube to provide hope for the future for LGBT youth viewers. They wanted supporters to tell LGBT youth that the difficult situation of bullying and harassment they are facing in school does get better in time. At the time of writing this chapter, there have been more than 25,000 user-created videos that have been viewed more than 40 million times. This has had a massive and unexpected impact internationally. The project has received submissions from celebrities, organisations, activists, politicians, sports clubs and media personalities including David Cameron, Anna Bligh, Barack Obama, Ellen DeGeneres and Lady Gaga. The project also published a best selling book entitled *It Gets Better: Coming Out, Overcoming Bullying, and Creating a Life Worth Living* (Savage and Miller, 2011).

It Gets Better provides powerful counternarratives because they are stories of resistance and triumph from LGBT youth and their advocates. They not only express their pain, grief, loss and suffering – but also stand in defiance to dominant heteronormative discourses that describe people who are LGBT as deviant and sick:

Don't misunderstand. I am not here bashing people who are homosexuals, who are lesbians, who are bisexual, who are transgender. We need to have profound compassion for people who are dealing with the very real issue of sexual dysfunction in their life and sexual identity disorders.[5] (Michele Bachmann, Republican Minnesota Congresswoman and candidate for the Republican nomination in the 2012 US Presidential election)

With 25,000 videos on YouTube, LGBT youth can – in ways never before possible – truly believe things might actually get better. Additionally, many of the videos acknowledge the inherent pleasure in gay sexuality, letting LGBT children and young people know there are unlimited possibilities for love and pleasure in a productive and fulfilling life:

OK Listen up people.

It gets better. You being here makes the world a more blessed place. There's art to be made. And there are songs to be sung. There's so much to learn about yourself. There are sexy people to make out with. Yeah. There's a joy coming from you. Stay with us. It gets better. (Jules Skloot, (From Savage and Miller, p10)

With many politicians like Abbot and Bachmann who, by their actions, power and access to the media, utilise and promote discourses that other and marginalise, the *It Gets Better Project* harnesses the internet – particularly YouTube – by providing a tactical intervention to resist, construct, disseminate, popularise and legitimise the lifeworlds and sexualities of LGBT youth and adults:

I don't know what it is like to be picked on for being gay. But I do know what it's like to grow up feeling that sometimes you don't belong. It's tough. And for a lot of kids, the sense of being alone or apart – I know can just wear on you. And when you're teased or bullied, it can seem like somehow you brought it on yourself for being different, or for not fitting in with everybody else. But what I have to say is this. You are not alone. You did not do anything wrong. You didn't do anything to be bullied. And there is a whole world waiting for you, filled with possibilities. (US President Barack Obama (from Savage and Miller, p19)

When I was young there was a time when I figured, the hell with it. I'd never even said the word *transgender* out loud. I couldn't imagine saying it, ever. I mean, please … I thought about my parents. I thought about the clear inescapable fact that I was female in spirit and how, in order to be whole, I would have to give up every dream I'd had, save one. It is hard to be gay, or lesbian. To be trans can be even harder … But in the years since I heard that voice – *Are you all right son? You're going to be all right* – I've found to my surprise, that most people have treated me with love. Some of the people I most expected to lose, when I came out trans, turned out to be loving, compassionate and kind. I can't tell you how to get there from there. You have to figure that out for yourself. But I do know that instead of going over that cliff, I walked back down the mountain that morning and instead began the long, long journey towards home. (Jennifer Finney Boylan) (from Savage and Millner, p27-8))

The overarching motive of both these projects is that telling stories – especially counternarratives in opposition to dominant discourses – can change lives and provide hope to LGBT youth for something better that what they are currently experiencing in schools, at work or even at home. Heteronormativity and its hegemonic and violent legacy are constitutive of a concentration of power that determines the lens through which LGBT youth are seen and often legitimises bullying and marginalisation. Authoring counternarratives, whether in writing, digitally or through art, creates spaces for resistant tactics to be actualised by those who are 'othered' (or those who stand in solidarity with them) to creatively and critically read and critique the world and re-write dominant master narratives. This brings us, collectively, a step closer to a more inclusive and equitable society.

Going viral: (re)including counternarratives as a tool within critical pedagogy

Practitioners across educational contexts can use counternarratives to address longstanding problems where individuals and groups of children and young people have become 'docile citizens' – where normative and dominant discourses act as gatekeepers in silencing their experiences and histories and demonising their identities and lifeworlds. Incorporating counternarratives into educational practices can be a strategic localised intervention or a more viral tactic of resistance that can spiral on YouTube with 40 million views like the *It Gets Better Project*. They are powerful because they destabilise, dislodge and, at times, counter dominant (false) truths and those discursive strategies that work to sustain the separation of people with disabilities from community life, maintain negative narratives of single motherhood and promote homophobic bullying.

There is a battle 'for truth', or at least 'around truth – it being understood once again that by truth I … mean … 'the ensemble of rules according to which the true and the false are separated and specific effects of power attached to the true', it being understood also that it's not a matter of a battle 'on behalf' of the truth, but of a battle about the status of truth and the economic and political role it plays. (Foucault, 1980:132)

Counternarratives allow practitioners to work with children and young people to read, critique and take critical action against systems of power which produce and sustain 'truth', through their discursive practices. Paramount to this endeavour is how counternarratives can come to occupy a space of permanence online and continue to work to challenge normative and dominant discourses related to practitioners' situationality across disciplines. As Toni Morrison reminds us, if the narrative or story does not exist, 'we must write it'. The examples presented here illustrate how counternarratives draw attention to the structural issues and institutional relations that continue to be inequitable, exclude and marginalise.

It is my hope that counternarratives can be (re)included and incorporated more widely within educational practices to resist cultural and ideological hegemony because they contest the political and institutional discourses of power circulating within master narratives. It is surely the ethical responsibility of practitioners to assist children and young people in rewriting oppressive narratives. The challenge is to do so and consistently support their active efforts of resistance against any normative beliefs and educational practices that marginalise them.

Source: *newly commissioned for this volume.*

Notes

1   'Toni Morrison – Nobel Lecture'. Nobelprize.org. 20 Nov 2011 http://www.nobelprize.org/nobel_prizes/literature/laureates/1993/morrison-lecture.html

2   Unsourced quote widely attributed to Toni Morrison http://www.goodreads.com/author/show/3534.Toni_Morrison

3   Passion Works Studio (2011). Performing (Dis)ability and Art Differently. Retrieved from http://www.test.passionworks.org/stories/performing-disability-and-art-differently/

4   Quote taken from "Tony Abbott puts gay views in order" in the *Herald Sun*, March 9, 2010. http://www.heraldsun.com.au/news/tony-abbott-gay-remarks-dangerous/story-e6frf7jo-1225838436495

5   Senator Michele Bachmann, speaking at the EdWatch National Education Conference, November 6, 2004. http://www.thebachmannrecord.com/thebachmannrecod.html

References

Ajandi, J. (2011) 'Single mothers by choice': Disrupting dominant discourse of the family through social justice alternatives', *International Journal of Child, Youth and Family Studies*, vols.3 and 4, p410-431

Barnett, R. (1997) *Higher Education: A Critical Business*. Society for Research into Higher Education and Open University Press

Collins, P.H. (1997) 'How much difference is too much? Black feminist thought and the politics of postmodern social theory', *Current Perspectives in Social Theory*, vol.17, p3-37

Foucault, M. (1978/1995) *Discipline and Punish: The Birth of the Prison*, New York: Vintage Books

Foucault, M. (1980) *Power/knowledge: selected interviews and other writings 1972–1977*, New York: Pantheon

Friere, P. (1940) *Pedagogy of the Oppressed*, New York: Continuum

Giroux, H., Lankshear, C., McLaren, P. and Peters, M. (eds) (1996) *Counternarratives: Cultural studies and critical pedagogies in postmodern spaces*, London: Routledge

Harter, L.M., Scott, J.A., Novak, D.R., Leeman, M. and Morris, J.F. (2006) 'Freedom through flight: Performing a counter-narrative of disability', *Journal of Applied Communication Research*, vol. 34, no.1, p3-29

Hillier, L., Turner, A. and Mitchell, A. (2005) *Writing Themselves in Again: 6 years on, The 2nd national report on the sexual health and well-being of same sex attracted young people in Australia*, Australian Research Centre in Sex, Health and Society (ARCSHS), La Trobe University Melbourne

Jones, J.R. (2010) *Making Safe Places Unsafe: A Discussion of Homophobia with Teachers*, Kendal Hunt Publishing

McKay, C.L. (2010) 'Community education and critical race praxis: The power of voice', *Educational Foundations*, vol.24, no.1-2, p25-38

Mills, S. (1997) *Discourse*. London: Routledge

Morgan, P. (1998) *Adoption and the Care of Children: The British and American Experience*, London: Institute for Economic Affairs

Rivers, I. (2011) *Homophobic Bullying: Research and Theoretical Perspectives*, New York: Oxford University Press

Savage, D. and Miller, T. (2011) *It Gets Better: Coming Out, Overcoming Bullying and Creating a Life Worth Living*, New York: Dutton

Scott, J.C. (1985) *Weapons of the Weak: Everyday forms of peasant resistance*, New Haven, CT: Yale University Press

Part 3

Taking a stance on issues and practice to transform learning

Chapter 12

Len Barton, inclusion and critical disability studies: Theorising disabled childhoods

Dan Goodley and Katherine Runswick-Cole

Introduction

Len Barton has always reminded us that spoken words, delivered with passion and humility, are the very stuff of critical research and research that aims to be political. As one of the pioneers of British disability studies, Len has often spoken out to challenge researchers and practitioners to remain critical about the assumptions they hold, the impact of their research and the need to keep questioning how they understand marginalisation. During one seminar in London in 2004, in a paper that introduced the day (Barton, 2004a), Len argued that social exclusion, of which disablism is one element, has many compounding forms of differing exclusions, is not a natural but a socially constructed process, has no single factor that can remove it and is in constant need of conceptual analysis. This chapter aims to address each of Barton's four points in specific relation to the contemporary societal position of disabled children, their families and key professionals that work around them, through four analytical themes:

1 We explore the ways in which disabled childhoods are imbricated with other forms of exclusion.
2 We consider the ways in which 'disability', 'impairment' and 'child' are consistently being reproduced in particular and often contradictory ways by disability discourses.
3 We consider the need to work with numerous forms of educational intervention that address the exclusion of disabled children.

4   In our conclusion we appeal to a critical disability studies that builds on the shoulders of (social model) greats – such as Len Barton – but in ways receptive to other transformative ideas from queer, feminist and postcolonial positions.

We hope that our exploration demonstrates the energising potential of Len Barton's words of wisdom to keep disability studies and inclusive education constantly on the lookout for new and responsive theories, ideas, politics and passions. [...]

Queer contributions to disability studies and inclusive education provide possibilities for recasting disability as a site of resistance and disabled children (and their allies) as transformative agents. Queer is against heteronormativity and homonormativity (McRuer and Wilkerson, 2003). Queer develops 'fugitive knowledges' to express what it means to be a transgressive subject: of centring queer and queering the centre (Vicars, 2008). Disabled children are queer children: with the potential to subvert, rethink and reject normative, narrow, dull, limiting, disablist, respectable, middle-of-the-road, conservative, traditional and exclusionary schools, classrooms and pedagogical practice. Queer transgresses the normal and normative ways of life. Sherry (2004) asks two questions: How is queerness evoked in the construction of disability and how is disability evoked in the construction of queerness? We seek to answer these questions through recognising the affirmative – or queering – nature of disabled children, their families and other allies (including teachers).

Barton's attraction to new ideas goes beyond theory – highlighting a further theme within his work – that of listening carefully to the accounts of the people we work with. In order to understand the dynamics of social exclusion and disability politics, researchers need to work with key stakeholders, including not only professionals but disabled children and their families, users of services and a host of community activists (Clough and Barton, 1995). There are risks, of course, of recreating the conditions of exclusion through presenting research accounts that emphasise the victim status of recipients of exclusionary practices (Barton and Clough, 1998). It is therefore crucial to keep in mind issues of how we re-present the people we work with. [...]

Disabled childhoods are imbricated with other forms of exclusion

Many of our interviews with parents have revealed the assumptions on the part of professionals and services about the good parent. While disabled children are expected to perform in ways in keeping with dominant assumptions about disability, as we shall see below, their parents are assessed in terms of what we might call heteronormative conceptions of parenting. The vast majority of the parents we have spoken to are mothers. This is an unsurprising finding as women are usually the ones involved as the primary care givers and advocates for their children. Consequently, as gender and disability intersected in the accounts we gathered, we were required to bring together analyses from feminist disability studies. For example, mothers reported to us numerous occasions when their care and parenting were judged in terms of expectations held by professionals:

I arrived at school at 10.30, the secretary was a bit surprised to see me as she had the social worker down to arrive at 10.30 and me at 11. The social worker clearly wanted to meet with the SENCO [Special Educational Needs Co-ordinator] before he met with me. I hadn't turned up early on purpose, I genuinely thought that the meeting was at 10.30, but was glad that it minimised the amount of time that they met without me. When I finally arrived in the room – they'd met for about 20 mins by then – I was surprised to find a male social worker. We had a long and heated (on my part) discussion about the assessment form [social work core assessment form for 'children in need', which social workers use to assess all families of disabled children who seek access to services]. I asked him how he was going to assess the sections of the form including 'warmth'. I asked what criteria he would use for assessing warmth. He was completely flummoxed. He assured me that he could see that I was 'committed' to my son. I thought that irrelevant and wanted to know how he'd come to that decision. (Imogen)

The assessment of parental (read 'maternal') warmth evokes psychological and psychoanalytic tropes associated with good enough mothering and attachment theories of mother and child. While these ideas are not explicitly accounted for – nor explained by the social worker – they recurred throughout our interviews. The discourses of '(not) good enough mother' and 'attachment separation' circulate in wider patriarchal discourses and have been widely used to assess the psychological health (or pathological illness) of all mothers (Ussher, 1991). The extent to which these labels might stick even more firmly to mothers who are parenting disabled children has not really been explored in feminist literature. Following disabled feminists such as Morris (1996), our sense is that mothers of disabled children are likely to encounter these discourses: a case of pathologies hunting in pairs. Fortunately, mothers like Imogen refuse to be assimilated into these disabling accounts of mothering. Imogen can be seen as queering normative measures of parenting by insisting that she and the professional interrogate concepts of 'warmth' and 'good enough' thus revealing their problematic nature. That said, mothering discourses are difficult to avoid in the context of parenting disabled children:

One incident, my daughter was on stage with some other children and she just went to the edge of the stage behind the other child and pushed the child off, and the child crashed to the floor and she just looked at him and thought, 'Well yeah, I've done that well,' and walked off with no understanding that this child was screaming with pain, I thought she'd broken something. I thought, 'Something's not right here'. So we went to the clinical psychologist not quite knowing what the problems were, but – and school saying as well, you know, her behaviour is bizarre, she doesn't relate to others, school had suggested autism, but we didn't know. So we went to the clinical psychologist, who basically seemed to think that I had a problem and not Lily, and I was some middle-class mother who was over-anxious about her daughter. So anyway I kept at it and we went back and had interviews and we went and visited and they didn't come up with anything particularly conclusive, they said she was mildly learning disabled with some autistic type characteristics. (Roberta)

The notion of the neurotic parent re-emphasises the responsibilities of the mother to remain dutiful and caring in her primary role. Mothers adopt the roles of advocate, carer, supporter, care manager and facilitator of the support of the extended family. They adopt such roles under the watchful eyes of professional others whose pseudo-scientific imperial processes colonise the social worlds of mothers (Shakespeare, 2000). We know from previous work that parents are subjected to the professional gaze in ways that they feel they have to respond to. The following pen portraits (taken from Goodley and McLaughlin, 2008:84) capture some examples of the ways in which parents are governed:

Governing the parent: 9 pen portraits

1   Sylvia made sure that she got up at the 'crack of dawn' to tidy the house in preparation for the health visitor 'assessing the suitability' of the home. She wanted it just right.

2   A physiotherapist discussed with the researcher a parent's 'struggles with controlling her weight'. They confided, 'They are bound to affect how she looks after her child'.

3   A professional had told Lesley she must fit locks on internal doors to prevent Stuart from 'going where he shouldn't'.

4   Mags was encouraged by the nurses in the special care baby unit to leave her child for a while 'to get some fresh air'. They were worried about the 'attachment problems' that might result from her spending too much time with Gerry. She had to 'let go'. Mags had had experiences of a couple of units and they differed in their approach. She had been allowed to bath Gerry at the first unit but in the second she was told 'oh no, he shouldn't be having baths yet.'

5   A number of mothers told us about feeling an intense pressure to dress their children up in the nicest clothes possible for hospital appointments so as to curb any possible inference that they were incapable of looking after their children.

6   Angela described how she adopted a business like demeanour for professional appointments, including wearing a suit, carrying a brief-case and consciously altering her speech pattern to neutralise her local accent.

7   Sharon joked, 'I didn't have time for my postnatal depression' because she had to demonstrate to professionals she was capable of being a parent.

8   Cheryl had initially felt that she could not ask for respite care to 'just' go to the Post Office because it seemed too trivial. She spoke of the relief she felt when a health visitor encouraged her to employ a support worker to sit with her son for an hour while Cheryl took a bath.

9   Sharon had been visited by Sure Start workers. She had been peeling onions when they arrived and answered the door with tears streaming down her face. The Sure Start people had left saying they would call at a more convenient time. In due

course, they alerted the Social Services and shortly afterwards a social worker had visited the family. This had incensed Sharon as she had not requested support from Social Services. She wondered if it was because she has appeared distressed during the Sure Start visit.

The challenges mothers face are further magnified by the socio-economic conditions that currently face those parenting a disabled child. While mothers are expected to sanely and rationally parent their children in ways akin to what might be seen as forms of (unpaid) professionalism or human resource management, they are expected to do so in ways that support the achievements of their children (Burman, 2008). Children – and their mothers – are caught up in the marketisation of education. Schools are stressful places. Teachers are held to greater accountability, more assessment and a loss of autonomy (Barton, 2004b). Teachers are implementers of decisions of others – like policy makers – and are assessed in terms of how well they implement these decisions. [...]

'Disability', 'impairment' and 'child' are reproduced in contradictory ways by disability discourses

A finding that we have developed in other papers relates to a parenting paradox: that in order to access potentially enabling support and services for families of disabled children, families have to re-present their disabled children in explicitly disabling ways. [...] Clearly, access to benefits is key to the financial and emotional well-being of disabled families. Disability Living Allowance (DLA) is a tax-free statutory benefit for individuals 'with long-term disability' in the UK. When their child reaches the age of three months, parents/carers of disabled children are able to claim DLA for their disabled child. Three children per hundred thousand children are eligible for DLA (Ellis *et al*, 2008). The DLA can be awarded for different periods of time before a reassessment is made – from one year to life (Ellis *et al*, 2008). It has two components: the care component and the mobility component. The care component is for help with 'personal care' and the mobility component is for help 'getting around' (Form: DLA1A Child). Personal care is defined as: 'needing assistance (over and above what would normally be expected of a child of their age) with: washing or bathing; dressing/undressing; using the toilet; eating; using stairs; getting in/out of bed; communicating with people; and using special equipment' (Form: DLA1A Child). It is possible to claim either or both components at the same time. The DLA recipient (or their parent/carer) must identify strongly with a ready-made deficient categorisation of disability.

In order to claim the support of the welfare state, parents of disabled children are asked to depict their children (and their families) in ways that emphasise deficiency, need and lack. [...] Claire explains:

So for instance with autism, there is a box you have to tick which says is your child physically disabled yes or no? If you tick no, which typically parents of autistic children do, you automatically rule out mobility. You may get the lower rate but you certainly won't get the higher rate. If you research all the rules, which is what I did which is why it takes so long, autism is a physical disability, because it is a brain injury which means it is a physical disability and every section of the form that you fill in you must say that they have this behaviour due to their physical disability which is a brain injury which causes that behaviour, and that's not how any right minded person is going to fill in the form.

Barton's (2004a) observation about the socially constructed character of exclusion is supported by the accounts of parents. Parents have to pathologise their children in order to access services. Such an enforcement is understandably experienced as problematic:

I know it's really hard to produce any kind of system that describes the impact of disability without doing that kind of detail but to make a parent write so many bad things about their child, is just cruel 'cos most parents throughout their child's life never write anything bad about their child. (Shelley)

This requirement to account for the child in terms of lack is found in other attempts to access support. The following is an account from another parent, Imogen:

I went to see the SENCO at my son Danny's school on Friday and we talked about getting a social worker to come to the 14+ review of his statement. So I rang the number and was taken through an assessment form that would be passed to the disabled children's team – they will then decide who will come out and do an assessment. I was asked to give a description of Danny. I was asked about how his disability affects him and how it affects us. I was asked to give details of his medical needs, and his personal care needs and I was asked about his mobility. I was asked about the rate of DLA and mobility he received. This meant that I had to describe Danny as 'autistic', talk about his epilepsy surgery and the 'strangenesses' he has now. I told them he has an IQ of 49. I had to explain that he couldn't do things that other children his age can do, that we can't leave him on his own, that he can't organise himself to get a meal, that he still needs help with his personal care, including washing his hair and wiping his bum, that we have to take him everywhere with us and that sometimes he doesn't want to go. She started to type 'he can't do things that normal fourteen-year-olds can do'. I said, 'I didn't say that he isn't "not normal"'. She apologised and said she didn't mean that she meant 'average'. I got off the phone and felt terrible. Partly because I'd been quite rude to the woman on the phone, partly because I'd described Danny in ways that I hate and because I feel like it is a betrayal of him. Partly because I'd had to talk about intimate care with a woman who sounded like she was talking about car insurance rather than a person. Partly because I've just described Danny's life and our family life in a way which makes it sound shit and it isn't – I feel like I've been dishonest because if I talk positively about him he won't get what he needs. I'm hoping that I'll be able to behave myself better if the SENCO is there and that she can take the role of describing Danny's difficulties rather than me having to do it. So now we just have to wait for them to get back to me!

This account illuminates the struggles of parents with the contradictory positions they are forced to adopt: fighting for their children whilst trying to 'behave' for professionals and emphasising deficiencies of a child to access support while recognising that a child exists behind the labels. [...] Mothers are expected to be compliant, appreciative and well behaved: 'good mothers'. Furthermore, we can see here the close alliances of dis/ability and ab/normality: and that one can collapse into the other very easily, in ways that threaten to turn an impairment label (autism) into a global descriptor of the child (not normal).

[...]

Working with numerous forms of educational intervention to address the exclusion of disabled children

She did go to Brownies for a few weeks until the leader said, 'Well a lot of parents are now keeping their children away because Lily's there, would you mind not bringing her anymore?' And we went to swimming and she was holding other children under the water, so the teacher said, 'Do you mind not bringing her anymore?' And so, you know what I mean, everything we've tried she was just sabotaging and running amok and so the school said, 'Do you mind if she doesn't come anymore?' So everything we've tried other than horse riding, which is working quite well at the moment, she just can't cope with and so we're not able to send her to anything. And now we're having a problem, and this is this week's kind of panic, now we're asking to go to the special school. (Roberta)

A number of parents reported to us that their communities were inaccessible for their children – not just in terms of the built environment but also because of the lack of enabling relationships. One of the advocates we spoke to during a focus group informed us that a girl in her teens who had 'handling and moving needs' was denied access to her local youth club unless her mother was present to 'take her to the toilet'. Back in school, we have collected complaints that disabled children are 'whisked off at lunchtime by their PAs [personal assistants] to room 101' (focus-group worker, Helen, for a disabled children's play organisation) while their non-disabled peers rush out to play in the playgrounds. We know, too, that disabled children often suffer exclusion from friendship groups of non-disabled children (Salmon, 2010). Consequently, disabled children and their kin often access what might be termed impairment-specific contexts as this example, taken from Katherine's ethnographic notes, describes:

I arrived at the sports centre close to the town centre. I met Brenda, a mother of a child with autism. Brenda is in her forties. Her son now attends residential special school. She set up the leisure club for children with autism six years ago. It has grown since and now the club provides training for the local authority and for other local authorities in the region. There is a social enterprise arm of the organisation, which is there to support the development of other clubs. The aim is to have a leisure club for children with autism in every town in the country. Brenda explained that the motivation for the club was the lack of services for children on the autism spectrum. She explained that there were sports opportunities for disabled children in the town, but that children with autism had been unable to access them. Children do not need a diagnosis of autism to access Brenda's club. She explained that it was difficult to get a diagnosis of autism in the town because the local paediatrician was reluctant to label children, so a child needed to be displaying autistic traits and their parents needed to be actively exploring a diagnosis of autism for them to access the club. Parents stay at the sessions. Brenda is clear that this is a 'co-production of leisure' and not a respite service.

When the children arrived with their parents, they confidently came in, chucked their coats under a table and went either to the soft play area or the trikes. The children knew to wait until their picture was on the board under 'now' to be able to trampoline. The board also had 'next' so that the children had some sense of when their turn was coming. The children greeted one another. There was a small group of children sitting on a piece of soft play apparatus having a chat, other children were bouncing and the parents sat nearby watching their children. Brenda came up to me and said, 'you can't tell, can you?' – meaning that autism was not on display. And she was right: they were just children playing. The sessions were very well planned and organised, the children knew what to expect and what was going to happen and when. The parents loved the sessions, they said that it had given them somewhere to go and they were able to share experiences with other parents 'going through the same stuff'. There were several dads there with their children, and one dad, in particular, enjoyed romping around on the soft play with his son. I could see exactly why Brenda has set up autism specific provision, it was a logical reaction to a gap in services in the town. However, I still felt uneasy about the idea of a club exclusively for children with autism. The activities are carefully planned with children with autism and all their stereotypical 'traits' in mind, but it is difficult to see why careful planning, visual timetables, precise language, 'showing as well as talking' isn't just good practice for all children. The children in the leisure centre looked 'just the same' because they were confident about the routines and the structures. So couldn't they be 'just the same' with children 'without autism' if those structures were in place? It seemed to me that there are two responses to inaccessible provision: one is to set up alternative provision as Brenda has done, and the other is to challenge and change the existing provision. What is difficult to know is whether the children themselves prefer to be with other children with autism. Brenda said that people with autism don't want forced integration, but what do the children want? Certainly the parents enjoy the club, they enjoy sharing experiences while their children play. They like being in an environment where no one stares or asks questions and where they feel they 'belong'.

Finally, I want to ask whether we should accept a sports hall full of children 'with autism'. What would we say about a sports hall full of black children and a social enterprise company that wants leisure clubs for black children in every town? If what we say about these two things is different, then what are the reasons why? (Katherine's ethnographic account)

We present this reflexive ethnographic account here because we feel it highlights Barton's (2004a) conviction that social exclusion has no single factor that can remove it. As Katherine's reflections towards the end of the piece highlight, we share an uncertain and troubled view of segregated leisure provision. As advocates of inclusive education, we view the practice of separating disabled and non-disabled children as highly problematic. For Booth (2002), inclusive education refers to the increasing participation of learners in the culture, curricula and communities of their neighbourhood centres of learning. For Booth, achievements of schools mean nothing if the community do not enhance the spirit of all teachers and pupils. In this sense, then, we could argue that the autism sports club provides a welcoming community to children (whether or not they are officially diagnosed with autism) whose leisure interests are not addressed by other elements of the community. Clearly, in response to Katherine's questions about ethnicity, there are groups and leisure activities that form in ways that respond to local communities. Indeed, the origins of the disabled people's movement, black civil rights and queer politics can be found in the development of counter-cultures that emerged as a consequence of being segregated from the disablist, racist and heterosexist mainstream. What we remain mindful of, though, is Barton's notion of their being no single factor: clearly, only having segregated forms of leisure will not address the community exclusion of different children. Indeed, in our exploration of the pastimes of disabled children we have unveiled inclusive aspects of mainstream communities:

Jack [Hattie's father] talks about taking Hattie to football. She started going with him this season. At the first match she cheered when both sides scored but she's learnt not to now! Jack says football is a great leveller; it is the only place that Hattie can truly be herself because she can cheer and shout and no one quietens her down. She is totally accepted by the people who sit around them. Jack says there are lots of other people with special needs there. (ethnographic notes)

Is the football stadium queer/enabling when compared with rigid heteronormative/ disabling characteristics of the typical classroom? Barton's (2004a) assertion that inclusion requires a multitude of sites feeds into wider considerations of community belonging, acceptance and recognition. At the heart of this is respect, beautifully captured by Fanon (1993):

We need to mutually recognise each other ... to educate man [sic] to be actional preserving in all his relations his respect for the basic values that constitute a human world, is the prime task of him who, having taken thought, prepares to act. (222)

Conclusion: developing critical disability studies

To conclude we want to take up a position that Barton has adopted in all his writings: of constantly questioning the viability of theories and seeking dialogue with other transformative positions. Barton's work in disability studies is often associated with the social model of disability and, specifically, a materialist analysis of the conditions of disablism (Barton, 2001, 2004c). This perspective reflects the influence of Marxist sociologies in the 1970s through which issues such as illness and disability were understood as products of capitalism. Key units of analysis include material conditions of labour, transport and leisure. Power is centred in the external, material world, not people's heads. Ideology is therefore a tool of ruling-class structures that maintain unequal means of production. Through our work with disabled children and their families we have found ourselves drawn to a critical disability studies that builds on the shoulders of (social model) thinkers like Barton but is receptive to the other transformative theories and non-material conditions of exclusion to be found in society and culture. For this section we say a little more about queer:

Northtown is a co-located special school. The deputy head told me that both the head of Northtown and the mainstream school head were keen to co-locate. They both saw this as an opportunity for inclusion but also saw the potential that sharing resources might have for improving provision for both schools. The schools share the sports facilities, canteen, school hall and theatre. The schools share one reception area but the special school is in one half of the building and the mainstream school in the other. The Deputy Head told me that the special school parents had accepted co-location as a positive step, partly because they could see that their children would have access to better resources and partly because the school moved a very short distance. Many children in the special school come from the local area and are therefore part of the local community, so there is a sense that they share a sense of community with peers. The Deputy Head said there had been concerns that the mainstream pupils would tease or stare at or name call the disabled pupils but this hasn't happened. He felt that this had been a very positive outcome of the re-location. The school itself is extremely well appointed with break out areas, interactive whiteboards, sensory room, huge accessible changing/toilet facilities, music, art, science rooms and soft play. The atmosphere in the school was incredibly calm and purposeful with children engaged in a range of practical activities. The art room was stunning and I met the art teacher who the Deputy Head described as 'bonkers' but brilliant. This seemed to be a bit of a theme among the staff. Another teacher was constructing a display that would use lighting to move from day to night and different creatures would emerge throughout the day. This was alongside his construction of a display which glows under UV lights. He uses projectors to display moving pictures of animals and UV paint to bring to life a huge ant. He explained how he had used a projector to take the children to the moon and that they had asked 'where are we?' then speculated on the fact that they couldn't live there because there was no water. He said that there was no way his pupils could have learnt this looking at books. The Deputy Head said that the science teachers from the mainstream school had said 'why can't we teach science like this?' The Deputy Head said that some of the staff had special school backgrounds but others had left mainstream and would probably find it difficult to get a job in mainstream again.

Is it possible to find inclusive practices within special schools? The above extract would suggest we can. In order to identify these practices we may need the tools of queer theory. A queer teacher, then, is someone who is prepared to take risks, to embrace their 'bonkers' style of teaching. Queer teachers are inclusive and creative teachers who offer opportunities for what McKenzie (2009) terms *possability*: a neologism to describe the ways in which disabled children demand imaginative and responsive forms of educational provision. Queer teaching has the development of creative pedagogies as its guiding interest – rather than normative teaching which emphasises competition and narrow notions of achievement. We wonder if queer teaching might contribute to what Lloyd (2008) terms the necessary denormalisation of school culture that subverts the marketisation of (inclusive) education and, instead, offers more imaginative approaches to teaching and learning. Clearly, for such transformations to occur then we need to look outside special provision and ask to what extent all schools can promote queer teaching and learning that respond well to difference and have inclusion at their very core. This imagination is at the heart of Len Barton's work, and the blending of disability and queer studies is one example of the development of critical disability studies that is responsive not only to exclusion but also attempts to promote resistance. Len Barton (2004b) argues that 'in this struggle [of disability politics and inclusive education], I do most passionately believe that a political analysis is now even more important and requires our most serious attention' (p74). We would share Len's view in relation to understanding and enabling the lives of disabled children. In order to craft these political analyses we require theoretical ideas that are responsive to the complex elements of exclusion outlined by Barton at the start of the chapter. We believe that such theoretical ideas can be found at the theoretical intersections of queer, postcolonial, feminist and disability studies and in the resistant accounts of parents of disabled children.

Source: Goodley, D. and Runswick-Cole, K. (2010) 'Len Barton, inclusion and critical disability studies: Theorising disabled childhoods', *International Studies in Sociology of Education*, vol. 20, no. 4, pp. 273-290, Taylor & Francis Group

References

Barton, L. (ed) (2001) *Disability, politics and the struggle for change*. London: David Fulton

Barton, L. (2004a) Social inclusion and education: Issues and questions. Paper presented at the ESRC seminar Towards Inclusion: Social Inclusion and Education, July 19, in London

Barton, L. (2004b) The politics of special education: A necessary or irrelevant approach? In *Ideology and the Politics of (In)exclusion*, (ed) L. Ware, 63-75. New York: Peter Lang

Barton, L. (2004c) The disability movement: Some personal observations. In *Disabling Barriers – enabling environments*, (ed) Swain, J, Finkelstein, V, French, S and Oliver, M. 285-90. London: Sage

Barton, L. and Clough, P. (eds) (1998) *Articulating With Difficulty: Research voices in special education*. London: Paul Chapman

Booth, T. (2002) Inclusion and exclusion policy in England: Who controls the agenda? In *Inclusive Education: Policy, contexts and comparative perspectives*, (ed) Armstrong, F, Armstrong, D and Barton, L. 78-98. London: David Fulton

Burman, E. (2008) *Developments: Child, image, nation*. London: Routledge

Clough, P. and Barton, L. (eds) (1995) *Making Difficulties: Research and the construction of special educational needs*. London: Paul Chapman

Ellis, J, Logan, S, Pumphrey, R, Tan, H.K, Henley, W, Edwards, V, Moy, R. and Gilbert, R. (2008) Inequalities in provision of the Disability Living Allowance for Down Syndrome. *Archive of Disease in Childhood* 93: 14-16

Fanon, F (1993) *Black skins, white masks*. 3rd ed. London: Pluto Press

Goodley, D, and McLaughlin, J. (2008) Productive parental alliances. In *Families Raising Disabled Children: Enabling care and social justice*, (ed) McLaughlin, J, Goodley, D, Clavering, E. and Fisher, P. 78-105. London: Palgrave

Lloyd, C. (2008) Removing barriers to achievement: A strategy for inclusion or exclusion? *International Journal of Inclusive Education* 12, no. 2: 221-36

McKenzie, J.A. (2009) Constructing the intellectually disabled person as a subject of education: A discourse analysis using Q-methodology. Unpublished PhD thesis, Rhodes University

McRuer, R. and Wilkerson, A. (2003) Cripping the (queer) nation. *GLQ: A Journal of Lesbian and Gay Studies* 9, no. 1-2: 1-23

Morris, J. (ed) (1996) *Encounters with strangers: Feminism and disability.* London: The Women's Press

Salmon, N. (2010) 'We just stick together': Centering the friendships of disabled youth. Unpublished PhD thesis, Dalhousie University

Shakespeare, T. (2000) *Help.* London: Cassell

Sherry, M. (2004) Overlaps and contradictions between queer theory and disability studies. *Disability & Society* 19, no. 7: 769-83

Ussher, J. (1991) *Women's madness: Misogyny or mental illness?* London: Harvester Wheatsheaf

Vicars, M. (2008) How queer! Insider research in educational settings. Paper presented to the Social Change and Well Being Seminar series, February 6, in Manchester, UK

Chapter 13

What to do about culture?

Kris D. Gutiérrez and Maricela Correa-Chávez

Understanding cultural variation in approaches to learning: that is, how to characterise regularities of individuals' approaches according to their cultural background has been a continuing and complex dilemma in the learning sciences. The persistent surge in immigration globally makes understanding this question more urgent as the intercultural nature of people's everyday lives has increased, as members of different cultural communities come into contact with one another with more regularity.

The phenomenon of interculturality, from our perspective, results from the boundary crossing that occurs as people move across the activities and settings of everyday life and encounter different forms of culturally organised practices. People may view these new forms of practice as more or less familiar to them depending on their own histories as participants in particular cultural communities, households, and various activity systems of which they are a part. However, not understanding the range and sources of variation in an individual and community's practices can often facilitate generalising about members of non-dominant communities and, thus, makes it more difficult to develop nuanced understandings about new cultural practices encountered.

It is this understanding of culture as practice and historically based that we wish to advance in this chapter, especially in relation to the effects of interculturality on non-dominant students, that is, students from communities who are not in positions of power – economically, sociopolitically, and socioculturally. More often, non-dominant students are new immigrants or members of historically marginalised communities whose intercultural navigation is complicated by poverty, racism, other forms of institutional and intergenerational stigmatisation, and inequitable access to social and educational supports (Center for the Study of Human Learning and Diversity, 2005).

We argue that the cultural-historical or cultural-practice-based approach to the cultural dimensions of learning utilised in our own work helps us account for the range of diversity that exists within cultural communities, and the range of ways individual members of those communities utilise resources to negotiate the various challenges of their lives. As researchers, we focus our attention on understanding the continuity and variability of cultural communities, their individual members, and their ways of organising learning. This approach can be contrasted with one that relies on comparing various cultural communities or subgroups with one another with little or no consideration of the history or logic leading to observable cultural patterns. We believe these various approaches have important consequences, both in terms of the rigour and validity of research on non-dominant communities, as well as material effects on individuals and these communities as a whole.

We return to our opening question: what to do about culture? That is, how should we conceive of the role of culture in learning when the existing body of scientific work has not yet demonstrated an understanding of how to avoid the common error of equating culture solely with race and ethnicity and conceiving of cultural communities as static, unchanging and homogeneous. Consider that many of the measures used in the study of learning and normative development have been normed with European-American or European middle class children. Little is known about their appropriateness for addressing similar questions among other populations. In addition, much of the research on children from non-dominant backgrounds has focused on risks or deviance rather than normative development that includes adaptive response to risks.

In this chapter, we will argue that a cultural-historical approach will help researchers to think about culture and learning in ways that we hope will discourage the tendency to homogenise or broadly categorise groups of people who may share a geographical, linguistic, and historical background or to assume that differences from middle-class practices imply deficits (Foley, 1997). We begin by discussing our view of culture that is based on people's shared practices and histories and then comment on several common ways culture has been historically examined in the literature that we believe promotes reductive and static understandings of culture: Culture as either attributes located in individuals or held uniformly across entire groups. We then chart how this has led to the idea or studying 'cultural learning styles' and their associated threats to developing dynamic views of individual and cultural communities.

Looking for regularities and variation

In our work, culture is not a single variable or something that can be identified directly by a person's appearance, race/ethnicity, or national origin. Rather, we view culture as something that is lived dynamically and reflected in people's participation in their community's practices, traditions and institutions. However, our dynamic view of culture does not mean that we stop looking for regularities in the ways members of cultural communities participate in everyday practices. Instead, we view the regularities in communities and the relatively stable characteristics of particular cultural environments as being in constant tension with the emergent goals and practices that participants construct. This conflict and tension help contribute to the variation and ongoing change in an individual and a community's practices (Engestrom, 1993; Gutiérrez, 2002; Guriérrez and Rogoff, 2003). And it is the regularity and variation, that is, stability and ongoing change in culture, people's membership in multiple communities, and the individual's adaptive responses to the developmental tasks at hand that make the study of culture both challenging and a rich area for study.

But looking for cultural regularities will be more fruitful – both for research and practice – if we focus our examination of differences on cultural processes in which individuals engage with other people in dynamic cultural communities, some of which involve ethnic or racial group membership in important ways. By cultural community we mean a coordinated group of people with some traditions and understandings in common, extending across several generations, with varied roles and practices and continual change among participants, as well as transformation in the community's practices. For example, people draw on concepts, practices, and resources that have been valued and used intergenerationally. Over time, such practices, including ways of talking and belief systems, can come to be associated with a particular cultural community both by its members and neighbours. However, it would be reductive to equate the use of these concepts, ways of talking, or belief systems with race or ethnicity – a practice that we see employed too often in research about members of non-dominant communities. To be sure, race matters in important ways in the analysis of non-dominant communities, but we are careful not to assume that members of particular racial or ethnic groups engage uniformly in the same set of cultural practices or do so in the same ways.

Consider the following examples from our work that illustrate how members of the same national or ethnic group vary depending on the institutions and practices in which they participate. In one Mayan town, differences have been found between Mayan children in how they pay attention to ongoing events that are related to family participation in the cultural institution of school and in traditional indigenous ways of organising teaching and learning (Chavajay and Rogoff, 1999; 2002; Correa-Chávez and Rogoff, 2005). Similar results have been found in a farmworking community of

Mexican descent in the US. Children of Mexican descent in this community exhibited attention patterns in learning that were related to how much schooling their mother had attained (Correa-Chávez, Rogoff, and Mejía Arauz, 2005; Silva, Correa-Chávez and Rogoff, 2006). In this community, a group of US Mexican heritage children whose mothers varied in their amounts of schooling, participated in a study where they learned how to construct some toys. The children whose mothers averaged seven years of schooling tended to pay attention to multiple events at a time and to pay attention to events not addressed to them more so than US Mexican heritage children whose mothers had twelve or more years of schooling. The authors of these studies argue that maternal participation in school and in historical Mesoamerican forms of organising teaching and learning that emphasise observation to ongoing activity are related to the attentional patterns observed in the children.

If our goal is to capture the cultural dimensions of learning, that is, how people appropriate cultural concepts, then we must argue against using culture as a proxy for race, ethnicity, or national group. In our work, we take it for granted that members of the same national or ethnic group will vary in important ways, including the institutions and practices in which they participate. Rather than hindering us, this variation allows us to examine how people's participation in cultural traditions and institutions are related to the patterns that interest us. This way of studying cultural patterns with close attention to people's participation in activity also provides the opportunity to consider variation as a window to understanding historical change.

Locating culture in individuals

One common way of conceptualising culture has been to attribute aspects of culture to individuals. In this view, culture is located inside individuals' heads as they navigate through the world, and any one member of a cultural community would be replaceable with any other member in regards to the particular questions under study. A notable example of this view of culture in the United States is found in the guidelines for the National Institute of Health that require inclusion of members of minority groups in all studies applying for funding. We concur with the NIH that research should not be based solely on European American male participants. However, there are several problematic assumptions at work here in the guidelines: variance exists between and not within groups, and variation is accounted for by including minority groups, even without an examination of the member's histories and practices.

Following this line of enquiry, an individual possesses cultural traits that remain constant: over time, independent of the tasks and contexts in which they participate. Likewise, contexts are treated as if they exist independently of the people active in creating and maintaining them, and individuals as though their characteristics are unrelated to the contexts in which they and their families have participated over recent generations. Further, within this logic, the dominant group remains the unexamined normative group (Gutiérrez, 2005).

Culture attributed to entire groups and learning styles

Another commonly held view of culture assumes that members of cultural communities participate in similar kinds of cultural practices and do so in the same way regardless of individuals and time. In other words, cultural characteristics are attributed to entire groups of individuals. For example, individuals from one group may be characterised as learning holistically, whereas individuals from another group may be characterised as learning analytically. Similarly, individuals may be divided into cooperative versus individualist learners on the basis of membership of a particular cultural group. This way of characterising learners overgeneralises whole groups of people and assumes that there is a built-in relationship between learning style and group membership (Dunn, Griggs and Price, 1993).

Approaches that accommodate instructional practice to group styles treat what is 'known' about a group and apply it to all individuals in the group and assume only one style per person according to the individual's group categorisation. This labelling makes it more likely that groups will be treated as homogenous, with fixed ways of doing things. Recall our example of the various ways US Mexican heritage children use their attention in learning activities. If educators followed a learning styles approach, they would be led to believe that all Mexican children approach learning in one particular way. Indeed, even saying that all Mexican children from this one farmworking community approach learning in the same way would be misleading.

Yet, current instructional practices for immigrant children in the US often employ that very approach in which most of the students who are English learners receive a one-size-fits-all instructional treatment (English only and a reductive literacy curriculum) despite their diversity in terms of life and schooling experience, literacy skills, parents' education, home practices, and subject matter knowledge (Gutiérrez, 2004). The homogenisation of English learners in California, primarily Spanish-speaking youth from Mexico and Central America, is a glaring example of how things go awry when we equate race/ethnicity or national origin with culture, when we assume regularity without accounting for variation, and attribute a one style approach to learning to entire groups based on their social categories rather than to a history of their experiences.

We contrast this approach with our design of learning environments for secondary school students from migrant farmworker backgrounds who are also largely immigrant and non-English speaking. Following a cultural-historical view of culture and development, our work with migrant students gives emphasis to creating a social situation of development in which the curriculum and its pedagogy are grounded in the historical and current particulars of the students' everyday lives. As we learn more about our students, we might expect to see some continuity in the cultural practices of students who share a history of participating in the same cultural community, as well as new or hybrid forms of activity resulting from immigration, transmigration, and intercultural experiences (Gutiérrez, 2005). So rather than focusing narrowly on students' English language skills, for example, we attempt to learn about the socio-historical influences on students' language and literacy practices to help us resist reductive curricular and instructional approaches, and instead to build robust learning activities.

What is common across these examples is attention to people's usual ways of doing things as a means to understanding individuals' history of involvement in the varied practices of the community, including different years of participation in the cultural institution of school. Thus, by focusing on individuals' and groups' varied ways of participating and experience in activities, we can begin to understand how people's engagement in their communities lead to observable patterns, while also accounting for variation between individuals and groups.

Put simply, we argue against the tendency to equate culture with race, ethnicity, language preference, or national origin, especially on the basis of stable characteristics such as surname or country of birth, as it results in weak, limited, and ahistorical understandings of both individuals and the community practices in which they participate (Gutiérrez, Asato, Santos and Gotanda, 2002).

Accounting for change and membership in multiple communities

Static notions of culture such as those found in some learning styles frameworks treat culture as unchanging at the level of the individual, the activity setting, or the community's cultural practices. This perspective, of course, makes it much easier to study culture. However, if we believe that culture is lived and experienced in local, face-to-face interactions, we begin to understand that cultural practices are necessarily and simultaneously dynamic, locally constrained, hybrid, and heterogeneous with respect to the cultural community as a whole, as well as to the parts of the entire toolkit experienced by a given individual (Gutiérrez, 2002). In this way, we expect to find change and continuity in individuals and their communities.

And because cultural communities are composed of individuals, as individuals change (for example by attending school for many years), communities change as well (and vice versa). One of our studies on schooling and children's everyday lives illustrated this phenomenon. This study examined the way that children's lives have changed over the course of 23 years in a Guatemalan Maya community, as school became a more prominent institution. The same 60 families participated in the study in 1976 and then in 1999. Three generations of family members provided demographic information regarding family size, schooling aspirations, and children's daily activities.

The results showed a number of related changes occurred, as schooling became an expected part of children's lives. Children's educational and occupational aspirations changed to ones where schooling and certification were prerequisites. As children spent more time at school they were less likely to contribute productively to family work. Children's interaction with peers of different ages was limited, as age-gradation at school became more restricted and family size shrunk. Increased maternal schooling was associated with a dramatic decline in the birth rate and infant mortality limiting the number of siblings with whom children engaged.

Thus, as we previously mentioned, when we account for variability in groups of people, we have already built in a way of tracking changes over time. And understanding this variability includes acknowledging not only the complexity of community membership, but also the understanding that individuals participate in and constitute multiple practices and communities at the same time. Our response as a research community has been to ignore this complexity or to dichotomise individuals' communities in ways that treat them as completely independent activity systems, and often in ways that privilege one over another.

One more notable example in educational research of a version of this 'one community per person' thinking is the traditional mismatch theories of home and school discontinuities used to describe the relationship between community and school for non-dominant students. We reject such mismatch frameworks, as they reinscribe deficit portraits of home in ways that compel us 'to fix' communities and their participants so that they match normative views and practices without regard to the students' existing repertoires of practice or the additional set of challenges non-dominant youth experience.

As we have written elsewhere, a more productive approach in our work has been to focus attention on how people, especially non-dominant youth, appropriate cultural concepts as they move in and across a range of social practices – attending to the ways boundary crossing reinforces, extends, and conflicts with individuals' dispositions and repertoires of practice, of understanding better what takes hold in this movement. This focus has helped us identify productive and unproductive aspects of learning cycles, to see the sites of possibility and contradiction, and to document the processes that lead to learning, that is, processes marked by new forms of participation and activity that change (Gutiérrez, 2005).

Consider that many children in urban cities today interact with a wide-range of people and engage in a range of activities in which they have ongoing opportunities to extend what they know and to appropriate new knowledge. For example, in our work with children in a diverse after-school club in Los Angeles, we see with regularity how interculturality plays itself out in everyday practice, as children participate in the new and different practices of children of other cultural communities without being themselves members of that group or its practices. For example, African American girls in the programme participate in conversations and practices around popular Latino television shows, even though the shows are in Spanish, a language that the girls do not speak. In these contexts, children, influenced by popular culture and their participation in new activities valued by their peers, develop new practices and become participants in new communities of practice (Nixon and Gutiérrez, 2006). A cultural style, cultural trait, or one community per person approach limits the ability to account for such daily practices that are meaningful to children.

Repertoires of practice

We propose a shift from a view of culture where regularities in groups are attributed to individuals and assumed constant in all group members to one where the focus is on people's practices in their cultural communities. By focusing on these varied practices we can come to understand the range, or repertoires, of cultural practices in which people engage which would involve characterising their experience and initiative in prior cultural activities (Rogoff, 1997; 2003). By focusing on repertoires of practice we can account for change, continuity and multiple community memberships. We would characterise people's repertoires in terms of their familiarity with engaging in particular practices on the basis of what is known about their own and their community's history.

A central and distinguishing thesis in this approach is that the structure and development of human psychological processes emerge through participation in culturally mediated, historically developing, practical activity involving cultural practices and tools (Cole, 1996). By taking the practice and historically based nature of culture into account, we would then be able to characterise a child's repertoires and dexterity in moving between approaches appropriate to varying activity settings. In the process, we would have a historical, developmental account of that child's or that community's familiar, value-laden experience, and we would be able to speak about the usual, customary, or even habitual approaches taken by individuals (and communities) in known circumstances.

Implications for research

As previously mentioned, we see the examination of cultural regularity, variation and change as important starting points for those interested in examining the relationship between culture, interculturality, and learning. We also would like to argue that it is nor enough to say that culture matters in learning (which leads us to make broad generalisations of large (often minority) groups), but rather that it is important to understand how it matters. Trying to understand how culture matters forces us to move away from the common approach to studying cultural communities that assumes that regularities in cultural communities are static, and that general traits of individuals are attributable categorically to ethnic or racial group membership.

It is our hope that the ideas and examples put forth in this chapter have provided direction in how one can examine learning and culture from a cultural-historical perspective – a view that highlights the dynamic nature of culture and, thus, cultural communities. We can think of few issues that are as important in our work as attending to the ways we examine and represent those we study in all their complexity, especially in a time of rapidly shifting demographics across the world. We would urge researchers studying non-dominant communities to persist in attending to variability in community practices across group members, and variability that exists in individual's repertoires. We believe these suggestions will be especially useful in the conduct of more thoughtful, careful, and valid research involving cultural communities, especially those different from our own.

Source: Gutierrez, D.K. and Correa-Chavez, M. (2006) 'What to do about Culture?', *Lifelong Learning in Europe*, vol. 11, no. 3, pp. 152-159, LLinE

References

Center for the Study of Human Learning and Diversity, 2005. Northwestern University

Chavajay, P. and Rogoff, B. (1999) Cultural variation in management of attention by children and their careglvers. *Developmental Psychology*, 35, 1079-91

Chavajay, P. and Rogoff, B. (2002) Schooling and traditional collaborative social organisation of problem solving by Mayan mothers and children. *Developmental Psychology*, 38,55-66

Cole, M. (1996) *Cultural Psychology: A once and future discipline*. Cambridge, MA: Harvard University Press

Correa-Chávez, M. and Rogoff, B. (2005, September) Variation in third party attending in Mayan children whose mothers vary in extent of school. In R. Mejía Arauz (Chair) *Children's learning through intent participation*. Symposium conducted at the meetings for the International Society for Cultural and Activity Research, Seville, Spain.

Correa-Chávez, M., Rogoff, B. and Mejía Arauz, R. (2005) Cultural patterns in attending to two events at once. *Child Development*, 76, 664-78

Dunn, R., Griggs, S.A. and Price, G.E. (1993) Learning styles of Mexican-American and Anglo-American elementary school students. *Journal of Multicultural Counseling and Development*, 21, 237-47

Engestrom, Y. (1993) Developmental studies of work as a test bench of activity theory: The case of primary care medical practice. In Chaiklin, S. and Lave, J. (eds), *Understanding practice: Perspective on activity and context* (pp64-103). Cambridge, UK: Cambridge University Press

Foley, D. (1997) Deficit thinking models based on culture: The anthropological protest. In Valencia, R. (Ed.). *The evolution of deficit thinking: Educational thought and practice* (pp113-31). Washington, DC: Falmer Press

Gutiérrez, K. (2005) White innocence: A framework and methodology for rethinking educational discourse. *International Journal of Learning*

Gutiérrez, K. (2005) Intersubjectivity and Grammar in the Third Space. Scribner Award Talk. Annual meeting of the American Educational Research Association, Montreal, Canada

Gutiérrez, K (2004) Literacy as laminated activity: Rethinking literacy for English Learners. *National Reading Conference Yearbook*. (101-14) Chicago, Illinois: National Reading Conference

Gutiérrez, K. (2002) Studying cultural practices in urban learning communities. Human Development, 45(4), 312-21

Gutiérrez, K., Asato, J., Santos, M. and Gotanda, N. (2002) Backlash pedagogy: Language and culture and the politics of reform. *The Review of Education, Pedagogy, and Cultural Studies*, 24(4), 335-51

Gutiérrez, K and Rogoff, B. (2003) Cultural ways of learning: Individual traits or repertoires of practice. *Educational Researcher*, 32(5), pp.19-25

Nixon, A. and Gutiérrez, K. (2006) From their own voices: Understanding children's identities through the literacy practices or digital storytelling. Paper presented at the annual meeting of the American Educational Research Association, San Francisco, CA

Rogoff, B. (1997) Evaluating development in the process of participation: Theory, methods, and practice building on each other. In Amsel, E. and Renninger, A. (eds), *Change and development: Issues of theory, application and method* (pp265-85). Hillsdale, NJ: Erlbaum

Rogoff, B. (2003) *The cultural nature of human development.* New York: Oxford University Press

Silva, K., Correa-Chávez, M. and Rogoff, B. (2010) Cultural variation in children's attention and learning in events not directed at them: Patterns in a US Mexican community. *Child Development*, 81(3), pp.898-921

Chapter 14

Toward a critical race theory of education

Gloria Ladson-Billings and William F. Tate IV

[...]

Understanding race and property

Our discussion of social inequity in general, and school inequity in particular, is based on three central propositions:

1 Race continues to be a significant factor in determining inequity in the United States

2 US society is based on property rights

3 The intersection of race and property creates an analytic tool through which we can understand social (and, consequently, school) inequity.

Here we expand on these propositions and provide supporting 'meta-propositions' to make clear our line of reasoning and relevant application to educational or school settings.

Race as a factor in inequity

The first proposition – that race continues to be a significant factor in determining inequity in the United States – is easily documented in the statistical and demographic data. Hacker's look at educational and life chances such as high school dropout rates, suspension rates, and incarceration rates echoes earlier statistics of the Children's Defense Fund.[1] However, in what we now call the post-modern era, some scholars question the usefulness of race as a category.

Omi and Winant argue that popular notions of race as either an ideological construct or an objective condition have epistemological limitations.[2] Thinking of race strictly as an ideological construct denies the reality of a racialised society and its impact on 'raced' people in their everyday lives. On the other hand, thinking of race solely as an objective condition denies the problematic aspects of race – how do we decide who fits into which racial classifications? How do we categorise racial mixtures? Indeed, the world of biology has found the concept of race virtually useless. Geneticist Cavalli-Sforza asserts that 'human populations are sometimes known as ethnic groups, or 'races'. They are hard to define in a way that is both rigorous and useful because human beings group themselves in a bewildering array of sets, some of them overlapping, all of them in a state of flux.'[3]

Nonetheless, even when the concept of race fails to 'make sense', we continue to employ it. According to Nobel Laureate Toni Morrison:

Race has become metaphorical – a way of referring to and disguising forces, events, classes, and expressions of social decay and economic division far more threatening to the body politic than biological 'race' ever was.

Expensively kept, economically unsound, a spurious and useless political asset in election campaigns, racism is as healthy today as it was during the Enlightenment. It seems that it has a utility far beyond economy, beyond the sequestering of classes from one another, and has assumed a metaphorical life so completely embedded in daily discourse that it is perhaps more necessary and more on display than ever before.[4]

Despite the problematic nature of race, we offer as a first meta-proposition that race, unlike gender and class, remains untheorised.[5] Over the past few decades theoretical and epistemological considerations of gender have proliferated.[6] [...] Roediger points out that 'the main body of writing by white Marxists in the United States has both 'naturalised' whiteness and oversimplified race.'[7]

Omi and Winant have done significant work in providing a sociological explanation of race in the United States. They argue that the paradigms of race have been conflated with notions of ethnicity, class, and nation because 'theories of race – of its meaning, its transformations, the significance of racial events – have never been a top priority in social science'. [...]

To mount a viable challenge to the dominant paradigm of ethnicity (ie. we are all ethnic and, consequently, must assimilate and rise socially the same way European Americans have), Omi and Winant offer a racial formation theory that they define as 'the sociohistorical process by which racial categories are created, inhabited, transformed and destroyed. ... [It] is a process of historically situated *projects* in which human bodies and social structures are represented and organised'. [...]

By arguing that race remains untheorised, we are not suggesting that other scholars have not looked carefully at race as a powerful tool for explaining social inequity, but that the intellectual salience of this theorising has not been systematically employed in the analysis of educational inequality.

Both Woodson and Du Bois[8] presented cogent arguments for considering race as *the* central construct for understanding inequality. Briefly, Woodson, as far back as 1916, began to establish the legitimacy of race and, in particular, African Americans as a subject of scholarly inquiry.[9] As founder of the Association for the Study of Negro Life and History and editor of its *Journal of Negro History*, Woodson revolutionised the thinking about African Americans from that of pathology and inferiority to a multitextured analysis of the uniqueness of African Americans and their situation in the United States. His most notable publication, *The Mis-education of the Negro*, identified the school's role in structuring inequality and demotivating African-American students:

The same educational process which inspires and stimulates the oppressor with the thought that he is everything and has accomplished everything worthwhile, depresses and crushes at the same time the spark of genius in the Negro by making him feel that his race does not amount to much and never will measure up to the standards of other people's.[10]

Du Bois, perhaps better known among mainstream scholars, profoundly affected the thinking of many identified as 'other' by naming a 'double consciousness' felt by African Americans. According to Du Bois, the African American 'ever feels his two-ness – an American. A Negro; two souls, two thoughts, two unreconciled strivings'. [...]

As a prophetic foreshadowing of the centrality of race in US society, Du Bois reminded us that 'the problem of the twentieth century is the problem of the colour line.'[11]

The second meta-proposition that we use to support the proposition that race continues to be significant in explaining inequity in the United States is that class- and gender-based explanations are not powerful enough to explain all the difference (or variance) in school experience and performance. Although both class and gender can and do intersect with race, as stand-alone variables they do not explain all of the educational achievement differences apparent between whites and students of colour. Indeed, there is some evidence to suggest that even when we hold constant for class, middle-class African-American students do not achieve at the same level as their white counterparts.[12] Although Oakes reports that 'in academic tracking ... poor and minority students are most likely to be placed at the lowest levels of the school's sorting system,'[13] we are less clear as to which factor – race or class – is causal. [...]

The property issue

Our second proposition, that US society is based on property rights, is best explicated by examining legal scholarship and interpretations of rights. To develop this proposition it is important to situate it in the context of critical race theory.

Monaghan reports that 'critical race legal scholarship developed in the 1970s, in part because minority scholars thought they were being overlooked in critical legal studies, a better-known movement that examines the way law encodes cultural norms.'[14] However, Delgado argues that despite the diversity contained within the critical race movement, there are some shared features:

an assumption that racism is not a series of isolated acts, but is endemic in American life, deeply ingrained legally, culturally, and even psychologically

a call for a reinterpretation of civil-rights law 'in light of its ineffectuality, showing that laws to remedy racial injustices are often undermined before they can fulfill their promise'

a challenge to the 'traditional claims of legal neutrality, objectivity, colour-blindness, and meritocracy as camouflages for the self-interest of dominant groups in American society'

an insistence on subjectivity and the reformulation of legal doctrine to reflect the perspectives of those who have experienced and been victimised by racism first-hand

the use of stories or first-person accounts.[15]

[...]

According to Bell, 'the concept of individual rights, unconnected to property rights, was totally foreign to these men of property; and thus, despite two decades of civil rights gains, most Blacks remain disadvantaged and deprived because of their race.'

The grand narrative of US history is replete with tensions and struggles over property – in its various forms. [...] We talk about the importance of the individual, individual rights, and civil rights while social benefits accrue largely to property owners.[16]

Property relates to education in explicit and implicit ways. Recurring discussions about property tax relief indicate that more affluent communities (which have higher property values, hence higher tax assessments) resent paying for a public school system whose clientele is largely non-white and poor.[17] In the simplest of equations, those with 'better' property are entitled to 'better' schools. Kozol illustrates the disparities:

Average expenditures per pupil in the city of New York in 1987 was some $5,500. In the highest spending suburbs of New York (Great Neck or Marihasset, for example, on Long Island) funding levels rose above $11,000, with the highest districts in the state at $15,000.[18]

But the property differences manifest themselves in other ways. For example, curriculum represents a form of 'intellectual property'.[19] The quality and quantity of the curriculum vary with the 'property values' of the school. [...]

The availability of 'rich' (or enriched) intellectual property delimits what is now called 'opportunity to learn'[20] – the presumption that along with providing educational 'standards'[21] that detail what students should know and be able to do, they must have the material resources that support their learning. Thus, intellectual property must be undergirded by 'real' property, that is, science labs, computers and other state-of-the-art technologies, appropriately certified and prepared teachers. Of course, Kozol demonstrated that schools that serve poor students of colour are unlikely to have access to these resources and, consequently, students will have little or no opportunity to learn despite the attempt to mandate educational standards.[22]

Critical race theory and education

With this notion of property rights as a defining feature of society, we proceed to describe the ways that the features of critical race theory mentioned in the previous section can be applied to our understanding of educational inequity.

Racism as endemic and deeply ingrained in American life

If racism were merely isolated, unrelated, individual acts, we would expect to see at least a few examples of educational excellence and equity together in the nation's public schools. Instead, those places where African Americans do experience educational success tend to be outside the public schools.[23] While some might argue that poor children, regardless of race, do worse in school, and that the high proportion of African-American poor contributes to their dismal school performance, we argue that the cause of their poverty in conjunction with the condition of their schools and schooling is institutional and structural racism. [...]

A reinterpretation of ineffective civil rights law

In the case of education, the civil rights decision that best exemplifies our position is the landmark *Brown v. Board of Education of Topeka, Kansas*. While having the utmost respect for the work of Thurgood Marshall and the National Association for the Advancement of Colored People (NAACP) legal defense team in arguing the *Brown* decision, with forty years of hindsight we recognise some serious shortcomings in that strategy. Today, students of colour are more segregated than ever before.[24] Although African Americans represent 12 per cent of the national population, they are the majority in twenty-one of the twenty-two largest (urban) school districts.[25] Instead of providing more and better educational opportunities, school desegregation has meant increased white flight along with a loss of African-American teaching and administrative positions.[26] [...]

Lomotey and Staley's examination of Buffalo's 'model' desegregation programme revealed that African-American and Latino students continued to be poorly served by the school system. The academic achievement of African-American and Latino students failed to improve while their suspension, expulsion, and dropout rates continued to rise. On the other hand, the desegregation plan provided special magnet programmes and extended day care of which whites were able to take advantage. What, then, made Buffalo a model school desegregation programme? In short, the benefits that whites derived from school desegregation and their seeming support of the district's desegregation programme.[27] Thus, a model desegregation program becomes defined as one that ensures that whites are happy (and do not leave the system altogether) regardless of whether African-American and other students of colour achieve or remain.

Challenging claims of neutrality, objectivity, colour-blindness, and meritocracy

A theme of 'naming one's own reality' or 'voice' is entrenched in the work of critical race theorists. Many critical race theorists argue that the form and substance of scholarship are closely connected.[28] These scholars use parables, chronicles, stories, counterstories, poetry, fiction, and revisionist histories to illustrate the false necessity and irony of much of current civil rights doctrine. Delgado suggests that there are at least three reasons for naming one's own reality in legal discourse:

1 Much of reality is socially constructed

2 Stories provide members of outgroups a vehicle for psychic self-preservation

3 The exchange of stories from teller to listener can help overcome ethnocentrism and the dysconscious conviction of viewing the world in one way.[29]

The first reason for naming one's own reality is to demonstrate how political and moral analysis is conducted in legal scholarship. [...]

Critical race theorists argue that political and moral analysis is situational – 'truths only exist for this person in this predicament at this time in history.'[30] For the critical race theorist, social reality is constructed by the formulation and the exchange of stories about individual situations.[31] These stories serve as interpretive structures by which we impose order on experience and it on us.[32]

A second reason for the naming-one's-own-reality theme of critical race theory is the psychic preservation of marginalised groups. A factor contributing to the demoralisation of marginalised groups is self-condemnation.[33] Members of minority groups internalise the stereotypic images that certain elements of society have constructed in order to maintain their power.[34] Historically, storytelling has been a kind of medicine to heal the wounds and pain caused by racial oppression.[35] The story of one's condition leads to the realisation of how one came to be oppressed and subjugated and allows one to stop inflicting mental violence on oneself.

Finally, naming one's own reality with stories can affect the oppressor. Most oppression does not seem like oppression to the perpetrator.[36] Delgado argues that the dominant group justifies its power with stories – stock explanations – that construct reality in ways to maintain their privilege.[37] Thus, oppression is rationalised, causing little self-examination by the oppressor. Stories by people of colour can catalyse the necessary cognitive conflict to jar dysconscious racism.

The 'voice' component of critical race theory provides a way to communicate the experience and realities of the oppressed, a first step on the road to justice. As we attempt to make linkages between critical race theory and education, we contend that the voice of people of colour is required for a complete analysis of the educational system. Delpit argues that one of the tragedies of education is the way in which the dialogue of people of colour has been silenced. [...]

A growing number of education scholars of colour are raising critical questions about the way that research is being conducted in communities of colour.[38] Thus, without authentic voices of people of colour (as teachers, parents, administrators, students, and community members) it is doubtful that we can say or know anything useful about education in their communities.

The intersection of race and property

We have argued that race is still a significant factor in determining inequity in the United States and that society is based on property rights rather than on human rights. In this section we discuss the intersection of race and property as a central construct in understanding a critical race theoretical approach to education.

Harris argues that 'slavery linked the privilege of Whites to the subordination of Blacks through a legal regime that attempted the conversion of Blacks into objects of property. Similarly, the settlement and seizure of Native American land supported White privilege through a system of property rights in land in which the 'race' of the Native Americans rendered their first possession right invisible and justified conquest'. But more pernicious and long lasting than the victimisation of people of colour is the construction of whiteness as the ultimate property. 'Possession – the act necessary to lay the basis for rights in property – was defined to include only the cultural practices of Whites. This definition laid the foundation for the idea that whiteness – that which Whites alone possess—is valuable and is property.'[39] [...]

Rights of disposition. Because property rights are described as fully alienable, that is, transferable, it is difficult to see how whiteness can be construed as property.[40] However, alienability of certain property is limited (eg. entitlements, government licences, professional degrees or licences held by one party and financed by the labour of the other in the context of divorce). Thus, whiteness when conferred on certain student performances is alienable.[41] When students are rewarded only for conformity to perceived 'white norms' or sanctioned for cultural practices (eg. dress, speech patterns, unauthorised conceptions of knowledge), white property is being rendered alienable.

Rights to use and enjoyment. Legally, whites can use and enjoy the privileges of whiteness. As Mcintosh has explicitly demonstrated, whiteness allows for specific social, cultural, and economic privileges.[42] Fuller further asserts that whiteness is both formative and pleasurable.[43] In the school setting, whiteness allows for extensive use of school property. Kozol's description of the material differences in two New York City schools can be interpreted as the difference between those who possess the right to use and enjoy what schools can offer and those who do not:

The [white] school serves 825 children in the kindergarten through sixth grade. This is approximately half the student population crowded into [black] P.S. 79, where 1,550 children fill a space intended for 1,000, and a great deal smaller than the 1,300 children packed into the former skating rink.[44]

This right of use and enjoyment is also reflected in the structure of the curriculum, also described by Kozol:

The curriculum [the white school] follows 'emphasises critical thinking, reasoning and logic'. The planetarium, for instance, is employed not simply for the study of the universe as it exists. 'Children also are designing their own galaxies,' the teacher says. [...]

In my [Kozol's] notes: 'Six girls, four boys. Nine White, one Chinese. I am glad they have this class. But what about the others? Aren't there ten Black children in the school who could *enjoy* this also?'[45]

Reputation and status property. The concept of reputation as property is regularly demonstrated in legal cases of libel and slander. Thus, to damage someone's reputation is to damage some aspect of his or her personal property. In the case of race, to call a white person 'black' is to defame him or her.[46] In the case of schooling, to identify a school or programme as non-white in any way is to diminish its reputation or status. [...]

The absolute right to exclude. Whiteness is constructed in this society as the absence of the 'contaminating' influence of blackness. Thus, 'one drop of black blood' constructs one as black, regardless of phenotypic markers.[47] In schooling, the absolute right to exclude was demonstrated initially by denying blacks access to schooling altogether. Later, it was demonstrated by the creation and maintenance of separate schools. More recently it has been demonstrated by white flight and the growing insistence on vouchers, public funding of private schools, and schools of choice.[48] Within schools, absolute right to exclude is demonstrated by resegregation via tracking,[49] the institution of 'gifted' programmes, honours programmes and advanced placement classes. So complete is this exclusion that black students often come to the university in the role of intruders – who have been granted special permission to be there. [...]

The limits of the multicultural paradigm

Throughout this chapter we have argued the need for a critical race theoretical perspective to cast a new gaze on the persistent problems of racism in schooling. We have argued the need for this perspective because of the failure of scholars to theorise race. We have drawn parallels between the way critical race legal scholars understand their position vis-a-vis traditional legal scholarship and the ways critical race theory applied to education offers a way to rethink traditional educational scholarship. We also have referred to the tensions that exist between traditional civil rights legislation and critical race legal theory. In this section we identify a necessary tension between critical race theory in education and what we term the multicultural paradigm. [...]

Current practical demonstrations of multicultural education in schools often reduce it to trivial examples and artefacts of cultures such as eating ethnic or cultural foods, singing songs or dancing, reading folk tales, and other less than scholarly pursuits of the fundamentally different conceptions of knowledge or quests for social justice.[50] At the university level, much of the concern over multicultural education has been over curriculum inclusion.[51] However, another level of debate emerged over what became known as 'multiculturalism'.

Somewhat different from multicultural education in that it does not represent a particular educational reform or scholarly tradition, multiculturalism came to be viewed as a political philosophy of 'many cultures' existing together in an atmosphere of respect and tolerance.[52] Thus, outside the classroom multiculturalism represented the attempt to bring both students and faculty from a variety of cultures into the school (or academy) environment. Today, the term is used interchangeably with the ever-expanding 'diversity', a term used to explain all types of 'difference' – racial, ethnic, cultural, linguistic, ability, gender, sexual orientation. Thus, popular music, clothes, media, books, and so forth, reflect a growing awareness of diversity and/or multiculturalism. Less often discussed are the growing tensions that exist between and among various groups that gather under the umbrella of multiculturalism – that is, the interests of groups can be competing or their perspectives can be at odds.[53] We assert that the ever-expanding multicultural paradigm follows the traditions of liberalism – allowing a proliferation of difference. Unfortunately, the tensions between and among these differences are rarely analysed, presuming a 'unity of difference' – that is, that all difference is both analogous and equivalent.[54]

To make parallel the analogy between critical race legal theory and traditional civil rights law with that of critical race theory in education and multicultural education we need to restate the point that critical race legal theorists have 'doubts about the foundation of moderate/incremental civil rights law.'[55] The foundation of civil rights law has been in human rights rather than in property rights. Thus, without disrespect to the pioneers of civil rights law, critical race legal scholars document the ways in which civil rights law is regularly subverted to benefit whites.[56]

We argue that the current multicultural paradigm functions in a manner similar to civil rights law. Instead of creating radically new paradigms that ensure justice, multicultural reforms are routinely 'sucked back into the system' and, just as traditional civil rights law is based on a foundation of human rights, the current multicultural paradigm is mired in liberal ideology that offers no radical change in the current order.[57] Thus, critical race theory in education, like its antecedent in legal scholarship, is a radical critique of both the status quo and the purported reforms.

Source: *Teachers College record* by Columbia University, copyright 2012. Reproduced with permission of Teachers College Record in the format textbook and other book via Copyright Clearance Center.

References

1 Andrew Hacker, *Two Nations: Black and White, Separate, Hostile, Unequal* (New York – Ballantine Books, 1992); and Marian Wright Edelman, Families in Peril: An Agenda for Social Change (Cambridge, Mass.: Harvard University Press, 1987).

2 Michael Omi and Howard Winant. 'On the Theoretical Concept of Race', in *Race, Identity and Representation in Education*, ed. C. McCarthy and W. Crichlow (New York: Routledge 1993), 3-10.

3 Luigi Luca Cavalli-Sforza, 'Genes, People and Languages', *Scientific American*, November 1991,104.

4 Morrison, *Playing in the Dark*, 63.

5 This assertion was made forcefully by the participants of the Institute NHI (No Humans Involved) at a symposium entitled 'The Two Reservations: Western Thought, the Colour Line, and the Crisis of the Negro Intellectual Revisited', sponsored by the Department of African and Afro-American Studies at Stanford University. Stanford, Calif., 3-5 March 1994.

6 See, for example, Nancy Chodorow, *The Reproduction of Mothering* (Berkeley: University of California Press, 1978); Simone de Beauvoir. *The Second Sex* (New York: Bantam Books, 1961); Vivian Gornick. 'Women as Outsiders,' in *Women in Sexist Society*, ed. V. Gornick and B. Moran (New York: Basic Books, 1971), 70-84; Nancy Hartsock, 'Feminist Theory and the Development of Revolutionary Strategy', *Capitalist Patriarcli and the Case for Socialist Feminism*, ed. Z. Eisenstein (London and New York: Monthly Review Press, 1979); and Alison Jagger, *Feminist Theory and Human Nature* (Sussex: Harvester, 1983).

7 David Roediger. *The Wages of Whiteness* (London: Verso, 1991), 6.

8 Carter C. Woodson, *The Miseducation of the Negro* (Washington, DC: Association Press, 1933); and W. E. B. Du Bois. *The Souls of Black Folks* (New York: Penguin Books, 1989; first published in 1903).

9 See John Hope Franklin, *From Slavery to Freedom*, 6th edn. (New York: Alfred A. Knopf, 1988).

10 Woodson, *The Miseducation of the Negro*, p. xiii.

11 Du Bois, *The Souls of Black Folks*, 5. Other people of colour, feminists, and gay and lesbian theorists all have appropriated Du Bois's notion of double consciousness to explain their estrangement from mainstream patriarchal, masculinist US culture.

12 See, for example, Lorene Cary, *Black Ice* (New York: Alfred A. Knopf, 1991); and Jeannie Oakes, *Keeping Track: How Schools Structure Inequality* (New Haven: Yale University Press, 1985).

13 Oakes, *Keeping Track*, 67.

14 Peter Monaghan, 'Critical Race Theory' Questions the Role of Legal Doctrine in Racial Inequity', *Chronicle of Higher Education*, 23 June 1993, A7, A9.

15 Delgado, cited in Monaghan, 'Critical Race Theory'. Quotations are from p. A7. For a more detailed explication of the first item in the list, see Bell, *Faces at the Bottom of the Well*.

?? Bell, *And We Are Not Saved*, 239.

16 Even at a time when there is increased public sentiment for reducing the federal deficit, the one source of tax relief that no president or member of Congress would ever consider is that of denying home (property) owners their tax benefits.

17 See, for example. Howard Wainer, 'Does Spending Money on Education Help?' *Educational Researcher* 22 (1993): 22-4; or Paul Houston, 'School Vouchers: The Latest California Joke' *Phi Delta Kappan* 75 (1993): 61-6.

18 Kozol, *Savage Inequalities*, 83-4.

19 This notion of 'intellectual property' came into popular use when television talk show host David Letterman moved from NEC to CBS. NEC claimed that certain routines and jokes used by Letterman were the intellectual property of the network and, as such, could not be used by Letterman without permission.

20 See, for example, Floraline Stevens, *Opportunity to Learn: Issues of Equity for Poor and Minority Students* (Washington, DC: National Center for Education Statistics, 1993): idem 'Applying an Opportunity-to-Learn Conceptual Framework to the Investigation of the Effects of Teaching Practices via Secondary Analyses of Multiple-case-study Summary Data', *The Journal of Negro Education* 62 (1993): 232-48; and Linda Winfield and Michael D. Woodard, 'Assessment, Equity, Diversity in Reforming America's Schools', *Educational Policy* 8 (1994): 3-27.

21 The standards debate is too long and detailed to be discussed here. For a more detailed discussion of standards see, for example, Michael W. Apple, 'Do the Standards Go Far Enough? Power, Policy, and Practices in Mathematics Education', *Journal for Research in Mathematics Education* 23 (1992): 412-31; and National Council of Education Standards and Testing, *Raising Standards for American Education: A Report to Congress, the Secretary of Education, the National Goals Panel, and the American People* (Washington. DC: Government Printing Office, 1992).

22 Kozol, *Savage Inequalities*.

23 Some urban Catholic schools, black independent schools, and historically black colleges and universities have demonstrated the educability of African-American students. As of this writing we have no data on the success of urban districts such as Detroit or Milwaukee that are attempting what is termed 'African Centered' or Africentric education. See also Mwalimu J. Shujaa, ed., *Too Much Schooling, Too Little Education: A Paradox of Black Life in White Societies* (Trenton, NJ: Africa World Press, 1994).

24 See, for example, Gary Orfield, 'School Desegregation in the 1980s', *Equity and Choice*, February 1988, 25; Derrick Bell, 'Learning from Our Losses: Is School Desegregation Still Feasible in the 1980s? *Phi Delta Kappan* 64 (April 1983): 575; Willis D. Hawley, 'Why It Is Hard to Believe in Desegregation', *Equity and Choice*, February 1988, 9-15; and Janet Ward Schofield, *Black and White in School: Trust, Tension, or Tolerance?* (New York: Teachers College Press, 1989).

25 James Banks, 'Teaching Multicultural Literacy to Teachers', *Teaching Education* 4 (1991):135-44.

26 See Karl Taeuber, 'Desegregation of Public School Districts: Persistence and Change', *Phi Delta Kappan* 72 (1990): 18-24; and H. L. Bisinger, 'When Whites Flee', *New York Times Magazine*, 29 May 1994, 26-33, 43, 50, 53-4, 56. On loss of professional positions, see Sabrina King, 'The Limited Presence of African American Teachers', *Review of Educational Research* 63 (1993): 115-49; and Jacqueline Irvine, 'An Analysis of the Problem of Disappearing Black Educators', *Elementary School Journal* 88 (1988): 503-13

27 Kofi Lomotey and John Statley, 'The Education of African Americans in Buffalo Public Schools' (Paper presented at the annual meeting of the American Educational Research Association, Boston, 1990).

28 Richard Delgado, 'Storytelling for Oppositionists and Others: A Plea for Narrative', *Michigan Law Review* 87 (1989): 2411-41.

29 See Richard Delgado *et al*, 'Symposium: Legal Storytelling', *Michigan Law Review* 87 (1989):2073. On dysconsciousness, see Joyce E. King, 'Dysconscious Racism: Ideology, Identity and the Miseducation of Teachers', *Journal of Negro Education* 60 (1991):135. King defines dysconsciousness as 'an uncritical habit of mind (including perceptions, attitudes, assumptions, and beliefs) that justifies inequity and exploitation by accepting the existing order of things as given. ... Dysconscious racism is a form of racism that tacitly accepts dominant White norms and privileges. It is not the absence of consciousness (that is, not unconsciousness) but an *impaired* consciousness or distorted way of thinking about race as compared to, for example, critical consciousness.'

30 Richard Delgado, 'Brewer's Plea: Critical Thoughts on Common Cause', *Vanderbilt Law Review* 44 (1991): 11.

31 For example, see Williams, *Alchemy of Race and Rights; Bell, Faces at the Bottom of the Well*; and Mari Matsuda, 'Public Response to Racist Speech: Considering the Victim's Story', *Michigan Law Review* 87 (1989): 2320-81.

32 Delgado, 'Storytelling'.

33 *Ibid.*

34 For example, see Crenshaw, 'Race, Reform, and Retrenchment'.

35 Delgado, 'Storytelling'.

36 Charles Lawrence. 'The Id, the Ego, and Equal Protection: Reckoning with Unconscious Racism', *Stanford Law Review* 39 (1987): 317-88.

37 Delgado *et al*, 'Symposium'.

38 At the 1994 annual meeting of the American Educational Research Association in New Orleans, two sessions entitled 'Private Lives. Public Voices: Ethics of Research in Communities of Colour' were convened to discuss the continued exploitation of people of colour. According to one scholar of colour, our communities have become 'data plantations'.

39 Cheryl I. Harris, 'Whiteness as Property', *Harvard Law Review* 106 (1993):1721.

40 See Margaret Radin, 'Market-Inalienability', *Harvard Law Review* 100 (1987):1849-906.

41 See Signithia Fordham and John Ogbu, 'Black Student School Success: Coping with the Burden of 'Acting White" *The Urban Review* 18 (1986):1-31.

42 Peggy Mcintosh, 'White Privilege: Unpacking the Invisible Knapsack', *Independent School*, Winter 1990, 31-6.

43 Laurie Fuller, 'Whiteness as Performance' (Unpublished preliminary examination paper University of Wisconsin-Madison, 1994).

44 Kozol, *Savage Inequalities*, 93.

45 *Ibid.* 96: emphasis added.

46 Harris, 'Whiteness as Property', 1735.

47 Derrick Bell, *Race, Racism and American Law* (Boston: Little, Brown, 1980).

48 We assert that the current movement toward African-centered (or Africentric) schools is not equivalent to the racial exclusion of vouchers, or choice programs. Indeed, African-centeredness has become a logical response of a community to schools that have been abandoned by whites, have been stripped of material resources, and have demonstrated a lack of commitment to African-American academic achievement.

49 Oakes, *Keeping Track*.

50 Banks, 'Multicultural Education'.

51 In 1988 at Stanford University the inclusion of literature from women and people of colour in the Western Civilisation core course resulted in a heated debate. The university's faculty senate approved this inclusion in a course called Cultures, Ideas, and Values. The controversy was further heightened when then Secretary of Education William Bennett came to the campus to denounce this decision.

52 In the 'Book Notes' section of the *Harvard Educational Review* 64 (1994):345-7, Jane Davagian Tchaicha reviews Donaldo Macedo's *Literacies of Power* (Boulder: Westview, 1994) and includes two quotes, one from noted conservative Patrick Buchanan and another from Macedo on multiculturalism. According to Buchanan, 'Our Judeo-Christian values are going to be preserved, and our Western heritage is going to be handed down to future generations, not dumped into some landfill called multiculturalism' (quoted in Tchaicha, 345). Macedo asserts that 'the real issue isn't Western culture versus multiculturalism, the fundamental issue is the recognition of humanity in us and in others' (quoted in Tchaicha, 347).

53 In New York City, controversy over the inclusion of gay and lesbian issues in the curriculum caused vitriolic debate among racial and ethnic groups who opposed their issues being linked to or compared with homosexuals. Some ethnic group members asserted that homosexuals were not a 'culture' while gay and lesbian spokespeople argued that these group members were homophobic.

54 Shirley Torres-Medina, 'Issues of Power: Constructing the Meaning of Linguistic Difference in First Grade Classrooms' (Ph.D. diss., University of Wisconsin-Madison, 1994).

55 Richard Delgado, 'Enormous Anomaly; Left-Right Parallels in Recent Writing about Race', *Columbia Law Review* 91 (1991):1547-60.

56 See Bell, *And We Are Not Saved*.

57 See Cameron McCarthy. 'After the Canon: Knowledge and Ideological Representation in the Multicultural Discourse on Curriculum Reform', in *Race, Identity and Representation*, ed. C. McCarthy and W. Crichlow (New York: Routledge. 1994), 290; and Michael Oineck, 'Terms of Inclusion: Has Multiculturalism Redefined Equality in American Education?', *American Journal of Education* 101 (1993): 234-60.

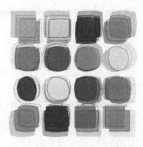

Chapter 15

Theory, values and policy research in education

Jenny Ozga

[...]

Theory and its uses

[...] Theories are useful, indeed essential, to researchers. Research and theorising are interdependent, and perhaps my approach to theories in education policy research becomes more comprehensible if we understand theories as statements about how things connect, and how things come to happen as they do.

Such a formulation stresses the everyday, routine nature of theorising. The necessity of theory and its accessibility are more evident if we recognise that we all 'theorise'. I suggest that we all attempt to make sense of our own situations as workers in education, and the ways in which that situation is constructed, negotiated and/or disputed – in other words, theory's relationship to policy.

Of course, the level of engagement with theory involved in analysing our own circumstances as an instance of education policy research will vary, depending on the resources available to us and our orientation towards the task; put differently, what sort of project we believe we are engaged in when we do this task. The explanation we reach for in conversation with a colleague may differ from the one we may adopt in completing a formal piece of work on the topic – a master's thesis, for example. In a hurried assessment, without reference to the rules of the discipline, we may seize on explanations that are partial or whose function may be to allocate blame, rather than increase understanding.

So the resources that we draw on, that we call theories, are not all of the same size, weight, complexity or quality. Theories may be quite limited in their scope; for example, they may explain individual cases (a burnt-out colleague, a recalcitrant pupil) or they may point to patterns of phenomena (high wastage rates among experienced teachers, low rates of pay in the 'caring' professions). We need to get to grips with theory because theories help us to sort out our world, and make sense of it. Beyond that, theories provide a guide to action and help to predict what may happen next. We should not, in my view, think about theorising as though it was an extraordinary or exceptional activity, to be engaged in only in certain conditions, and those to be as far removed as possible from 'normal' life. Nor should we hand over responsibility for theorising, or for developing perspectives informed by theory, to some specialised group of researchers who are disconnected from educational practice.

This argument about theory should come as no surprise; it is part of the overarching argument about the entitlement and responsibility of those engaged in educational work. It also, self-evidently, contributes to my disagreement with the relationship with research (and by implication theorising) that is contained in current policy for teachers. It is not so difficult to imagine theory as accessible if we acknowledge that we construct theories routinely. We do this by thinking about information we routinely collect, categorising it and considering whether or not it may be understood as an instance of some larger pattern. It is, therefore, both inappropriate and impossible to attempt to divorce 'theorising' from research, or to put the two in separate compartments; for example, understanding research as something we do to establish facts that we then make sense of. Rather, the intention is to stress the need to look at what we find out, and what we define as a 'problem' or topic, in a self-conscious, theorised way, while being open and explicit about our theoretical 'hunches'.

Understanding theory in this way underlines the need for explicitness that I advocated above. This is a dynamic and reflexive relationship that prevents us from undertaking research in order to demonstrate the correctness of some static 'grand theory' that dictates the story, but it also prevents research from falling into the contrasting trap of endless accumulation of evidence that tells no story at all. [...]

Values in policy research

At this point I return to choice, and to values. [...] I turn to values, as these help us to decide which narrative is most convincing and engaging, both as an account of how things are and as a statement of how we want things to be. Researchers are inevitably influenced in their choices about theory by their ideas about how things ought to be. This has been described as an *engaged subjectivity* in the research. As Stanley and Wise put it:

Our experiences suggest that 'hygienic research' is a reconstructed logic, a mythology which presents an oversimplistic account of research. It is also extremely misleading, in that it emphasises the 'objective' pressure of the researcher and suggests that she can be 'there' without having any greater involvement than simple presence. In contrast, we emphasise that all research involves, as its basis, an interaction, a relationship between researcher and researched. (Stanley and Wise, 1993:161)

My primary relationship as a researcher is with teachers: as they have been, as they are and as I would like them to be. My ideas about that future state shape how I interpret the past and the present. This illustrates how value positions form the broad background against which theoretical positions are developed or selected, and these in turn affect all aspects of research design, including the selection and interpretation of evidence. We need to remind ourselves of differences in purpose among policy researchers; different projects rest on different values and result in different choices of research topic, research relationships and research design. The ways in which values are carried into theory are well set out in Cox's well-known elaboration of the differences between problem-solving theory and critical theory:

Theory is always *for* someone and *for* some purpose. All theories have a perspective. Perspectives derive from a position in time and space. The world is seen from a standpoint definable in terms of national or social class, of dominance or subordination, of rising or declining power, of a sense of immobility or of present crisis, of past experience, and of hopes and expectations for the future. Of course, sophisticated theory is never just the expression of a perspective. The more sophisticated a theory is, the more it reflects upon and transcends its own perspective, but the initial perspective is always contained within a theory and is relevant to its explication. There is, accordingly, no such thing as theory in itself, divorced from a standpoint in time and space. When any theory so represents itself, it is more important to examine it as ideology, and to lay bare its concealed perspective ...

Theory can serve two distinct purposes. One is a simple, direct response, to be a guide to help solve the problems posed within the terms of the particular perspective which was the point of departure. The other is more reflective upon the process of theorising itself, to become clearly aware of the perspective which gives rise to theorising, and its relation to other perspectives (to achieve a perspective on perspectives), and to open up the possibility of choosing a different valid perspective from which the problematic becomes one of creating an alternative world. Each of these purposes gives rise to a different kind of theory ...

The first purpose gives rise to *problem-solving theory*. It takes the world as it finds it, with the prevailing social and power relationships, and the institutions into which they are organised, as the given framework for action. The general aim of problem-solving is to make these relationships and institutions work smoothly by dealing effectively with particular sources of trouble ...

The second purpose leads to critical theory. It is critical in the sense that it stands apart from the prevailing order of the world and asks how that order came about. Critical theory, unlike problem-solving, does not take institutions and social and power relations for granted but calls them into question by concerning itself with their origins and how and whether they might be in the process of changing. It is directed towards an appraisal of the very framework for action, or problematic, which problem-solving theory accepts as its parameters. Critical theory is directed to the social and political complex as a whole rather than to the separate parts, As a matter of practice, critical theory, like problem-solving theory, takes as its starting point some aspect or particular sphere of human activity. But whereas the problem-solving approach leads to further analytical sub-division and limitation of the issue to be dealt with, the critical approach leads towards the construction of a larger picture of the whole of which the initially contemplated part is just one component, and seeks to understand the processes of change in which both parts and whole are involved. (Cox, 1980:128-30)

Critical theory and social justice

The adoption of critical theory results from a particular value position and resonates with a social science project, though not, perhaps, with pessimistic versions of postmodernism. Its adoption also has certain consequences; it is evident that critical theory in education policy is not implicated in the solution of problems, or at least not in the solution of problems defined exclusively by administrators and policy makers. Working within a critical frame places requirements on the researcher to pursue ethical research principles and to assess research activity in relation to what might be broadly termed social justice concerns (Gewirtz and Ozga, 1994). As a result, researchers are placed under an obligation to ask certain questions about the work they intend to do, questions that go back to the core preoccupation with purpose.

Such questions might include consideration of whether the work implies consent to or approval of policies that support the maintenance, justification and legitimisation of regulatory institutions that restrict the capacity for autonomous, independent educational development. Other questions might explore whether the planned research offers any potential contribution to freedom from arbitrary, coercive power. Does it support the development of human capacity, respect for human dignity and worth, a more equitable distribution of economic and social goods, and an expansion of economic opportunity to meet need? These are all rather abstract and grandiloquent concerns, and might imply that critical theorists have rather inflated expectations of the outcomes of policy research, and of their own significance.

However, I would argue that research can make a contribution to the goals embedded in these questions, particularly if the potential exists for it to be engaged with by the professional community in these terms, rather than in a restricted, technical mode. Research has the potential to contribute in three ways. First, it can draw attention to and challenge the taken-for-granted or dominant assumptions informing policy: for example, that we must mirror global competition by enhancing competitiveness in our schools. It can also expose the effects of policy on the ground: for example, by highlighting the recent increase in stress among very young pupils following early testing (Jensen, 1998). More generally, it may examine how and where policies increase inequality and affect particular groups (for example, pupils with special educational needs who are not selected by schools in competition for market advantage; see Gewirtz 1995). Second, research can set out to explore how injustices and inequalities are produced, reproduced and sustained, in order that we better understand how such processes may be challenged. Third, as Harvey (1990) and Troyna (1994) remind us, research can provide an illumination of injustice and inequity that may assist educationalists in working for change, and helps to challenge 'common-sense' assumptions about the desirability and rationality of the official logic of outcomes and indicators. [...]

To adopt such a position is to acknowledge that the value position will have a considerable impact on the policy problem chosen for research purposes and on the pursuit of the enquiry itself. Yet it is not only those who clearly and overtly identify their value position and seek to connect it explicitly to a theoretical orientation who are working within a value-laden framework in doing research on education policy – we all are, researchers and policy makers alike. Values are assumptions or beliefs about what is desirable and about how things are. They thus have a powerful impact at the level of pretheoretical thinking (Dale, 1989) or in the formation of subsets of beliefs and assumptions about the world.

[...] Values are contested, they do not have universal currency. Values pervade and infuse our activities as researchers, as they pervade all aspects of social life. I have already argued that they shape our purposes in doing research, but it is necessary also to consider the question of explicitness. By this I mean that values may be so well integrated into our thinking that they shape it in subtle and implicit ways. Their pervasiveness and taken-for-grantedness, along with the assumption in some research traditions that they can be put to oneside in the pursuit of objectivity, serve to obscure the differences between analysis and prescription. Some research traditions are quite clear that they are developed from a value position, others seek to be free of such subjectivity, while a considerable amount of research on education does not consider this issue at all, and apparently assumes that there is no connection between theory and values, or that the adoption of particular techniques will ensure objective enquiry.

However, I would argue that our assumptions about how things are or ought to be construct our choices about what it is possible to find out, and about how to find it out. [...] Here, I am anxious to emphasise the interrelatedness of values and methodology, so that the case for explicitness about informing assumptions is made still clearer.

Another 'worked example' might help. I have chosen an extract that connects pretheoretical assumptions and 'gut preferences' to the ways in which different theoretical perspectives on the state are constructed. As well as illuminating my arguments, the extract provides a useful summary of alternative positions on a topic that is of central importance in education policy research, namely the state and what we mean by it. The extract is from Dunleavy and O'Leary's *Theories of the State*, in which they explore the ways in which value positions influence conceptions of the state and its operation:

There are five components of values relevant to theories of the state:

1   Views about 'human nature' (also known as 'philosophical anthropologies') lie at the heart of each theory of the state. They crystallise convictions about the basic make-up and driving force of the human character, such as the proposition that 'man is a social animal' or that 'man is born free but everywhere he is in chains'.

2   Core moral values indicate how particular theories of the state are related to wider systems of morality.

3   Political associations indicate how theories of the state connect with practical political movements.

4   Selections of social phenomena as 'interesting' or 'problematic' indicate how writers in different analytic approaches select aspects of the political process for explicit consideration. Where theories of the state disagree about the importance of being able to explain various phenomena, their disputes often cannot be reconciled by theoretical or empirical arguments.

5   'Gut' preferences for particular styles of explanation reflect competing methodological priorities. (Dunleavy and O'Leary, 1987:337-8)

Dunleavy and O'Leary usefully point up the possibility of incoherence in value positions that underlie theoretical choices. Clear acknowledgement of values – indeed, articulation of them – may assist in developing coherence in the chosen 'project'. Within the social science/critical theory project that I am advocating here, it may mean that when we engage in research activity which takes as its central focus the scrutiny of particular policies and their implementation, there should be a tighter articulation of concerns about the exclusionary, divisive and socially unjust intentions and consequences of such policies, as Power (1993) has argued.

The principle of choice

I want now to focus the discussion on the question of making choices. We have considered choice in policy research in relation to values and their impact on the selection of theoretical resources. I want now to put those together with other factors that contribute to choice, in order to make a case for explicitness in research in policy. In this discussion [...] researchers on policy should pursue explicitness in their research choices; as Seddon argues, following Howell, choice is inevitable in research, so that if other researchers are to understand fully the principles informing a research project, there must be a commitment to as great a degree of explicitness as possible. Seddon quotes Howell as follows:

There must be more to policy-oriented research than self-consciously eclectic and wide ranging suggestions. There must be some principle of choice, some justification for drawing the line in one place rather than another. One must have some formulated idea of what to look for, and how and where to look for it. (Howell, 1990:242)

In considering the implications of that call, and my own discussion of the need to focus on the source, scope and patterning of education policy (Ozga, 1990), Seddon identifies a number of contributory factors that make the articulation of the principles of choice in policy research both complex and necessary.

The first issue is the state of theoretical development: that is, the kinds of theoretical resources that are available to students of education policy. We have already seen that there are tensions and divisions among research projects in this field, these tensions broadly reflecting the differences between the competing theoretical paradigms that dominated the area until the early 1990s. The debate encapsulated the differences between policy science or policy analysis and critical social science. The first paradigm was very much informed by pluralistic assumptions: that is, there was an implicit or explicit adherence to the view that policy was made through negotiation and compromise among those who had an interest in it. In education policy this was usually government at local and central levels, organised teachers, parents, pressure groups and business interests. Research in that tradition was generally preoccupied with finding the best solution to a given problem; this is a version of the social administration project discussed earlier.

The second paradigm in policy research, within the critical social science framework, was heavily influenced by Marxist theory, and was thus pre-occupied with structural inequality and its reproduction through education policy. The debate, as Seddon points out, and as I indicated above in stressing the diversity of social science and some turning away from projects, has moved on. Both pluralism and Marxism have been reworked in response to changing social conditions and changes in social theory, while theories of postmodernity emphasise discontinuities, contingency and the absence of a dominant narrative. A simple polarity of pluralism and Marxism is no longer sufficient to capture the kinds of choices of theoretical resource available to researchers. This is not to say that the projects outlined above are no longer relevant. I believe that they do offer researchers ways of considering their orientation towards a research task. [...]

Dealing with complexity

Seddon's discussion contextualises the particular problems of education policy research within this wider framework of change in social theory, thereby making the current diversity and uncertainty of the field more comprehensible. The problem, as she sees it, is not just that of dealing with the revision of hitherto accepted theories, revisions that tend to emphasise the contingent and the fragmented, but is also that of considering the possibility of quite new social relations and new experiences of social life, which require new forms of explanation. These explanatory forms seem to me to be most convincing when they bring together structural analyses with sophisticated and detailed understanding of the human agent. [...]

Seddon goes on to explain the implications of this recognition of the rootedness of research work, and the processes involved in creating what she calls 'a lacework of meaning'. These are connected to my earlier discussion of seeking to identify research purpose, so that the obligation on the researcher to reveal the principle of choice involves:

an elaboration of the principles which guide our selection of research resources, a clarification of what counts as principled research practice in our appropriation of these resources and in the formation of conceptual frameworks; and the justification of these principles and processes of intellectual work. (Seddon, 1996:199)

I have tried to identify some of the ways in which it might be possible to make these choices explicit and I revisit some of the points in that discussion here. First of all, I assumed that it is possible and desirable to seek robust and transferable explanations of education policy, and that these may be at a level of abstraction that enables generalisations and comparisons to be made, but are not so far removed from the detail or substance of any given policy as to have nothing relevant to say about it. I also argued that these explanations should be couched as sustainable propositions that linked education policy to the institutions and discourses of wider society. This involves identifying what is to be studied, clarifying the researcher's orientation to what is studied and indicating the perspective from which the research is undertaken.

Answering the 'what' question produces, for me, a set of necessary characteristics of any education policy that may then be explored in relation to a particular case. That is, I argue that any education policy must have a source (or sources), a scope and a pattern. That is, any education policy has to originate somewhere, it has to contain, however implicitly, some notion of what it is desirable and possible for education systems to achieve, and it has to carry within it some awareness of the workings of the education system and of the potential for change. [...]

If we then look at the 'how' question, this requires an elaboration of the theoretical framework which shapes the researcher's orientation to what he or she studies. This requires choices; in making these choices we reduce possibilities (it is impossible to keep the 'how' question open indefinitely). The choices we make will depend on the intellectual traditions from which we draw resources, and from our particular use of these resources.

The intention is not to advocate a rigid model, but to suggest that research on education policy adopts certain principles of design that require explicitness in relation to what is being studied, why it is being studied and how. There are many problems with categorising and interpreting theory, and most researchers solve these problems by drawing on insights from across a range of theories, and by working 'at the margins of theories or in the interstices of them' (Seddon, 1996:200). A condition of genuine exchange in research based on such work is that researchers not only clarify the intellectual traditions within which they are located but also make clear the particular ways in which they are using those traditions. [...]

There has been some turbulence in the formation of the 'collective biography' of education policy researchers in recent years. Paying attention to that, and to its consequences, emphasises the distance between this conceptualisation of research and positivist assumptions about research. I argued above for acceptance of the researcher's engagement with a research agenda, and against the idea of 'hygienic' research. The emphasis on values and orientation is part of the same argument. Here I am taking further the implications of understanding research (and perhaps particularly research on policy) as a process of knowledge production that is shaped in relationship with changes in society, and reflects them while reflecting on them. Researchers and the resources that they bring to research cannot be ignored as contributory factors in the framing and performance of the research. The research problem is not 'out there' in some world that is external to the researcher; nor, indeed, can we accept the existence of an external world that can be captured and reduced to verifiable fact. Critics of positivism have come from different intellectual traditions to argue against its assumptions and to raise questions about the nature of the relationship between researchers and the empirical world that they investigate, and the knowledge and language that they use as resources.

As a consequence, the issue of choice and explicitness in education policy research becomes ever more complex. In a research culture that was dominated by positivist research, the principle of choice was a given, built into the formula of introduction, literature review and methodology. The formula obliged you to provide sufficient information to other researchers so that they could replicate your study, or at least understand how you had arrived at your conclusions and make some judgement on the adequacy of your findings (Seddon, 1996:211). This neat formula has been overturned, but there is no obvious substitute that allows for productive research exchange. In my view, that absence (which is understandable, because there is no simple substitute) has left the policy research community, and perhaps the more general education research community, with silences or differences where productive continuing conversations should be. This in turn prevents researchers from extending their conversations with practitioners, and may leave the field open to denigration by policy analysts, who want to deny complexity and restore simplicity. [...]

I am arguing here that changes in the policy context have an impact on how researchers develop ideas about explaining those changes (often at the level of pretheoretical assumptions), and may influence their choice of project and hence their theoretical resources.

References

Cox, R. W. (1980) Social forces, states and world orders, Millennium; *Journal of International Studies*, 10(2): 126-55

Dale, R. (1989) *The State and Education Policy.* Milton Keynes: Open University Press

Dunleavy, P. and O'Leary, B. (1987) *Theories of the State: The Politics of Liberal Democracy.* London: Macmillan

Gewirtz, S. (1995) Choice, equity and control in education. Paper presented to the Second Comparative Education Policy Seminar, Sweden and England, Umea University

Gewirtz, S. and Ozga, J. (1994) Interviewing the education policy elite, in Walford, G. (ed) *Researching the Powerful in Education.* London: UCL Press

Goldstein, H. (1998) *How can we evaluate Educational Research?* London: Institute of Education

Harvey, L. (1990) *Critical Social Research.* London: Unwin Hyman

Howell, D. (1990) Some thoughts on researching grant-maintained schools. *Journal of Education Policy,* 5(3): 242-4

Jensen, T. (1998) Stress in the Primary School, *The Guardian,* 11 May

Ozga, J. (1990) Policy research and policy theory: a comment on Fitz and Halpin, *Journal of Education Policy,* 5(4): 359-62

Ozga, J. and Gewirtz, S. (1994) Sex, lies and audiotape: interviewing the education policy elite, in D. Halpin and B. Troyna (eds) Researching Education Policy: *Ethical and Methodological Issues.* Lewes: Palmer Press

Ozga, J. and Lawn, M. (1981) Teachers, Professionalism and Class. Lewes: Falmer Press

Power, S. (1993) The detail and the bigger picture: the use of state-centred theory in researching education policy and practice. *International Studies in the Sociology of Education,* 6(3):77-92

Seddon, T. (1996) The principle of choice in policy research. *Journal of Education Policy,* 2(2):200-14

Stanley, L. and Wise, E. (1993) *Breaking Out Again.* London: Routledge

Troyna, B. (1994) Critical social research and education policy, *British Journal of Educational Studies,* 42(1): 52-71

Chapter 16

Co-participative transformation:
Creative learning conversations

Anna Craft

This chapter explores creative learning conversations as methodological devices for transformational change. It draws on three co-participative initiatives exploring educational futures in the South-West of England, each involving emancipatory change. At the heart of each is the development of the creative learning conversation, characterised in terms of spatiality and dialogue. Using Lefebvre's (1991) conceptualisation of Lived Space, and Bakhtin's (1984) work on open-ended dialogue, the chapter theorises creative learning conversations as producing 'living dialogic space' (Chappell and Craft, 2011). The chapter explores why living dialogic space is necessary to transformational change.

The frame: co-participative transformation in education

The twenty-first century is a time of rapid change which brings special challenges for educators. Economic, social, technological, environmental and spiritual uncertainty for young learners demands of them creativity, confidence and capability as they navigate both independently and with others. As digital technology opens up learning contexts in new ways, and as the demand for creativity is counterbalanced with political demands for ever higher achievement, schools face the question of the probable future with regard to curriculum, learning and assessment as well as the wider question of their purpose and mode of operation. This tension between creativity – the capacity to shift with ease from what is to what might be – and performativity, where student achievement is linked with school performance and reward, is seen in many parts of the world (Ball, 2003; Craft and Jeffrey, 2008). At the same time, a potential chasm is exposed between the highly participative, immersive and attractive social cultural, and digital environments in which young people (and adults) are engaged outside formal education, and approaches to learning and teaching in schools (Craft, 2011). The need for transformation in schools toward creative and co-participative engagement is clear.

Wise humanising creativity

The initiatives and approaches explored in this chapter were developed by a research team concerned with creative development, based mainly at the University of Exeter. The team, whose work was informed broadly by a Critical Theory perspective – seeking not simply to understand (eg. McCarthy, 1991) but to critique and change through their research – aimed to open up a potentially transformative space between the creativity discourse which had begun to emerge globally from the late 1990s, and the simultaneously emergent performative discourse (discussed by Cochrane *et al*, 2008). The Exeter team valued creativity – working with possibility – in its own right, adopting the democratic creativity stance proposed by the policy paper published by the National Advisory Committee on Creative and Cultural Education (NACCCE, 1999). The team's focus was therefore on nurturing creative co-participation in research focused on improving or transforming learning and teaching. Their work acknowledged the performative environment yet foregrounded creativity, viewing creativity as a social good, and as ubiquitous as well as democratic (Banaji *et al*, 2010).

The expansion of co-enquiry space between the two poles of creativity and performativity, encouraged students, teachers and others to engage in 'what if?' and 'as if' thinking and behaviour (Craft, 2010) as living provocations against a risk-averse wider performative culture (Cochrane and Cockett, 2007). The sorts of creativity nurtured in this co-enquiry space fused two conceptualisations of creativity (Chappell, 2008; Craft, 2008) into a newly-formed concept of *wise humanising creativity*. Wise humanising creativity is informed by recognition that even the creativity pole can be conceived of as individualised and marketised (Craft, 2005), and that childhood, youth and education can therefore be shaped by values which highlight competition, acquisition and individualism (Craft, 2008).

Wise humanising creativity focuses on collective action rather than individual action. It emphasises expression rather than competition and is ethically grounded, rather than being driven by the marketplace. Wise humanising creativity questions performativity rather than accepting it. It is informed by the notion of 'humanising creativity' (Chappell, 2008) which emphasises that creativity occurs individually, collaboratively and communally and that communal creativity is important to the humanising process through its strong focus on shared ownership, group identity and empathy. Humanising creativity emphasises the emotional journey of lows as well as highs, and of conflict as well as shared struggles; it reveals how valuable new ideas emerge from working creatively together. Wise humanising creativity is also informed by the notion of wise, creative trusteeship (Craft, 2008) positioned against marketised, individualised and culture-blind creativity and embracing creative stewardship toward the collective good, thus is focused on nurturing creativity with wisdom.

A quiet revolution for emancipatory change?

In a world where schools and other educating systems seek to find their way from a Victorian mode of cohort-based educating where authority and power are located in the adults responsible for the institution, and where performative measures drive the activities and concerns of teachers and others, to approaches which may better meet the needs of students and society in offering greater agency and enabling greater engagement (Wrigley, Thomson, Lingard, 2012), wise humanising creativity seeks to offer a 'quiet revolution' (Chappell *et al*, 2011). Such a revolution is both critical yet ethically grounded and aligns personal with wider values, seeking sustainability through emotional, physical and aesthetic as well as virtual learning.

Ultimately such a quiet revolution may yield power to rebalance change in transactions, decision-making, expression of learning and outcomes involving shifting the balance of emphasis. Such *emancipatory* change means extending voice and participation beyond the traditional power hierarchy of the school community to include students, parents and external partners, and offers new, shared freedoms rather than control. This is a daunting agenda, but starts with imagining and bringing to fruition possibilities in one's immediate situation.

Three initiatives

This chapter draws on three development and research projects of differing lengths, undertaken in English primary and secondary schools and in community education, through the University of Exeter, over a period of five years from early 2007. Each project is framed by Critical Theory. Each sought to initiate emancipatory educational change by generating space between creativity and performativity for rich engagement between students and adults. Each prioritised wise humanising creativity (Chappell, 2008; Craft, 2008).

Aspire: this development and research initiative has many funders. It offers school students, together with their teachers, ways of researching their schools so as to support transformational change. (http://elac.exeter.ac.uk/aspire/index.php). Co-participation (Fielding, 2001) and 'person-centred' engagement (Fielding, 2007) are emphasised, with student voice being at the heart of change. In each primary and secondary school involved in the programme (around twenty so far) is a lead team comprising students, staff and often parents and external partners, using qualitative methods to co-research a collectively-generated question (Craft and Chappell, 2010). Their focus is on collaboratively making transformational change in schools reflecting how they learn best. Examples of research questions asked in the schools include, 'what are students learning in lessons?', 'how is deep learning fostered in lessons?', 'how can homework be more effective?', 'how do students experience the pastoral care in our school?' and 'what role could mobile learning technology play in our learning?' Aspire seeks to transform school climate, through a facilitation team from the university who help to open the co-enquiry space but then also research what occurs. Their qualitative research is guided by the question: 'How can we characterise transformation in Aspire schools?' Analysis has led to the characterisation of creative learning conversations (Chappell and Craft, 2009, 2011).

Dance Partners for Creativity (DPC): this study, funded by the Arts and Humanities Research Council from 2008-2011, explored the fostering of student creativity through creative partnerships between dance artists and teachers in lower secondary school dance (http://education.exeter.ac.uk/dpc). Dance education researchers, teachers and artists co-researched the overarching question: What kinds of creative partnership are manifested between dance-artists and teachers in co-developing the creativity of 11-14 year olds in dance education, and how do these develop? The study was established in response to concern that creativity in dance was being stifled by a performative culture in schools, as discussed above. It sought to respond to government initiatives which highlighted the possible role of creative partnership in addressing this issue (Roberts, 2006; DCMS, 2006). The qualitative project involved university-based and school-based researchers (teachers and dance-artists) working in collaboration within four school sites. They focused on dance partnership initiatives with students aged 11-14, developing student creativity over up to five school terms. In each site, the overarching question guided the research and development under way, and each site team developed their own, locally-guiding research questions as well. For full details of all sites and research questions see (http://education.exeter.ac.uk/projects.php?id=343).

Imagining Possibilities: this much shorter yet similar initiative was funded by the Museums, Libraries and Archives Council (MLA). Co-ordinated by educational charity Devon Arts in Schools Initiative (Daisi), this half-day process held at the University of Exeter in early 2011 formed the concluding part of the one-year MLA Young People's Project. It sought, through immersive, participative, exploratory techniques of co-enquiry including creative writing, three collaboratively-designed research questions, to span the concerns of the cultural and heritage sectors and demonstrate the value of using this kind of workshop. It involved staff from museums, libraries and cultural centres such as Exeter Cathedral, from across the South-West of England. A film of the event can be found at: (http://vimeo.com/21640950).

All three projects were established with the combined intention of investigating how we conceive of and work for creative futures. Each therefore has sought both to understand creativity and also to action change in pedagogy, learning and curriculum. Each initiative therefore extends what educators typically engage in.

Creative learning conversations

Central to the initiatives are 'creative learning conversations': methodological devices for participatory creative change. Involving co-investigation by researchers, teachers, artists and students, the projects were developed by university researchers to flatten hierarchies, opening spaces promoting equality and oriented toward action. They were intentionally devised as distinct from the usual power structures expected in schools and universities. The creative learning conversations held in each initiative sought to engage participants in their investigations of creative educational futures, with enquiry and change at their heart.

Emerging organically over time, the team's understanding, both practical and theoretical, of creative learning conversations has involved re-analysis of data and processes within the projects in which creative learning conversations have mainly been used. We have looked for recurrent defining characteristics of creative learning conversations. Through cycles of analysis it has become clear that these conversations are distinct from the usual hierarchical, top down power conversations expected within schools and in their relationships with universities. Creative learning conversations take place between and amongst students, teachers, parents and external partners and different aspects of the same person's role in a project can be led by any of these. Thus, in Imagining Possibilities, collaborators in the Young People's Project articulated lived experience of others in their work through creative writing, sharing these in a dynamic, exploratory space with others, yielding new perspectives on participants in their programmes. In Aspire schools, students and staff collaborate in both critiquing and exploring practice and in developing provision. In Dance Partners for Creativity (DPC), enquiry-focused conversations between students, partner researchers and university staff revealed distinct differences in perspective.

Creative learning conversations, then, are a way of contributing to change which moves us towards an education future fit for the twenty-first century. They are the ongoing process without forced closure of those in the role of university academic, teacher, artist, student, co-participatively researching and developing knowledge of their 'lived space' together. Given the customary lethargy in the educational system as a whole, commitment to changing education for better futures demands active involvement in living dialogic space, where our humanity both emerges from and guides our shared learning.

Early articulation of the nature of creative learning conversations (Chappell and Craft with Jonsdottir and Clack, 2009) initially emphasised two elements: repositioning (ie. flattening the usually-experienced hierarchies) and listening-actioning (ie. emphasising the shift to action and not simply the expression of points of view).

Later analysis of data (Chappell and Craft, 2011) revealed that the repositioning and listening-actioning were the conditions in which the characteristics of creative learning conversations as spaces for co-research emerged. Creative learning conversations which emerged in co-research spaces shared the following characteristics:

- partiality (recognition that expression and interpretation of actions is partial ie. only a lens on lived experience and not 'the truth')
- emancipation (empowerment, or freeing from possible oppression)
- working from the bottom up (valuing perspectives of all and especially those who have least power)
- participation (opportunities for high involvement)
- debate and difference (expression of difference, thus openness to possible conflict of perspective)

These were experienced in a culture of openness to action, involving embodied and verbalised idea exchange.

The Critical Theory contextualising of all three initiatives foregrounds the shift from research to action in each. In the case of Aspire, the shift toward action focuses on change in school so as to improve the learning experiences of all. One example of a change made in an Aspire school was the introduction of mobile phone technology into homework for modern foreign languages, enabling students to record and upload material consolidating oral work done in class. In the case of Dance Partners for Creativity, an example of a shift to action came when a dance artist partnering a teacher recognised the need to offer students opportunities to generate choreographic ideas. And in Imagining Possibilities, an example of a shift to action was the acknowledgement by a museum educator of the multiple and valuable perspectives brought into museum learning by volunteers.

The Exeter research team recognises a spectrum of critical theory perspectives, from modernist to postmodern approaches, and leans toward post-modern critical theorising. This means that each of the projects discussed here acknowledge Ellsworth's (1989) warning of unintentional disempowerment implicit in what de Sousa Santos (1999) later called 'Celebratory Critical Theory' which reveals but does not lead to change. The research team was sensitive to Ellsworth's argument that knowledge of another person's or group's experience can never be complete and is always therefore 'partial'. Consequently, all three projects sought to adopt 'Oppositional Critical Theory' which, de Sousa Santos argues, recognises knowledge as emancipatory. In practice this meant opening space for the sharing and comparison of lived experience between all those engaged in the co-enquiry in each site, thus making visible conflict as well as harmony. All three initiatives thus shared a potential dynamic in the expression and interpretation of perspectives, which we came to understand as living dialogic space.

Living dialogic space at the heart of transformational change

The emancipatory expression and interpretation nurtured in each of these projects was positioned as distinct from 'scientific' and 'evidence-based' approaches to educational research and practice and drew on critiques from the UK (eg. Biesta, 2007) and the US (Denzin *et al*, 2006) which highlight a form of fundamentalist truth-seeking inherent in these movements. Instead we sought to build reciprocal, collaborative, mutually accountable and trusting relationships with those studied in each project, with an emphasis on recognising distinctive meanings rather than detecting truths. Consequently, the creative learning conversations nurtured in each of the three initiatives, honouring partiality, emancipation, participation, debate and difference, openness to action and embodied and verbalised exchange of ideas, generated multiple perspectives which exposed and fostered tensions and conflict as well as shared understandings and harmonious agreement.

Creative learning conversations – and the living dialogic space they open – can be conceptualised in terms of social spatiality and dialogue (Chappell and Craft, 2011). This framing draws on Massey, Allen and Sarre (1999) who, coming from a human geography perspective, emphasise reciprocity between social and spatial (ie. the social as spatially constructed and the spatial as socially constructed). The Exeter team has worked with two theoretical resources in underpinning their work, one set of ideas on spatial practice from Lefebvre, and the other set of ideas on dialogic interaction from Bakhtin. These are now briefly explained in relation to creative learning conversations.

The social and spatial reciprocity in the living dialogic space of creative learning conversations is further informed by Lefebvre's (1991) spatial discussion of thinking, in which he distinguishes between perceived, conceived and lived space. For Lefebvre, *perceived space* is equivalent to spatial practice – the observable reality of everyday routines such as those inherent to pupil-teacher relationships, partnership practices in dance education or routines associated with museum, library or cultural venue learning. Lefebvre's *conceived space* refers to 'representations' – systems of verbal signs and abstracted principles – and is a dominant controlling influence over how we understand, experience, explain and practice our human spatiality. Lefebvre recognises that perceived and conceived space are insufficient on their own, but require the complexity and possibly unknowable mystery of *lived space* which involves an open, fluid, dynamic, actioned representation of bodily experience directly lived through images and symbols. For Lefebvre, this is the location of passion and the making manifest of multiple possibilities.

It is this quality of lived space, which requires openness and enables the extrapolation of potentiality, co-constructed through social and physical sharing of space, which informs the 'living' aspect of the dialogic space theory embraced by the Exeter team. Learning conversations generate 'living space' (Chappell and Craft, 2011:380) which recognises 'the inhabiting, the embodiment, openness, lack of closure and thus capacity for change' (*ibid*:380). The 'dialogic' aspect of living dialogic space is informed by Bakhtin's approach to participatory action research and his recognition of the role of open-ended dialogue in shared enquiry to inform social change.

Wegerif's (2010) work on Bakhtin emphasises the role of continuous listening, mind-changing and arguing against one's own earlier position within the space of dialogue. This chain of exploration is embedded within the three projects discussed here, as is a recognition also highlighted by Wegerif (2007) of the role of silent and internal dialogue. So, in Imagining Possibilities for example, participants in the project engaged in their own internal dialogues with actual and imagined people and perspectives, through embodied activities including large scale Snakes and Ladders invested with meaning by individuals working silently alongside one another and building into debate, and also through creative writing. In layering one activity over the other, participants deepened their understandings and exploration of key points of view and opened up others, changing their minds about priorities and possibilities while reinforcing others.

Thus, as collaborators in all three projects – Aspire, DPC and Imagining Possibilities – undertake co-analysis of data pertinent to their shared enquiry, they expose different and sometimes conflicting perspectives including their own changing points of view over time. The way forward is not always clear, but the impetus is always to struggle towards further understandings through internal and externalised dialogue, recognising that it is not necessary or possible always to agree, yet that transformation occurs through openness and engagement. Clearly, the approaches in each project contrast markedly with the perhaps more common school practice of fixing things and moving on. Our contention is that deeper transformation is resonant with all of those involved, and can mean abandoning and re-examining what appear to be 'solutions'.

Wise humanising transformation

Utilising Lefebvre's (1991) conceptualisation of Lived space and Bakhtin's (1984) work on open-ended dialogue, and drawing on three change-oriented educational initiatives, this chapter has theorised creative learning conversations as producing living dialogic spaces. These social and spatial engagements offer ways of contributing to change through open, enquiry-oriented, multiple-voiced processes which avoid forced closure or artificial unison. Creative learning conversations, then, by their nature assume co-participative engagement in developing understandings of shared 'lived space' and are oriented, through this knowledge-in-action, toward transforming them. The contention of the team that has evolved creative learning conversations is that such living dialogic spaces may challenge what Claxton (2008) refers to as the lethargy in current education systems, and may yield possibilities for twenty-first century-oriented provision, transcending the non-commensurability which seems inherent in the current tension between creativity and performativity.

Perhaps most importantly, creative learning conversations are, in their essence, oriented toward wise, humanising creativity. They seek very practically to harness individual, collaborative and communal creativity towards emergent ways of learning, teaching and structuring education that enable shared ownership, multiple forms of group identity, and they recognise the role of empathy. They are situated in tension with marketised narratives for creative educational futures, seeking simplicity in humanising the educative process.

Source: *newly commissioned for this volume.*

Acknowledgements: these concepts have collaboratively developed with many colleagues, in particular Dr Kerry Chappell, University of Exeter. A fuller explanation can be found in Chappell, K. and Craft, A. (2011) 'Creative learning conversations: producing living dialogic spaces', *Educational Researcher*, vol.53, no.3, p363-85. Grateful thanks are due to all involved, and to the funders of each initiative detailed above.

References

Bakhtin, M.M. (1984) *Problems of Dostoevsky's Poetics* (edited and trans. by Caryl Emerson), Minnieapolis: University of Michigan Press.

Ball, S. J. (2003) 'The teacher's soul and the terrors of performativity', *Journal of Education Policy*, vol.18, no.2, p215-28.

Banaji, S., Burn, A. and Buckingham, D. (2010) *The Rhetorics of Creativity,* London: Arts Council England (2nd edition).

Biesta, G. (2007) 'Why 'what works' won't work: evidence-based practice and the democratic deficit in educational research', *Educational Theory*, vol.57, no.1, p1-22

Boyd, B. (2005) 'Caught in the headlights', paper presented at ESRC Seminar, Documenting Creative Learning, Strathclyde University, October 2005. http://opencreativity.open.ac.uk/recent.htm#previous_papers

Chappell, K. (2006) 'Creativity within late primary age dance education: unlocking expert specialist dance teachers conceptions and approaches', Ph.D. thesis, Laban, London. http://kn.open.ac.uk/public/document.cfm?documentid=8627

Chappell, K. (2008) 'Towards humanising creativity', *UNESCO Observatory E-Journal Special issue on Creativity, policy and practice discourses: productive tensions in the new millennium*, vol.1, no.3, December 2008. http://www.abp.unimelb.edu.au/unesco/ejournal/vol-one-issue-three.html

Chappell, K. and Craft, A. (2009) 'What makes a creative learning conversation?', presentation prepared for British Educational Research Association conference, Manchester, September 2009

Chappell, K. and Craft, A. (2011) 'Creative learning conversations', *Educational Research*, vol.53, no.3, p363-85

Chappell, K., Craft, A. with Jonsdottir, S., Clack, J. (2008) *Aspire South West, Report to Qualifications and Curriculum Authority,* December 2008

Chappell, K., Craft, A., Rolfe, L., Jobbins, V. (2009) 'Dance partners for creativity: choreographing space for co-participative research into creativity and partnership in dance education', *Special Issue of Research in Dance Education on Creativity,* vol.10, no.3, p177-98

Chappell, K., Rolfe, L., Craft, A., Jobbins, V. (2011) *Close Encounters*, Stoke on Trent: Trentham Books

Claxton, G. (2008) *What's the Point of School?* Oxford: OneWorld

Cochrane, P. and Cockett, M. (2007) *Building a Creative School*, Stoke on Trent: Trentham Books

Cochrane, P., Craft, A., Jeffery, G. (2008) 'Mixed messages or permissions and opportunities? Reflections on current policy perspectives on creativity in education', in Sefton-Green, J. (ed) (2008) *Creative Learning*, p27-39, London: Creative Partnerships

Craft, A. (2005) *Creativity in Schools: Tensions and Dilemmas*, Abingdon: Routledge

Craft, A. (2010) 'Teaching for possibility thinking. What is it and how do we do it?', *Learning Matters*, vol.16, no.1, p19-23

Craft, A. (2011) *Creativity and Education Futures*, Stoke on Trent: Trentham Books

Craft, A. (2008) 'Tensions in creativity and education: enter Wisdom and Trusteeship?' in Craft, A., Gardner, H., Claxton, G. *et al* (2008) *Creativity, Wisdom and Trusteeship. Exploring the role of education*, p16-34, Thousand Oaks: Corwin Press

Craft, A. and Chappell, K. (2010) 'Co-creating possible educational futures', presentation to ESRC Seminar on Educational Futures, University of Exeter, March 2010

Craft, A. and Jeffrey, B. (2008) 'Creativity and performativity in teaching and learning: tensions, dilemmas, constraints, accommodations and synthesis', *British Educational Research Journal,* vol.34, no.5, p577-84

de Sousa Santos (1999) 'Oppositional Postmodernism', in Munck, R., O'Hearn, D. (eds) *Critical Development Theory: Contributions to a new paradigm,* London: Zed Books

Denzin, N.K., Lincoln, Y.S. and Giardina, M.D. (2006) 'Disciplining qualitative research', *International Journal of Qualitative Studies in Education*, vol.19, no.6, p769-82

DCMS (2006) *Government Response to Paul Roberts' Review on Nurturing Creativity in Young People,* London: DCMS

Ellsworth, E. (1989) 'Why doesn't this feel empowering? Working through the repressive myths of critical pedagogy', *Harvard Educational Review*, vol.59, no.3, p297-324

Fielding, M. (2001) 'Target setting, policy pathology and student perspectives', in Fielding, M. *Taking Education Really Seriously: Four years' hard labour*, London: Routledge Falmer

Fielding, M. (2007) 'The human cost and intellectual poverty of high performance schooling: Radical philosophy, John MacMurray and the remaking of person-centred education', *Journal of Educational Policy*, no.22, p383-409

Lefebvre, H. (1991) *The Production of Space*, Oxford: Wiley-Blackwell

Massey, D., Allen, J. and Sarre, P. (1999) *Human Geography Today*, Cambridge: Polity Press

McCarthy, T. (1991) *Ideals and Illusions: On reconstruction and deconstruction in contemporary critical theory*, Cambridge: The MIT Press

National Advisory Committee on Creative and Cultural Education (1999) *All Our Futures: Creativity, culture and education*, Sudbury, Suffolk: Department for Education and employment

Roberts, P. (2006) *Nurturing Creativity in Young People*, London: DCMS

Thomson, P., Lingard, B., Wrigley, T. (2012) 'Reimagining school change: the necessity and reasons for hope', in Wrigley, T., Thomson, P., Lingard, B. (eds) *Changing Schools: Alternative ways to make a world of difference*, Abingdon: Routledge

Wegerif, R. (2007) *Dialogic Education and Technology: Expanding the space of learning*, Lausanne: Springer

Wegerif, R. (2010) *Mind Expanding: Teaching for thinking and creativity in primary education*, Maidenhead: Open University Press

Part 4

Issues for 21st century practice

Chapter 17

Death to critique and dissent? The policies and practices of new managerialism and of 'evidence-based practice'

Bronwyn Davies

New managerialism, which is also referred to as neo-liberalism in the UK [...] is a system of government of individuals invented during the Thatcher and Reagan years. [...] Neo-liberalism is characterised by Thatcher's 'death of society' and the rise of 'individuals' who are in need of management, surveillance and control.

Management, surveillance and control are not new of course. Foucault (1977, 1980) analysed the panopticon as a form of government in which 'relatively few officials control large numbers of [workers] by foregrounding both hierarchy and visibility' (Schmelzer, 1993:127). The new panopticon, however, that can be observed in new managerialist worksites, works quite differently. Schmelzer observes that it is invisible and operates through *multiple eyes* at every level – eyes whose gaze is finely tuned to the inflow and outflow of funding and to the multitude of mechanisms that have been generated to manipulate those flows. This *multiplied gaze* works in such a way that it seems natural and makes us blind to its effects. It enables, according to Schmelzer (1993:127):

meticulous control over the network of power relations that produce and sustain the truth claims of an institution by means of an economical surveillance.

[...]

Now, as Schmelzer (1993) shows, instead of ... (more or less) benign leaders who could rely on our own internalised gaze to monitor our own work, we have the multiplied gaze of the workers on each other, their gaze shaped by the policies and practices emanating from management. The multiplied gaze infiltrates and shapes the way

work is understood. Little or no attention is paid to the actual effects on the work that this new panopticism might have, other than to monitor the meeting of institutional objectives. As long as objectives have been specified and strategies for their management and surveillance put in place, the nature of the work itself is of little relevance to anyone. If the auditing tools say that the work has, on average, met the objectives, it is simply assumed that the work has been appropriately and satisfactorily tailored according to the requirements of the institution (and often of the relevant funding body).

Within new managerialist systems, the individual's sense of their own value is no longer primarily derived from responsible self-conduct and competent knowledge and practice of professional knowledge. And yet, at the same time, new managerialism relies on habitual, internalised surveillance, through which the conduct of conduct is carried out to press subjects into making and remaking themselves as legitimate and appropriate(d) members of the latest shift within their particular new managerialist systems. The requirement of 'continuous improvement', and documented individual commitment towards and striving for it, is one of the strategies for creating this continually changing individual.

Within the terms of the new system individuals will be presented with an often overwhelming range of pressing choices and administrative tasks for which they are responsible. But any questioning of the system itself is silenced or trivialised. The system itself is characterised as both natural and inevitable. Resistance to it by individuals (and that includes critiques such as this) is constituted as ignorance of what the 'real' (financial) 'bottom-line' issues are, as sheer cussedness, or as a sign reminding management of individual workers' replaceability. As Hammersley (2001:9) points out, '[D]emands for 'transparent' accountability' (along with many other managerialist terms) are made into imperatives that are in turn justified as a response to severely limited financial resources. The fact that much of the resource base that was previously available to support professional work has been redirected into surveillance and auditing somehow remains invisible, or at least is generally not spoken about, or subjected to critique. [...]

New managerialism relies on a complex combination of the two forms of morality that Foucault observed, the first requiring compliance and the second driven by individuals' desires to shape their own directions. It works, on the one hand, to gain compliance, relying on that form of morality driven by 'obedience to a heteronomous code which we must accept, and to which we are bound by fear and guilt' (Rose, 1999:97). On the other hand, it partially disguises the coercion by placing increased emphasis on 'personal responsibility' within the new system, an emphasis that flows in part from the abdication by government and governing bodies from their former role in taking care of aspects of the social fabric. [...]

Dennis (1995), writing in the North American context, puts his finger on a central problem of new managerialism. He says that through an emphasis on measurable outcomes, on goals defined by management at the highest levels and on the systems through which such goals are achieved, new managerialism is always dangerously at risk of cutting its populace adrift from moral and political debate.[...]

Given all these negatives (the reduction in critical thought and responsible dissent, the pervasive subliminal fear and anxiety, the sense of personal pressure and responsibility combined with a devalued sense of self, the shift of value away from personal and professional considerations towards the single consideration of the economy), it is relevant to ask why so many of us have willingly worked towards the installation and maintenance of new managerialist systems. Individuals involved in implementing or simply caught within new managerialist systems are often seduced by their rhetoric of efficiency and accountability, and by their morally ascendant promise of a desired comeuppance for those perceived to be faulty or inadequate in conducting their own conduct. [...] Feminists, for example, were drawn to the possibility of breaking up old networks of power that held them on the margins and in low-status positions. The idea of a new system that could bring about change, breaking up old hegemonies and mandating equity, was seductive and appealing.

Those working to implement new managerialism set up systems in which everyone (subtext: specifically, those who did not satisfactorily conduct their own conduct under previous systems) will have to work harder to be 'good enough', to meet the exacting standards required of them. What they do not anticipate is that the constant threat of external punitive surveillance potentially erodes the professional judgement of everyone (including those who have, until now, successfully conducted their own conduct). The personal dynamic that is set up is potentially exhausting and debilitating, since it is likely that no one can experience themselves as 'good enough' when the basis of assessment is externalised, constantly escalating, subject to change, and often at odds with the professional knowledge on which previous good practice was based. [...]

Ironically, the reduction of freedom, the loss of a moral base in favour of an economic base, the celebration of the new macho individual, are presented within new managerialism as fundamental to the new morally ascendant position – the only position any reasonable person could have. That morally ascendant view has, as its fundamental tenet, survival of the imposed systems. Dissent, just like dissent amongst soldiers in times of war, cannot be tolerated. [...]

It is in part because of its apparently virtuous and morally ascendant language that otherwise critical professionals may be blind to the necessity for critique of the new managerialist discursive framework through which they are about to be, or are being, constituted. They may also be drawn into the sticky net of managerialism's agenda if they find themselves in policy-making positions where they can place their political demands, such as equal educational opportunity or gender reform, on the agenda. [...]

So how do managerialist agendas play out in schools, and in particular how might the new push towards evidence-based practice be understood in this context?

A critique of the concept of 'evidence-based practice'

Hammersley (2001) provides a critique of evidence-based practice, also analysing it as a new managerialist strategy. He points out that managerialism is based on an assumption that professional practice:

should take the form of specifying goals explicitly, selecting strategies for achieving them on the basis of objective evidence about their effectiveness, and then measuring outcomes in order to assess their degree of success (thereby providing the knowledge required for improving future performance). (2001:5)

These are not, when it comes to teaching, individually set goals, but the goals of the institution, or even of the state. While individual teachers may be responsible for providing the 'objective evidence', and may be held individually accountable if their evidence does not provide the institution with what it needs to make an acceptable account of itself to government, the definition of what is 'effective', of what counts as 'success', will not be something they have any control over. When HTO Davies *et al* (2000:2) observe that

in contrast to the preceding culture of largely judgement-based professional practice, there has risen the important notion of evidence-based practice as a means of ensuring that what is being done is worthwhile and that it is being done in the best possible way

we can be sure that it is not the teachers who are being asked to judge what is worthwhile, nor what might be regarded as the 'best possible way'. Of course, 'consultations' with representative teachers may have taken place, but those consultations will have been undertaken in such a way that the representatives will have acquired the new discourse and so become party to its dissemination, the only alternative being to be marginalised or replaced. Neither the teachers, nor their representatives, will have had freedom to dispute or resile from the institution's or state's criteria of effectivity and success, since both their own livelihoods and the funding of their institutions may well be tied in whole or in part to their satisfactory fulfilment. As Grundy points out:

Leaders will be expected to exercise control so that the objectives of the organisations, clearly defined and articulated, will be achieved. There will be a division of labour between the leader who plans (or who receives and interprets plans imposed from elsewhere) and the practitioners who implement the plans. The language of administrative planning will be 'end-directed', with criteria for the achievement of the objectives being articulated along with the plans. It will be the leader who is responsible for the training of the practitioners, and such training will be oriented towards the development of skills. It will also be the responsibility of the leader to motivate and enthuse practitioners to embrace the specified objectives and work for their achievement. (Grundy, 1993:168)

To this end, the language of managerialism cleverly cannibalises the liberal humanist terms in vogue during the period of high modernity that seem, on the face of it, indisputably virtuous and desirable. Take 'literacy', for example. Who can dispute the desirability of every child achieving a minimum standard of literacy and thus achieving not only the potential to be active citizens of democracy but also the potential to survive in the new information-technology-driven global world? The means of achieving this may actually be at the expense of the teaching strategies through which critical literacy or any other critical/analytic skills are taught. They may also draw massive resources away from teaching itself and into the bureaucracy that stages and evaluates the testing and other strategies through which the 'new' objectives are to be achieved. Individual resistance to the strategies through which these new/old ideals are implemented is likely to be read as inflexible, or conservative, or, worse, as motivated by individual incompetence or laziness. Resistance may well position you as one of those whom the systems are supposedly designed to catch out.

The proponents of evidence-based practice propose an unproblematic relationship between research and practice, and also amongst policy, research and practice. At first glance, the idea of evidence-based practice appears to be so obviously desirable (like universal literacy or continuous improvement) that it might be regarded as a truism. Who could argue against the idea that professional practice should be based on evidence? Its opposite, teaching without evidence, or against the evidence, sounds absurd. Read in this way, a move towards evidence-based practice seems impossible to disagree with. But another reading can be produced if we understand evidence-based practice as a product of new managerialism and as no more than a means of implementing managerialist agendas.

To get beyond the obviousness of the first reading it is useful to focus on the 'based' of evidence-based and ask, *which evidence should be the base, and who selects it?* In what ways, we might then ask, are the choices and decisions teachers make in the classroom and playground based on the evidence, not only that someone else provides, but that someone else (another someone, located in the bureaucracy) selects. Are those who produce the evidence and those who select it members of the profession of teaching? How have they chosen what counts as evidence, and how have they selected the particular evidence that is to be acted on? And, finally, how are the links to the everyday practice of teaching to be accomplished? How is the teacher to alter her/his practices of teaching in light of this 'evidence'? Such questions immediately alert us to a possible hidden agenda – to a plan to change what it is that teachers produce through the adoption of a language and a system that guarantees its sense of inevitability. The question we might then go on to ask is: are the practices of teaching so susceptible to this kind of subterfuge?

The right to be taught is now being framed through new managerialist strategies, in terms of measured outcomes, and yet at the same time relies on the very professional base of the teachers knowing her/his subject that new managerialism potentially undermines. Instructions from bureaucrats to produce specific outcomes (instructions backed by 'evidence') can only (logically speaking) be interpreted/ practised in terms of the teachers' already (per)formed, and (per)forming, profession-in-practice. But that profession-in-practice is what made sense in high modernity [pre new managerialism] when there was a personal and professional commitment to the pursuit of knowledge inside mutually respectful relations amongst colleagues and between teachers and students. So the profession-in-practice – or professional knowledge – is both relied on and undermined by new managerialist strategies such as the implementation of evidence-based practice.

So how are we to make sense of what it is that evidence-based practice sets out to achieve and its methods for doing so? There are two major considerations that I elaborate here that are relevant to this questioning of an ideal, or real, connection between evidence and practice. These relate to the interpretation and use of experimental evidence by the advocates of evidence-based practice and to the necessity for an underlying philosophy of the profession of teaching.

Interpreting Statistical/Experimental Evidence
As Hammersley (2001) points out, the proponents of evidence-based practice, for example Blunkett (2000), argue that statistically based, experimental research is to be preferred by evidence-based practitioners since it is less biased by the interests of the researcher. This trust in the objectivity of experimental research is embarrassingly naive. Experimental researchers, even those gazing down a microscope, are as capable of finding what they expect to find, or want to find, as anyone else. [...]

Experiments do not remove the subjectivity of researchers; they simply work to conceal it. 'Findings' are not guaranteed – they are more like working propositions that make sense within particular frameworks of assumptions and of practice.

Yet it is in order to give an appearance of an unchallengeable link between evidence and practice that the advocates of evidence-based practice rely on experimental research. They engage the authority of 'hard science' to give weight to their propositions. Although the words 'evidence-based practice' might be read as if there is an immediate connection between the individual practitioner and the selection, reading and interpretation of evidence, teachers are not allocated time (let alone given appropriate library resources) to read the research being produced relevant to their practice (Davies *et al*, 1996). Nor are they trained to interpret research evidence and to work out the relations between research and practice. There is thus an invisible sleight of hand embedded in the term itself which makes invisible the managers and policy-makers who will select what is relevant, and who will dictate how it is to be audited and deemed to have been put into practice.

An apparent (invisible) assumption is made by the advocates of evidence-based practice that bureaucrats and policy-makers do have the skills and resources to read all the possible available research, select what is relevant to particular schools and classrooms and teachers and to the particular problems they encounter, and then to assess whether or not the teachers have understood the implications of the selected research and acted accordingly. Since this is such an absurd assumption, we can guess immediately that this is not how evidence-based practice will work. Through an understanding of how new managerialism works, we can guess that the objectives will come first and that the 'experimental research evidence' will be generated to justify them. As long as the objectives have been met (according to the auditors), then questions about the appropriateness of the evidence for good teaching or the capacity of teachers to act on it can be left unasked and unanswered. Critique, in this model, becomes irrelevant.

Since the desire to meet the objectives has already been generated through the systems of surveillance and management and the subliminal fear and anxiety they can generate, there is no need to worry about how teachers managed to make the links between evidence and practice. Withdrawal of funds from schools and programmes is one of a battery of manipulative strategies to ensure that the appropriate fear and guilt, through the operation of the multiplied gaze, are generated to ensure the meeting of the objectives.

Am I being too cynical, you might ask? Is it possible that the processes of evidence-based practice might lead to better teaching?

My own work with teachers would suggest that it takes years of concerted effort for teachers to learn to read research and to generate new teaching practices based on that research. I have worked collaboratively with individual teachers, often over several years, guiding them in becoming reflexive researchers who can read both the assumptions and theoretical frameworks that inform research findings, and the details of their own practices. Only after such intensive work, driven by the teachers' own desire to develop their own capacity for critique and analysis, would I be willing to claim with any confidence that a productive link between research and practice can be established (see, for example, Davies *et al*, 1996; Davies and Hunt, 2000; Laws and Davies, 2000). If, in contrast, teachers are presented with 'research findings' and policy objectives as a guide to practice, along with a range of surveillance strategies to monitor their performance, there can be no assumption of a straightforward link between research and practice. Nor can we assume there should be – that the experimental research that is deemed to be relevant would, if acted on, lead to better teaching.

Evidence-based practice's preference for experimental evidence reveals either a naivety about research, or a hidden, managerialist agenda that has little to do with research findings and their implications for practice.

The Underlying Philosophy of the Profession of Teaching

The idea that professionals can be shaped by 'evidence' legitimated by managers and funding bodies and by coercive policies that mandate action on the basis of that evidence belies the complexity of professional work. As Derrida points out in *Who's Afraid, of Philosophy?* (2002:69), the relations of power and the lines of force acting on teaching are heterogeneous and marked by agonistic struggles:

The structures of a pedagogical institution, its forms, norms, visible or invisible constraints, settings, the entire apparatus ... that, appearing to surround it, determines that institution right to the centre of its content, and no doubt from the centre, one carefully conceals the forces and interests that, without the slightest neutrality, dominate and master – impose themselves upon – the process of teaching from within a heterogeneous and divided agonistic field racked (sic) with constant struggle.

The teachers who work in pedagogical institutions are multiply inscribed, subjected to discursive lines of force pushing and pulling in contradictory directions. Multiple discourses operate in a palimpsest of overlapping meanings that do not totally occlude each other. Teachers work in and through the dynamic tensions of these multiple discourses and relations of power to produce that complex set of processes that we call teaching.

Any new discourse (such as that encoded as 'evidence-based' and related to policy imperatives) necessarily jostles alongside other discourses that make up the discursive field of teaching (see Honan, 2001) for teachers' reflections on how they accommodate and resist new curricula). Many teachers tenaciously hold on to the philosophies that inform their teaching: their teaching is, in effect, the construction of that philosophy. We might even go so far as to say that their teaching cannot exist without that, implicit or explicit, philosophy. When teaching has been deserted by such philosophical bases, we find, according to Derrida, the perfect seeding ground for new managerialism: the ultimate manifestations of *phallogocentric hegemony*. He describes such places as 'places that have apparently been deserted by philosophy and that are therefore occupied, preoccupied, by empiricism, technocracy, moralism, or religion (indeed, all of them at the same time)' (2002:73-4). This occupation and abandonment comes from a belief, he says, that 'one can no longer defend the old machine (a machine one has even contributed to dismantling)' (2002:74). Derrida's analysis, while based on university teaching, is compatible with the observations that I have made about the implementation of new managerialism in schools (Davies *et al*, 1996). But the abandonment of the philosophies that are accomplished by particular teaching practices and that are developed out of philosophical commitments are, even when one has been critical of them, not so easy to abandon, even if teachers wish to do so. New managerialism's requirements must be managed, and held in tension with what teachers know and accomplish in their everyday practices. Teachers cannot become automatons who parrot the new practices dictated by the phallogocentric practices driven by new managerialism's passion for empiricism, technocracy and moralism, since the teaching enterprise requires much more of them than that. The specific requirements of evidence-based practice can only exist as one of the heterogeneous forces acting on teachers. Their philosophies of teaching, even if apparently erased, will nonetheless be visible in the palimpsest of meaning making and practices that make up classroom practice.

The importance of critique and debate is fundamental to the kind of teaching that might be called professional. This is particularly true as successive world leaderships move to the right and occupy a space devoid of any considerations other than the plays of power and economy. And while it is true that teaching exists as a palimpsest of competing and agonistic discourses, and that one discourse is unlikely to completely dominate teachers' thinking, the potential conflict between ethical reflections and managerialism's agenda is a dangerous one, if only because of managerialism's power to eclipse other discourses (Dennis, 1995) and to both normalise its practices and to silence dissent.

A first and necessary step in counteracting the force of any discourse is to recognise its constitutive power, its capacity to become hegemonic, 'to 'saturate' our very consciousness, so that the ... world we see and interact with, and the commonsense interpretations we put on it, become the world *tout court*, the only world' (Apple, 1979:5). By denaturalising new managerialism, by making its assumptions and mechanisms visible, we open up the possibility of new cultural narratives or collective stories with transformative potential (Richardson, 1990:25-26). [...] If and when we dismantle new managerialism and recuperate the resources that are currently ploughed into surveillance and control, we will have to find creative ways to recuperate the social and our places in it. This cannot mean a return to some idyllic dreamed-of past, since the faults of the past were what we have been caught up in moving beyond. We must turn our collective minds to active contemplation of just what a post-new-managerialist society might look like. Just what are the collective stories we might tell ourselves about this period of our history and about why and how it is another world that we want to live in?

Source: Davies, B. (2003) 'Death to critique and dissent? The policies and practices of new managerialism and of 'evidence-based Practice', *Gender and Education*, vol. 15, no. 1, pp. 91-103, reprinted by permission of the publisher, Taylor & Francis Ltd, http://www.tandfonline.com

References

Apple, M. (1979) *Ideology and Curriculum,* London, Routledge and Kegan Paul

Blunkett, D. (2000) Influence or irrelevance: can social science improve government? *Research Intelligence,* 71, pp.12-21

Davies, B. (2000) Troubling gender, troubling academe, University Structures, Knowledge Production and Gender Construction Conference, University of Copenhagen, March

Davies, B. and Hunt, R, (2000) Classroom competencies and marginal positionings, in: Davies, B. *A Body of Writing 1989-1999,* Walnut Creek, AltaMira Press

Davies, B. (1996) *Power/Knowledge/Desire: changing school organisation and management practices,* Canberra, Department of Employment, Education and Youth Affairs

Davies, H.T.O., Nutley, S.M. and Smith, P.C. (eds) (2000) *What Works? Evidence-based Policy and Practice in the Public Services,* Bristol, Policy Press

Dennis, D. (1995) Brave new reductionism: TQM as ethnocentrism, *Education Policy Analysis Archives,* 3(9)

Derrida, J. (2002) Who's afraid of philosophy? (trans. Jan Plug), Stanford, CA, Stanford University Press

Foucault, M. (1977) *Discipline and Punish: the birth of the prison,* New York, Vintage

Foucault, M. (1980) *Power/Knowledge: selected interviews and other writings. 1972-1977,* New York, Pantheon

Grundy, S. (1993) Educational leadership as emancipatory praxis, in: J. Blackmore and J. Kenway (eds) *Gender Matters in Educational Administration and Policy* (London, Falmer Press)

Hammersley, M. (2001) Some questions about evidence-based practice in education, Annual Conference of the British Educational Research Association, Leeds, September

Honan, E. (2001) (Im)Plausibilities: a rhizo-textual analysis of the Queensland English Syllabus, PhD thesis, James Cook University, Townsville

Laws, C. and Davies, B. (2000) Poststructuralist theory in practice: working with 'behaviourally disturbed' children, in: B. Davies, *A Body of Writing 1989-1999,* Walnut Creek, AltaMira Press

Richardson, L. (1990) *Writing Strategies. Reaching Diverse Audiences,* Newbury Park, CA, Sage

Rose, N. (1999) *Powers of Freedom,* Cambridge, Cambridge University' Press

Schmelzer, M. (1993) Panopticism and postmodern pedagogy, in: J. Caputo and M. Yount (eds) *Foucault and the Critique of Institutions,* University Park, PA, Pennsylvania State University' Press

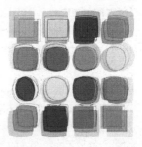

Chapter 18

Early childhood education as an evolving 'community of practice' or as lived 'social reproduction': Researching the 'taken-for-granted'

Marilyn Fleer

Introduction

[...] we must become reflective with regard to our own discourses of learning and to their effects on the ways we design for learning. (Wenger, 1998:9)

Early childhood education has developed a specialised discourse to allow individuals within the profession to communicate effectively about all matters associated with the design and implementation of learning programmes for children from birth to eight years. Yet have we locked ourselves into a self-perpetuating set of values and practices that makes it difficult to move thinking forward? Have we positioned ourselves so strongly within the rhetoric of the profession that it is difficult to introduce new ideas, or indeed, think of 'other ways of doing things?'

Our profession, with its own codes of practice, its own discourse and its own theoretical perspectives, has built itself into an institution that has taken on a life of its own. Anecdotal evidence suggests that our specialised field will only allow newcomers in when they have mastered the language and have understood the codes of practice. From time to time our profession has been criticised for being misunderstood or precious or for grounding itself in practices (eg. play-based programmes) that mean very little to anyone outside the profession. Indeed, it is difficult for anyone to communicate effectively within the profession without the appropriate knowledge of the discourse. Those who do not master the language of the practice are positioned as 'not being early childhood'.

It is timely that we critically examine our own profession and question what we have inherited from our forebears, the histories that we re-enact with each generation of early childhood teachers, and deconstruct the taken-for-granted practices that plague our field. The institution of early childhood education is in need of close examination:

For the structure of human exchanges, there are precise foundations to be discovered in the *institutions* we establish between ourselves and others; institutions which implicate us in one another's activity in such a way that, what we have done together in the past, *commits* us to going on in a certain way in the future. ... The members of an institution need not necessarily have been its originators; they may be second, third, fourth, etc generation members having 'inherited' the institutions from their forebears. And this is an important point, for although there may be an intentional structure to institutional activities, practitioners of institutional forms need have no awareness at all of the reasons for its structure – for them, it is just 'the-way-things-are-done'. The reasons for the institution having one form rather than another are buried in its *history*. (Shotter, cited in Rogoff, 1990:45)

The history we have inherited includes structures such as learning centres or areas within a preschool (eg. block corner), beliefs such as child-centredness, pedagogical practices such as play-based programmes, adult-child interactional patterns such as holding infants to face the adult for maximum communication, and using active questioning with five-year-olds to find out what they know. However, are these taken-for-granted views and beliefs about best practices in early childhood education relevant to all children from all cultures (see Rogoff, 1990, 1998; Chavajay and Rogoff, 1999; Dahlberg *et al*, 1999; Goncu, 1999; Mosier and Rogoff, 2000; Mejia-Arauz, 2001)? Although there are many areas that could be analysed, only four taken-for-granted assumptions are considered in this chapter. They are:

- how is the child situated – inside or external to the adult world?
- the orientation of children to learning
- individual and social orientation
- conversations as 'add-ons' or as part of the adult world.

How is the child situated: inside or external to the adult world?
Many English-speaking countries take great pride in the richness of their communities through their multicultural populations. Child-centredness, so highly valued in Western countries and in early childhood education, can have many different meanings. In Western communities children are placed central to curriculum – their interests, their needs, and their perspectives are privileged in programme planning. This child-centred view is foregrounded in most introductory early childhood textbooks (eg. Arthur *et al*, 1996). [...]

Yet consider the following, as noted by Rogoff (1990):

At home, young children in an age-segregated community such as the US middle class seldom have much chance to participate in the functioning of the household, and may be segregated from human company by the provision of separate bedrooms, security objects, and attractive toys. Middle-class infants are in the usual situation (speaking in worldwide terms) of being entirely alone for as much as 10 hours of a 24-hour-day, managing as best they can to handle their hunger or thirst with a bottle and their need for comforting with a pacifier or blanky or teddy, and working, as Margaret Mead put it, to establish their independence in the transitions to sleep and waking in the night and at naptime. (p124)

Rogoff (1990) argues that in Western communities, infants are not seen as central to everyday life. They are positioned as 'other' to the day-to-day life of families by being put into segregated spaces, and are given toys and materials that do not relate to real-world activities. In creating child-centred programmes in our centres, we have further removed children from the day-to-day world and placed them in an artificial world – one geared to their needs, where they are central, but separated from the real world. We have created an artificial world – with child-sized furniture and home equipment, materials such as thick paint brushes, blocks and puzzles, and an outdoor area with carefully designed climbing equipment for safety. These isolationist practices are common in most Western communities and fit within the child-rearing practices found in Western families for orienting children to their world (see Rogoff, 1990; Goncu, 1999). This perspective contrasts strongly with what takes place in some other cultures:

In societies in which children are integrated in adult activities, the children are ensured a role in the action, at least as close observers. Children are present at most events of interest in the community, from work to recreation to church. ... As infants, they are often carried wherever their mother or older siblings go, and as young children they may do errands and roam the town in their free time, watching whatever is going on. (Rogoff, 1990:124)

In these communities children are situated within the family and community as central beings. They are a part of all the activities of the community. They witness what takes place, they interact with community experiences and they are included within the day-to-day adult world. This approach to situating children within the adult world does reveal the inadequacies of a Western view of child-centredness. The child is already embedded within the community. These communities do not have the need to artificially centre the child to give importance to their role in the community – as many from the West must do, since they already situate the child outside the community. 'Child embeddedness' is a richer and more sophisticated concept than the term 'childcentredness'. [...]

What is important is the reconsideration of the way we have organised the spaces and the way we have created traditional areas such as the block corner, the home corner or the outdoor area. Much recognition for new ways of thinking about our [Australian]early childhood centres has taken place in recent years as a result of perspectives gained from Reggio Emilia (Edwards *et al*, 1998; Giudici *et al*, 2001).

Within this different cultural orientation to learning, there are three important differences. Firstly, the boundary of the learning environment extends well into the community – indeed, the centres were created with a community orientation in mind; secondly, the spaces within the centres do not follow the traditional early childhood environment; and thirdly, the equipment and materials available to children are real, representing what is available in the adult world. Our Froebel-inspired kindergartens have served a useful purpose for many generations of children. It is timely that other ways of thinking about and planning for children's learning are needed – ways that feature the diversity of cultures that represent Australia.

The orientation of children to learning

One day when my eight-year-old daughter was watching some girls her age play a game in the house where we were staying, she turned to the [Inuk] mother who spoke English and said:

Anna: How do I play this game? Tell me what to do. What are the rules?

Inuk Mother: (gently) Watch them and you'll see how it goes.

Anna: I don't know how to learn by watching, can't you tell me?

Inuk Mother: You'll be able to know by watching.

(Crago, cited in Mejia-Arauz *et al*, 2001:5)

Early childhood education is grounded in a belief that 'doing' is very important. Contributions from Piaget, Montessori, Froebel and others have instilled within our discourse the notion that learning occurs through the manipulation of concrete materials. We organise environments so children can choose materials and actively learn through blocks, construction kits, puzzles, and dress-ups with miniature home equipment. In centre-based care, we find the adult's role involves a significant amount of talking to children as they handle these materials. However, there is one interactional pattern that takes on less importance, and that is the modelling by adults and the corresponding observation by children. For example, in a recent study by Fleer and Richardson (2003), an analysis of twelve months of documentation collected by early childhood teachers indicated that staff recorded child behaviours in isolation from adults. No teacher modelling was recorded and only a limited amount of non-verbal interaction featured in the documentation. The traditional early childhood practice of observing children had privileged an individual orientation and did not include what adults were doing or saying.

However, as the teachers framed their observations from a sociocultural perspective (following professional development), they noted an increase in observations featuring adult modelling, extensive interactions between staff and children, and deliberate planning for working within the children's zone of proximal development. The reframing of staff perspectives in taking observations of children allowed more non-verbal communication to feature.

Learning within an observational context was no longer silenced as teachers were looking for and recording from a broader sociocultural perspective.

In many cultures adults and children learn by observation. In Rogoff's (1990) meta-analysis of the cross-cultural literature in this area, she stated:

the method of learning to use the foot loom in a weaving factory in Guatemala is for the learner (an adult) to sit beside a skilled weaver for some weeks, simply observing, asking no questions, and receiving no explanations. The learner may fetch a spool of thread from time to time for the weaver, but does not begin to weave until, after weeks of observation, the learner feels competent to begin. At that point, the apprentice has become a skilled weaver simply by watching and by attending to whatever demonstration the experienced weaver has provided. (p129) [...]

Fleer and Williams-Kennedy (2002) found that learning through observation was an important learning tool for the indigenous families who participated in the study. The families had videotaped observational learning and discussed their documented video recording as evidence of its importance, noting that 'doing' was more important than 'telling'. [...]

Since children are embedded within the community, they have numerous opportunities to observe real-world activities that are important in that community. As observers of ongoing and frequent community activities, they have plenty of time to watch. They have many opportunities to participate in aspects of community activity, and they have many family and community members on hand to support their efforts. The full performance of the community activity and the repetition of these performances provide time and space for children to observe and develop observational skills (Collier, 1988; Briggs, 1991; Lipka, 1991; Stairs, 1991; Chavajay and Rogoff, 1999; Fleer and Williams-Kennedy, 2002). In this way it is possible to see how observation is not necessarily a passive and therefore less useful approach to learning for young children. For some children, learning by observation is very important in their culture. To foreground active exploration through activity and adult narration would mean some children's modes of learning are not catered for in early childhood education – in effect they are silenced. [...]

At present there is a disjunction between children and communities who value observation as a vehicle for learning, and the beliefs and practices in early childhood education in many Western communities. [...] We need to move from a 'one approach to learning model', to a 'many approaches to learning model' in early childhood education.

Individual and social orientation

Autonomy (independence, personal agency, free will) and responsibility (cooperation with a small group, interdependence) are often treated as conflicting or even opposite (Mosier and Rogoff, 2000):

Ethnographic research suggests that in some communities, the goal is autonomous responsibility, in which individuals choose by their own will to cooperate with others – a different concept than the polarity of freedom from others or obedience to authority. Rather than autonomy and cooperation being in opposition, autonomy with personal responsibility for decision making can be compatible with values of interdepenence and cooperation among group members (Kim and Wibowo, 1996; Lamphere, 1977; White and LeVine, 1986; Oerter, Oerter, Agostiani, Paradise, 1994; Yau and Smetana, 1996) (p.3)

Early childhood education has always been geared to focusing on the individual child. We observe the child, we document what we observe (gather data), we analyse that data and then we make inferences which inform our planning for particular individuals. We have prided ourselves in concentrating upon the individual (Arthur *et al*, 1996). Yet not all communities value this focus (Rogoff, 1990). For instance:

Marquesan (South Pacific) mothers actively arrange infants' social interactions with others; if babies appear to get self-absorbed, mothers interrupt and urge attention to the broader social environment. (Rogoff, 1990:133)

and:

in Japan, autonomy and cooperation are compatible qualities that both fall under the definition of the term 'sunao'. (Mosier and Rogoff, 2000:4)

Fleer and Williams-Kennedy (2002) note in their research that some indigenous communities from Australia value a social orientation and find the individual focus in schools and centres to be very difficult for their children. [...]

As represented in Western education, an individualistic approach that encourages children to become independent workers actively works against the culture of some children. As such, thought needs to be given to fostering interdependence among children. [...]

Group membership is more highly valued than being an individual for some indigenous communities in Australia. It is part of the basic fabric of early childhood education to work with individual children's sense of self and praise their efforts in this process. Yet for some children, this works against the importance they place on being a group member. Excelling above other group members and having this highlighted by the teacher is culturally inappropriate for some cultures in Australia. [...]

Many of our interactional patterns in early childhood are tied up with observing the individual and moving thinking and development forward (Arthur *et al*, 1996). Yet for some children this effort is misguided. Our focus for these children should be how we can build upon the interdependence and social obligation that have been developed so thoughtfully in these communities. For example:

In everyday activities, (Marquesan) babies are usually held facing outward and encouraged to interact with and attend to others (especially slightly older siblings) instead of interacting with their mothers. (Rogoff, 1990:133)

The child-rearing practices of Marquesan families contrast with those espoused within many Western communities. Most child development books and curriculum documentation directed to carers who are working with infants in many English-speaking countries promote the view that babies should be held facing the adult who is holding them. This would be deemed as very important and an appropriate practice for communicating effectively and responding appropriately to infants (eg. Fleer and Linke, 2002). Yet this approach to adult-infant interaction is based upon a belief that an individual orientation is important (Rogoff, 1990), whilst for Marquesan families being oriented toward the group is more important. [...]

There is a growing body of literature that is beginning to question whether Western early childhood assumptions should be viewed as universal (Dahlberg *et al*, 1999). In deconstructing assumptions in early childhood education, how do we reconstruct in ways that reflect the diversity of multicultural Australia? How can we change our orientation from an individualistic perspective to a more socially focused view? Changing early childhood discourse so that it is more inclusive of other worldviews is an important beginning point. For instance, talking about planning for individuals should also be accompanied by planning for interdependence. We could begin by reappraising written material such as central curriculum, state-based curriculum, national accreditation documentation, early childhood textbooks for graduate and undergraduate students, licensing requirements and legislation documentation, teacher handbooks, centre and department websites, teacher education course material, centre policy statements, professional associations documents – these are but a few of the commonly available materials that all privilege an individual orientation in Australia today. In order to change public documentation to be more inclusive in its language, many conversations are needed. These conversations provide the beginning point for examining issues of diversity at a fundamental rather than a superficial level.

Conversations as 'add-ons' or as part of the real world?

If we go back to earlier arguments about how many Western families isolate their infants by placing them in their own bedroom, in their own cot and provide them with pacifiers, we can see that it is necessary to organise conversational opportunities during wakeful periods. If we now also consider how the child is generally not part of the adult world – but how, rather, a child's world with toys and friends is created, we can see how as children grow older further conversational opportunities must also be created. Rogoff (1990) has suggested that:

In cultures that adapt situations to children (as in middle-class US families), caregivers simplify their talk, negotiate meaning with children, cooperate with them in building propositions, and respond to their verbal and nonverbal initiations. (p123)

As part of creating these conversational opportunities, particular conversational genres are produced. One of the distinctive features of these interactional patterns is the use of questioning. These conversational patterns tend to be mirrored in many early childhood centres and schools. For instance, many early childhood teachers (see Fleer and Williams-Kennedy, 2002):

- ask questions about things to which they already know the answers
- ask questions to find out what children know
- ask questions to keep the conversation going
- ask questions as a social greeting (eg. how are you?)
- ask questions when they really don't want an answer (rhetorical questions)
- use questioning as a link between ideas and activities in the classroom or centre
- use questioning as a control technique
- use a variety of question types – (eg. why, when, how, who)
- expect children to ask questions and to know how to do this.

The last point reflects a belief that all children learn these conversational patterns in their home or community prior to beginning early childhood education. However, conversational patterns do not necessarily evolve in this way for all children (Goncu, 1999). As Rogoff (1990) stated:

In cultures that adapt children to the normal situations of the society (as in Kaluli New Guinea and Samoan families), caregivers model unsimplified utterances for children to repeat to a third party, direct them to notice others, and build interaction around circumstances to which the caregivers wish the children to respond. (p123)

In Australia, some indigenous people have challenged the use of questioning as part of the conversational genre valued in early childhood education. For instance:

My grandmother she believes you don't ask questions, you should just watch and listen. In some communities you only watch and listen. In some communities it is bad manners to ask too many questions. I was always taught by my grandmother that you don't ask questions, you watch and you learn; you don't question things; copying rather than asking questions (Laura). (Fleer and Williams-Kennedy, 2002:57)

The privileging of a question-based pattern of interaction in early childhood centres and schools has meant that some children are faced with the task of not just learning the content, but also the codes for participating effectively in the learning practices to have access to the content. Vicky explains:

When I was at school, I didn't learn the things I wanted to learn because I was too afraid to ask the questions or didn't know the questions to ask. I never learnt the things I wanted to know; if I was worried about spelling or reading or something like that, I never asked or questioned as a child; so I want Gregory [five year old son] to be able to learn things by asking questions (Vicky). (Fleer and Williams-Kennedy, 2002:57)

Hill *et al* (1998), in citing Delpit (1988), demonstrate the importance of not only making these schooling processes explicit, but actively teaching them:

[...] Delpit (1988) states that all students must be taught the codes needed to participate fully in mainstream life, not by being forced to do mundane pointless exercises but in meaningful endeavours. [...]

We can no longer assume that the taken-for-granted practice of asking questions should be privileged. Being aware of the particular interactional style normally exhibited by the teacher is the first step to realising inclusivity. The second step is to think beyond one interactional style and begin to develop a range of ways of interacting – a diversity of ways that reflect the diversity of the children. Privileging one way of interacting in effect silences other ways of interacting.

Maintaining the status quo or moving early childhood education forward?

In many English-speaking countries, early childhood education has developed routines, practices, rituals, artefacts, symbols, conventions, stories and histories. Many of our taken-for-granted practices have become traditions. Wenger (1998) used the term 'reified' to explain how these traditional practices become named, and a specialist and truncated discourse emerges. Yet what has become valued within the profession of early childhood education is essentially a Western view of childhood. We have assumed that:

- notions of high quality 'Western' interactional patterns between adults and infants are universal (that is, we all hold our babies to maximise adult-child interaction) (Rogoff, 1990)
- the best way to learn is through activity and not sitting and watching – since watching is considered a passive activity (Rogoff, 1998)
- question-asking by children and teachers is an important technique for learning for children (Mejia-Arauz *et al*, 2001).

We have created educational outcomes for early childhood education based on what has historically been perceived as needed for Western children, such as child-centredness, to compensate for the fact that infants and children are not embedded within community practices. We have created conversational opportunities and patterns of interaction, such as the use of questioning, to compensate for children's disembeddedness. We have channelled our efforts and discourse into an individualistic framework at the expense of interdependence, thus disenfranchising some children and positioning them as failures when they do not succeed on their own. Our early childhood community of practice that we have inherited from our forebears requires some reanalysis.

Ironically, we can use the notion of communities of practice as a vehicle for this process of reanalysis since it is also a useful analytical tool:

For many of us, the concept of learning immediately conjures up images of classrooms, training sessions, teachers, textbooks, homework, and exercises. Yet in our experience, learning is an integral part of our everyday lives. It is part of our participation in our communities and organisations. The problem is not that we do not know this, but rather that we do not have very systematic ways of talking about this familiar experience. (Wenger, 1998:8; emphasis added)

Communities of practice as a theoretical tool help illuminate how the taken-for-grantedness of early childhood education takes place:

What is taken for granted fades into the background – but the tacit is no more individual and natural than what we make explicit to each other. Common sense is only commonsensical because it is sense held in common. Communities of practice are the prime context in which we work out common sense through mutual engagement. (Wenger, 1998:47)

Meaning in communities of practice is possible only when ideas are jointly understood and enacted within a particular community. Meaning does not reside in an individual or even in printed matter, but, rather, meaning exists through a dynamic process of living in the world. Early childhood curriculum cannot exist unless a community gives it meaning and brings it into existence. [...]

Wenger (1998) warns that often the reification process results in slogans – such as 'Children learn through play' – which simplify complex understandings and hide broader meanings. As such, these terms become embedded within our community of practice, transcending time and cultures, forming part of our histories. For example, in thinking about children learning through play, what sort of play are we talking about and what sort of learning do we think happens? Have the reified ideas inherent in early childhood education reduced our profession to a community of practice built upon many slogans and with little capacity to reinvent itself? Have our reified and very precious ideals masked their culture-specific beginnings? Can we think differently about early childhood education and critically examine existing reified cultural tools?

In order to move forward, we need to look back and analyse what we have inherited. We also need to reify new cultural tools, such as child embeddedness, and give these terms meaning so that we can think differently and change our community of practice. When we do this, we see that we no longer reproduce ourselves in the next generation of teachers, but, rather, we speak openly about the cultural tools we are using and model the analysis required to ensure that those tools are still appropriate for the next generation of children attending our early childhood centres. In this sense we move beyond social reproduction.

Source: Fleer, M. (2003) 'Early Childhood Education as an Evolving 'Community of Practice' or as Lived 'Social Reproduction': researching the 'taken-for-granted", *Contemporary Issues in Early Childhood*, 4(1), 64-79. http://dx.doi.org/10.2304/ciec.2003.4.1.7

References

Arthur, L., Beecher, B., Dockett, S., Farmer, S. and Death, E. (1996) *Programming and Planning in Early Childhood Settings*, 2nd edn. Sydney: Harcourt Brace.

Briggs, J.L. (1991) Expecting the Unexpected: Canadian Inuit training for an experimental lifestyle, *Ethos*, 19, pp259-87.

Chavajay, P. and Rogoff, B. (1999) Cultural Variation in Management of Attention by Children and their Caregivers, *Developmental Psychology*, 35, pp1079-90

Collier, J. Jr (1988) Survival at Rough Rock: a historical overview of Rough Rock Demonstration School, *Anthropology and Education Quarterly*, 19, pp253-69

Dahlberg, G., Moss, P. and Pence, A. (1999) *Beyond Quality in Early Childhood Education and Care: postmodern perspectives*. London: Falmer Press

Edwards, C., Gandini, L. and Forman, G. (1998) *The Hundred Languages of Children. The Regio Emilia Approach – advanced reflections*, 2nd edn. London: Ablex

Fleer, M. and Linke, P. (2002) Babies: good beginnings last forever. *Research in Practice Series*, 6(2), 2nd edn. Canberra: Australian Early Childhood Association

Fleer, M. and Richardson, C. (2003) Collective Mediated Assessment: moving towards a sociocultural approach to assessing children's learning, *Journal of Australian Research in Early Childhood Education*, 10, pp. 41-55

Fleer, M. and Williams-Kennedy, D. (2002) *Building Bridges: researching literacy development for young Indigenous children*. Canberra: Australian Early Childhood Association

Giudici, C., Rinaldi, C. and Krechevsky, M. (2001) *Making Learning Visible: children as individual and group learners*. Reggio Emilia: Reggio Children Sri

Goncu, A. (ed) (1999) *Children's Engagement in the World: sociocultural perspectives*. Cambridge: Cambridge University Press.

Hill, S., Comber, B., Louden, B., Rivalland, J. and Reid, J. (1998) *100 Children Go to School. Connections and Disconnections in Literacy Development in the Year Prior to School and the First Year of School*, vols 1-3. Canberra: Department of Education, Training and Youth Affairs.

Lamphere, L. (1977) *To Run after Them: cultural and social bases of cooperation in a Navajo community*. Tucson: University of Arizona Press.

Lipka, J. (1991) Toward a Culturally Based Pedagogy: a case study of one Yup'ik Eskimo teacher, *Anthropology and Education Quarterly*, 22, pp203-23

Mejia-Arauz, R., Rogoff, B. and Paradise, R. (2001) Cultural Variation in Children's Observation during Demonstration, unpublished paper

Mosier, C.E. and Rogoff, B. (2000) Privileged Treatment of Toddlers: cultural aspects of autonomy and responsibility, unpublished paper

Oerter, R., Oerter, R., Agostiani, H., Kim, H-O. and Wibowo, S. (1996) The Concept of Human Nature in East Asia: etic and emic characteristics, *Culture and Psychology*, 2, pp9-51

Paradise, R. (1994) Interactional Style and Nonverbal Meaning: Mazahua children learning how to be separate-but-together, *Anthropology and Education Quarterly*, 26, pp156-72

Rogoff, B. (1990) *Apprenticeship in Thinking: cognitive development in social context*. New York: Random House

Rogoff, B. (1998) Cognition as a Collaborative Process, in W. Damon (Chief Editor), D. Kuhn and R.S. Siegler (volume eds) *Cognition, Perceptions and Language*, 5th edn, *Handbook of Child Psychology*, pp679-744 New York: John Wiley and Sons.

Stairs, A. (1991) Learning Processes and Teaching Roles in Native Education: cultural base and cultural brokerage, *Canadian Modern Language Review*, 47, pp280-94.

Wenger, E. (1998) *Communities of Practice: learning, meaning and identity*. Cambridge: Cambridge University Press

White, M.L. and LeVine, R.A. (1986) What is an Ii Ko (good child)? in H. Stevenson, H. Azuma and K. Hakuta (eds) *Child Development and Education in Japan*, pp56-62. New York: W.H. Freeman and Co.

Yau, J. and Smetana, J.G. (1996) Adolescent-Parent Conflict among Chinese Adolescents in Hong Kong, *Child Development*, 67, pp1262-1275.

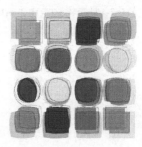

Chapter 19

Even in Sweden? Excluding the included: Some reflections on the consequences of new policies on educational processes and outcomes, and equity in education

Girma Berhanu

A number of educational reforms have been devised and implemented in Sweden in the 1990s, the consequences of which have yet to be mapped out and evaluated. The reforms revolve around the political management of schools, including a decentralisation of school management that empowers municipalities to be in charge of school affairs within their jurisdiction. Marginalisation and segregation of socially disadvantaged and ethnic minority groups has increased. Resultant resource differences have widened among schools and municipalities, and among pupils. The paradox is that all these trends that work against inequity are happening while, at the same time, the rhetoric advocating a school for all and inclusive education have become policy catchwords. As Skidmore (2004) observed, based on his experiences in the UK, inclusion has become a buzzword in educational discourse. Although inclusion has been adopted as a policy goal, to date much of the Swedish debate has amounted to little more than the trading of abstract ideological positions, which has little connection with the daily realities in schools. In practice, the trend may be described as *excluding the included.* [...]

The process of exclusion and marginalisation: Challenges and responses to inclusive education

[...] Sweden has adopted inclusive education as a guiding principle to guarantee equality of access in education to all and also as part of a human rights approach to social relations. The values involved relate to a vision of a whole society, of which education is a part. Issues of social justice, equity, and choice are central to the demands for inclusive education. This vision is concerned with the well-being of all pupils and with making schools welcoming institutions. [...]

Swedish efforts in the past to promote equity through a variety of educational policies have been fascinating. Those early educational policies, including the macropolitical agenda, focused on a social welfare model that has helped diminish the effects of differential social, cultural, and economic backgrounds on outcomes. Studies have also shown that inequalities in Swedish society have diminished over the last century in the sense that the influence of a number of background factors important for educational attainment – parents' class or social position, cultural capital, type of community, and gender – has been reduced (Wildt-Persson and Rosengren, 2001:299). This may be described mainly as the result of a combination of educational policies and welfare policies that have been the central features of the cultural, historical, and political heritage in Nordic societies. The main question is how this critical equity issue can be addressed in a decentralised educational system that was introduced about eighteen years ago.

Many of the social and educational changes made in the early 1990s were dramatic. Observers might ask why there was such a huge shift from the traditional inclusive, collective frame of reference and social justice towards individual rights, parental choice, and market oriented policies. Signs of such changes could be observed already in the late 1980s. But the landmark was the accession to power of the right wing party in 1991 (Coalition government headed by Conservative Carl Bildt during 1991-94). The country was in deep recession and employment rates fell, followed by a sharp decrease in social expenditure and a move towards further socio-economic inequalities. The situation abated in the mid-1990s. In consequence of this political change, however, education was increasingly regarded as a private rather than a public good. Rationales for educational attainment changed from an emphasis on collective values and social community to a focus on individual rights, academic progress, and choice. A new financial system was introduced that essentially moved resource allocation from the national to the local level, combined with a new type of steering and control mechanism (Wildt-Persson and Rosengren, 2001; Englund, 2005; OECD, 2005; Arnesen and Lundahl, 2006; Dahlstedt, 2007). This was not an accidental phenomenon. It is part and parcel of global phenomena in our late modernity (Bauman, 1992), high modernity (Giddens, 1990), and late capitalism, phenomena that are deeply entrenched with values of effectiveness, competition, standardisation, freedom of choice, and increasingly individualist and elitist culture.

The impact of the decentralised educational policy on equity is pervasive. Two studies cited by OECD (2005:17) confirm that:

... educational expenditure per student (measured in terms of money or teacher density) has fallen rather dramatically during the 1990s – followed by a slight increase after the turn of the millennium. According to Björklund *et al* (2004), the teacher/student ratio has decreased by 18.7 per cent during the 1990s. Whether this can be directly attributed to the decentralisation or to the impact of the economic downturn of the 1990s remains an open question. (Björklund, Edin, Frederiksson, and Krueger, 2004; Ahlin and Mörk, 2005 cited in OECD 2005)

The number of pupils placed in educational programmes for learning for disabled students has increased. In general, the number of children defined as special needs has shown a steady increase. In addition, there has been a dramatic increase in the number of private schools. Variances between schools and municipalities and student achievement including segregation and persistent socio-economic differences among the school populations have been the post decentralisation policy phenomenon. All the indicators of the National Agency for Education compiled through evaluations, case studies, and supervision, testify to this fact. This situation has worsened since the Conservative party took power in 2006. One may question whether decentralisation and equity are contradictory or incompatible. One might also argue that it is the Conservative party that is against equity and for differentiation, as always, rather than something connected to decentralisation. Decentralisation is part of a policy package that increases differences in internal and external performances, but it doesn't cause them (Berhanu, 2009).

It is clear that there are differences between municipalities and large differences in the type of provision they have made. Most of the reports on inclusion practices indicate that inclusion is happening. However, up-to-date and reliable time series data and data on the number of pupils who are included in the ordinary classroom, and data on the occurrence of exclusionary special units (classes) are lacking. Even the definition or construction of special needs is shifting and is fluid. There seems to be no effective mechanism installed to monitor inclusive/exclusionary processes at regional and national levels (see, eg. Heimdahl Mattsson, 2006; Nilholm, 2006a), which makes it difficult to document equity in inclusive education.

While the influence of a number of background factors significant to educational attainment, such as parental social position, cultural capital, type of community, and gender, may have diminished over the last century (Jonsson, 1993; Wildt-Persson and Rosengren, 2001), there is cause for concern for how long such declines will persist, and caution is needed if the traditional model is to survive. While there are signs that inclusive education as envisaged in the Salamanca declaration is being exercised at different levels, gaps in research and follow-ups are most noticeable in this area. [...]

Ethnic minority and socially disadvantaged students

It is obvious that the education system has come under serious pressure during the past two decades due to massive migration. This exogenous shock has changed the ethnic landscape and composition dramatically and has ushered Sweden into an era of multiculturalism and globalisation. On the negative side, this rapid demographic

TRANSFORMING PRACTICE: CRITICAL ISSUES IN EQUITY, DIVERSITY AND EDUCATION

change has also brought with it ethnic segregation and inequalities, particularly in large cities, on top of already existing inequalities between municipalities and social groups due to decentralisation and competition. This presents a major challenge to policymakers in terms of social integration generally, and educational inclusion specifically unless targeted positive discriminatory measures are put in place. Such measures, however, are anathema to Swedish policy principles (OECD, 2005).

A recent report by Gustafsson (2006:93) concludes that between 1992 and 2000 a consistent and linear increase occurred in school segregation in relation to immigration background, educational background, and grades. A national tracking system enables observation of variable achievement among groups of students. Students with foreign backgrounds receive lower average grades than do their peers, fewer qualify for higher education, and they have a higher dropout rate from upper-secondary education. There are also differences in achievement between girls and boys. Girls receive higher average grades in the majority of subjects in compulsory and upper-secondary school (OECD, 2005; Barnomsorg och skola i siffror, 2000, cited in Wildt-Persson and Rosengren, 2001:306). Results from national examinations in compulsory and upper-secondary schools demonstrate this difference in the subjects of Swedish and, to some extent, English, but show no difference in results in mathematics (*ibid*).

Oswald, Coutinho and Best (2000) proposed two general hypotheses on the phenomenon of disproportionality, the first one being tied to real differences in socio-economic outcomes between social groups, that is, that some groups (or minority students) are deeply disadvantaged (in social and economic experiences), marginalised, susceptible to diseases, and are more likely to have disabilities. The second hypothesis is that a significant portion of the over-representation problem may be a function of inappropriate interpretation of ethnic and cultural differences as disabilities (p2). There is sound evidence to support the second hypothesis with regard to disproportionality in Sweden (see also Dyson and Gallannaugh, 2008, for a similar observation in England).

While there is no conclusive evidence to suggest that over-representation of minority pupils or pupils with immigrant backgrounds or socially disadvantaged groups of students in special educational placements is nationwide, the phenomenon can be identified in large cities where there are concentrations of immigrants. The over-representation is not a new phenomenon. What is new is that new forms of exclusionary measures are taking place while the force of rhetoric toward inclusive measures is gaining substantial momentum in the pedagogical discourse. [...]

Evaluation and diagnostics procedures
[...] The proportion of Swedish pupils who fail in core subjects when leaving compulsory education and face problems finalising their upper-secondary education

has increased steadily. The number of young people who are more or less permanently left in a no-man's-land between education and work is high (SOU, 2003:92, in Arnesen and Lundahl, 2006; Skolverket, 2004).

According to Bel Habib (2001), who used quantitative methods to map out the magnitude of the problem of over-representation, the majority of the Swedish students (native/white Swedes) in special schools have clear, visible, medically proven or concretised functional handicaps, whereas the researcher, working from diagnosis and referral files, found that minority students who are assigned to these special schools were categorised in diffused, vague, symptom-based and pedagogical-related terms such as concentration and behavioural problems, speech and language difficulties, unspecified poor talent, or developmental retardation.

As is the case elsewhere (see, eg. Losen and Orfield, 2002; Harry and Klinger, 2006; Dyson and Gallannaugh, 2008), the special educational placement pattern for ethnic minority pupils is that these students are fairly represented (or in other words their representation is comparable to their number in the general society) in low incidence disabilities (eg. visual, hearing, multiple, and physical disabilities) and they are over-represented in high incidence disabilities (eg. emotional/behavioural disorder and learning disabilities). That means the observed over-representation is in subjective cognitive disability categories rather than in hard/visible disability categories (see Losen and Orfield, 2002). [...]

Foucault (1979, 1984) consistently argued that institutions, in this case schools, function to maintain and even advance the practice of normality and deviance through instruments of power and knowledge relations that not only exclude a segment of the student population but also serve as instruments to construct identities and labels such as students with special educational needs (see also Allan, 1995).

The analysis indicates how the structure of schools as organisations creates special educational needs rather than differences or diversity between individual pupils. The lack of holistic, contextual, and ecological perspectives is visible because the measures used to send these children to special schools emerge from being entirely concerned only with pupils' cognitive, emotional, and pathological problems. [...]

Both the statistical and qualitative analyses, compiled in Losen and Orfield (2002:xviii) suggest similar observations in the USA as in Sweden, although the statistical figures and the magnitude of the problem in these two countries vary considerably. These American studies suggest that racial, ethnic, and gender differences in special educational placements are due to many complex interacting factors, including unconscious racial bias on the part of school authorities, large resource inequalities that run along lines of race and class, unjustifiable reliance on IQ and other evaluation tools, educators' inappropriate responses to the pressures of high-stakes testing, and power differentials between minority parents and school officials.

The problem surrounding the over-representation of ethnic minorities in special educational arrangements in Sweden is complex, and some of the evidence presented here and in Berhanu's article (2008) also points to problems surrounding the home environment, including poverty; sociocultural related problems, family factors, and language problems; the lack of parental participation in decision making and the huge power distance between parents and school authority; institutional intransigence and prejudices; and large resource inequalities that run along lines of race and class. [...]

Future studies in Sweden should systematically evaluate the following area of problem or research questions (see Losen and Orfield, 2002):

– What is the chain of events that sets certain students, from various backgrounds, in certain school districts, on the road to special education placement or special schools?
– Is there one or many patterns?
– By what criteria do those responsible for special education placements evaluate students for these programmes? (see Dagens Nyheter, 2007; Rosenqvist, 2007)
– How is this cycle initiated and how can it be stopped?
– What are the students actually like?
– What are the criteria for referral and special educational placements?
– What is the parental role or role of culture in this process, and how do parents perceive their responsibility?
– To what extent do social factors override (special) educational efforts intended to rectify school failures?

There are some signs that at least the school authorities are aware of the problem. The public media and several researchers have dealt with the phenomenon of disproportionality, and that has led to increased awareness of the problem. Data from a recent study do not support the existence of disproportionality at a national level, although it does appear to be concentrated in large cities. The distribution of disproportionality suggests the dubious nature of the diagnostic procedure and the assessment culture (Rosenqvist, 2007).

The road forward
The fragmentation of educational policymaking that we have witnessed in the past two decades has particularly affected already vulnerable groups such as the disabled, ethnic minority students, and socially disadvantaged segments of the population. On the basis of a large number of indicators, we can presume that over the next decade Swedish society will become increasingly multiethnic and multilingual, and the number of disadvantaged children will increase substantially. [...]

The challenge in Sweden is to meet these changes and still guarantee equivalence in the education system. Sweden has developed a broad follow-up system and quality indicators in order to monitor changes within the system. However, the indicator systems do not specifically show the nature, extent, and processes of inclusive and exclusionary processes within the regular system. Since a return to the former centralised management system is unlikely, constant flow of monitoring, evaluation, and inspection, and a stronger partnership between the central system and the local level, between parents and schools, as well as between municipalities, must be established in order to mitigate variance and inequalities. Stronger central government authority over educational priority funding will be critical for at-risk groups, either in the form of targeted central budgets, or in terms of regulatory power over municipal education outlays (OECD, 2005).

Sweden is a wealthy, highly educated, and healthy society with one of the highest standard of living in the world. In comparison even to many well-developed countries, Sweden is one of the leading countries at successfully combining equity and social inclusion with high economic efficiency. The tradition of universalism and comprehensiveness with minimisation of streaming and tracking has been the hallmark of the Swedish education system. Redistribution policies underpinned by high levels of taxation and public spending still appear to have strong social consensus. Sweden has, however, undergone a dramatic transformation within the past two decades. The changes are framed within neoliberal philosophies that place greater emphasis on devolution, marketisation (driven by principles of cost containment and efficiency), competition, standardisation, individual choices and rights, development of new profiles within particular school units, and other factors that potentially work against the values of diversity, equity and inclusion. [...]

The justification for inclusive education is based in part on the ideals of social justice and the fact that the social justice goals and inclusive education are inextricably intertwined. However, social justice views in inclusion discourses vary. Social justice views can be classified as individualistic or communitarian; both perspectives permeate the discourses on inclusion (Artiles, Harris-Murri and Rostenberg, 2006: 262). The authors argue that we must move from a traditional social justice discourse in inclusive education (individualistic/communitarian) to a transformative model of social justice. The values involved relate to a vision of a whole society, of which education is a part. Issues of social justice, equity, and choice are central to the demands for inclusive education. This vision concerns the well-being of all pupils, and making schools welcoming institutions through, for instance, measures examining ideological and historical assumptions about difference, critiquing marginalisation, debunking merit-based cultures, deliberating/negotiating programme goals, tools, and practices, and so on (Artiles *et al*, 2006). I also believe that a fundamental change in our educational system and core of educational practice may mitigate the dilemmas. As Elmore (1996) succinctly put it, this core of practice includes:

How teachers understand the nature of knowledge and the student's role in learning, and how these ideas about knowledge and learning are manifested in teaching and class work. The 'core' also includes structural arrangements of schools, such as the physical layout of classrooms, student grouping practices, teachers' responsibilities for groups of students, and relations among teachers in their work with students, as well as processes for assessing student learning and communicating it to students, teachers, parents, administrators, and other interested parties. (p23)

Source: Berhanu, G. (2010), 'Even in Sweden? Excluding the included: Some reflections on the consequences of new policies on educational processes and outcomes, and equity in education', *International Journal of Special Education*, vol. 25, no. 3.

References

Allan, J. (1995) *Pupils with Special Educational Needs in Mainstream Schools: A Foucauldian Analysis of Discourses*. University of Stirling, Department of Education

Arnesen, A. and Lundahl, L. (2006) Still social and democratic? Inclusive education policies in the Nordic welfare states. *Scandinavian Journal of Educational Research*, 50(3), 285-300

Artiles, A., Kozleski, E., Dorn, S. and Christensen, C. A. (2006). Learning in inclusive education research: Re-mediating theory and methods with a transformative agenda. Review of Research in Education, 30: 65-108

Artiles, A.J., Harris-Murri, N. and Rostenberg, D. (2006). Inclusion as social justice: Critical notes on discourses, assumptions and the road ahead. *Theory into Practice*, 45, 260-68

Bauman, Z. (1992) *Intimations of post modernity*. London: Routledge

Bel Habib, I. (2001) *Elever med invandrarbakgrund i särskolan: specialpedagogik eller disciplinär makt*. [Pupils with immigrant background in education for intellectually disabled]. Kristianstad: Högskolan i Kristianstad. Enheten för kompetensutveckling.

Berhanu, G. (2006) *Framgångsfaktorer för delaktighet och jämlikhet*. [Favourable factors to enhance participation and equality]. Specialpedagogiska institutet: Sweden (Monograph)

Berhanu, G. (2008) Ethnic minority pupils in Swedish schools: Some trends in overrepresentation of minority pupils in special educational programs. *International Journal of Special Education*, 23(3), 17-29

Berhanu, G. (2009) Challenges and Responses to Inclusive Education in Sweden: Mapping issues of equity, participation and democratic values. Presented at Research Forum: A Comparative Analysis of Equity in Inclusive Education. Centre for Advanced Study in the Behavioural Sciences (CASBS), Stanford University. Palo Alto, California, USA, February 1-5, 2009

Björklund, A., Edin, P.A., Frederiksson, P., and Krueger, A. (2004). Education, equality and efficiency. An analysis of Swedish school reforms during the 1990s. IFAU Report No. 1

Dagens Nyheter (2007) Invadrarelever skrivs felaktigt in i särskolan[Immigrant pupils are wrongly placed in special schools] Tuesday, June 12, 2007. (*The Swedish Daily*)

Dahlstedt, M. (2007) "I val(o)frihetens spår: Segregation, differentiering och två decennier av skolreformer", [In the direction of choice and freedom: Segregation, differentiating and two decades of school reforms]. In *Pedagogisk Forskning i Sverige*, 12 [1]; 20-38

Dyson, A. and Gallannaugh, F. (2008) Disproportionality in special needs education in England. *Journal of Special Education*, 42(1), 36-46

Elmore, R. F. (1996) Getting to scale with good educational practices. *Harvard Educational Review*, 66(1) 1-25

Englund, T. (2005) The discourse on equivalence in Swedish education policy. *Journal of Education Policy*, 20(1), 39-57

Foucault, M. (1979) On governmentality. *Ideology and Consciousness*, 6, 5-21

Giddens, A. (1990) *The contradictions of modernity*. Cambridge: Polity Press

Gustafsson, J.-E. (2006) *Barns utbildningssituation. Bidrag till ett kommunalt barnindex* [Children's educational situation. Contribution to a local child index; in Swedish]. Stockholm, Sweden: Rädda Barnen.

Harry, B. and Klinger, J. (2006) *Why Are so Many Minority Students in Special Education? Understanding Race and Disability in Schools*. New York: Teachers College Press, Columbia University

Heimdahl Mattsson, E. (2006) *Mot en inkluderande skola*. [Towards inclusive school] Stockholm: HLS Förlag

Jonsson, J. O. (1993) Persisting inequalities in Sweden. In Y. Shavit and H. P. Blossfeld (eds), *Persistent inequality. Changing educational attainment in thirteen countries* (pp101-132). Boulder: Westview Press

Losen, D. J. and Orfield, G. (2002) *Racial inequity in special education*. Cambridge, MA: Harvard Education Press

Nilholm, C. (2006) *Including av elever 'I behov av särskilt stöd' – vad betyder det och vad vet vi?* [Including children with special needs – what does it mean? what do we know?]. Myndigheten för Skolutveckling: Forskning i fokus nr. 28

OECD (2005) *Equity in education: Thematic review*. Sweden, Country Note. Paris: OECD (Organisation for Economic Cooperation and Development)

Oswald, D. P., Coutinho, M.J., and Best, A. M. (2000, November 17) Community and school predictors of overrepresentation of minority children in special education. Paper prepared for the Harvard University Civil Rights Project Conference on Minority Issues in Special Education, Cambridge, MA

Rosenqvist, J. (2007) *Specialpedagogik i mångfaldens Sverige: Om elever med annan etnisk bakgrund än svensk i särskolan* [Special education in multicultural Sweden: Ethnic minority pupils in education for intellectually disabled] (Ett samarbetsprojekt mellan Specialpedagogiska institutet och Högskolan Kristianstad (HKr), Specialpedagogiska institutet

Skidmore, D. (2004) *Inclusion: The dynamic of school development*. Milton Keynes: Open University Press

Skolverket (2004) *Skolverkets lägesbedömning av förskoleverksamhet, skolbarnsomsorg, skola och vuxenutbildning* [The evaluation of the situation in preschools, after-school childcare, schools and adult education; in Swedish]. Rapport 249. Stockholm, Skolverket

SOU (2003:35) *För den jag är. Om utbildning och utvecklingstörning.* [For who I am: On Education and Developmental Disability] Stockholm: Skolverket

Wildt-Persson, A. and Rosengren, P. G. (2001) Equity and equivalence in the Swedish school system. In W. Hutmacher (ed), *In pursuit of equity in education. Using international indicators to compare equity policies* (pp288-321). Hingham, MA: Kluwer Academic Publishers

Chapter 20

Feminist class struggle

bell hooks

Class difference and the way in which it divides women was an issue women in the feminist movement talked about long before race. In the mostly white circles of a newly formed women's liberation movement the most glaring separation between women was that of class. White working-class women recognised that class hierarchies were present in the movement. Conflict arose between the reformist vision of women's liberation which basically demanded equal rights for women within the existing class structure, and more radical and/or revolutionary models, which called for fundamental change in the existing structure so that models of mutuality and equality could replace the old paradigms. However, as the feminist movement progressed and privileged groups of well-educated white women began to achieve equal access to class power with their male counterparts, the feminist class struggle was no longer deemed important.

From the onset of the movement women from privileged classes were able to make their concerns 'the' issues that should be focused on, in part because they were the group of women who received public attention. They attracted the mass media. The issues that were most relevant to working women or most women were never highlighted by mainstream mass media.

Betty Friedan's *The Feminine Mystique* (1963) identified 'the problem that has no name' as the dissatisfaction females felt about being confined and subordinated in the home as housewives. While this issue was presented as a crisis for women it really was only a crisis for a small group of well-educated white women. While they were complaining about the dangers of confinement in the home a huge majority of women were in the workforce. And many of these working women, who put in long hours for low wages while still doing all the work in the domestic household, would have seen the right to stay at home as 'freedom'.

It was not gender discrimination or sexist oppression that kept privileged women of all races from working outside the home, it was the fact that the jobs that would have been available to them would have been the same low-paying unskilled labour open to all working women. Elite groups of highly educated females stayed at home rather than do the type of work large numbers of lower-middle-class and working-class women were doing. Occasionally, a few of these women defied convention and worked outside the home performing tasks way below their educational skills and facing resistance from husbands and family. It was this resistance that turned the issue of their working outside the home into an issue of gender discrimination and made opposing patriarchy and seeking equal rights with men of their class the political platform that chose feminism rather than class struggle.

From the outset, reformist white women with class privilege were well aware that the power and freedom they wanted was the freedom they perceived men of their class enjoying. Their resistance to patriarchal male domination in the domestic household provided them with a connection they could use to unite across class with other women who were weary of male domination. But only privileged women had the luxury to imagine working outside the home would actually provide them with an income which would enable them to be economically self-sufficient. Working-class women already knew that the wages they received would not liberate them.

Reformist efforts on the part of privileged groups of women to change the workforce so that women workers would be paid more and face less gender-based discrimination and harassment on the job had a positive impact on the lives of all women. And these gains are important. Yet the fact that the privileged gained in class power while masses of women still do not receive wage equity with men is an indication of the way in which class interests superseded feminist efforts to change the workforce so that women would receive equal pay for equal work.

Lesbian feminist thinkers were among the first activists to raise the issue of class in the feminist movement, expressing their viewpoints in an accessible language. They were a group of women who had not imagined they could depend on husbands to support them. And they were often much more aware than their straight counterparts of the difficulties all women would face in the workforce.

In the early '70s anthologies like *Class and Feminism*, edited by Charlotte Bunch and Nancy Myron, published work written by women from diverse class backgrounds who were confronting the issue in feminist circles. Each essay emphasised the fact that class was not simply a question of money. In 'The Last Straw', Rita Mae Brown clearly stated:

Class is much more than Marx's definition of relationship to the means of production. Class involved your behavior, your basic assumptions, how you are taught to behave, what you expect from yourself and from others, your concept of a future, how you understand problems and solve them, how you think, feel, act.

These women who entered feminist groups made up of diverse classes were among the first to see that the vision of a politically based sisterhood where all females would unite together to fight patriarchy could not emerge until the issue of class was confronted.

Placing class on feminist agendas opened up the space where the intersections of class and race were made apparent. Within the institutionalised race, sex, class social system in our society black females were clearly at the bottom of the economic totem pole. Initially, well-educated white women from working-class backgrounds were more visible than black females of all classes in the feminist movement. They were a minority within the movement, but theirs was the voice of experience. They knew better than their privileged-class comrades of any race the costs of resisting race, class, and gender domination. They knew what it was like to struggle to change one's economic situation. Between them and their privileged-class comrades there were ongoing conflicts over appropriate behaviour, over the issues that would be presented as fundamental feminist concerns. Within the feminist movement women from privileged-class backgrounds who had never before been involved in leftist freedom fighting learned the concrete politics of class struggle, confronting challenges made by less privileged women, and also learning in the process assertiveness skills and constructive ways to cope with conflict. Despite constructive intervention many privileged white women continued to act as though feminism belonged to them, as though they were in charge.

Mainstream patriarchy reinforced the idea that the concerns of women from privileged-class groups were the only ones worthy of receiving attention. Feminist reform aimed to gain social equality for women within the existing structure. Privileged women wanted equality with men of their class. Despite sexism among their class they would not have wanted to have the lot of working-class men. Feminist efforts to grant women social equality with men of their class neatly coincided with white supremacist capitalist patriarchal fears that white power would diminish if non-white people gained equal access to economic power and privilege. Supporting what in effect became white power reformist feminism enabled the mainstream white supremacist patriarchy to bolster its power while simultaneously undermining the radical politics of feminism.

Only revolutionary feminist thinkers expressed outrage at this co-optation of feminist movement. Their critique and outrage gained a hearing in the alternative press. In her collection of essays, *The Coming of Black Genocide* (1993), radical white activist Mary Barfoot boldly stated:

There are white women, hurt and angry, who believed that the '70s women's movement meant sisterhood, and who feel betrayed by escalator women. By women who went back home to the patriarchy. But the women's movement never left the father Dick's side. ... There was no war. And there was no liberation. We got a share of genocide profits and we love it. We are Sisters of Patriarchy, and true supporters of national and class oppression. Patriarchy in its highest form is Euro-imperialism on a world scale. If we're Dick's sister and want what he has gotten, then in the end we support that system that he got it all from.

Indeed, many more feminist women found and find it easier to consider divesting of white supremacist thinking than of their class elitism. As privileged women gained greater access to economic power with men of their class, feminist discussions of class were no longer commonplace. Instead, all women were encouraged to see the economic gains of affluent females as a positive sign for all women. In actuality, these gains rarely changed the lot of poor and working-class women. And since privileged men did not become equal caretakers in the domestic household, the freedom of privileged-class women of all races has required the sustained subordination of working-class and poor women. In the '90s collusion with the existing social structure was the price of 'women's Liberation'. At the end of the day class power proved to be more important than feminism. And this collusion helped destabilise the feminist movement.

When women acquired greater class status and power without conducting themselves differently from males, feminist politics were undermined. Lots of women felt betrayed. Middle- and lower-middle-class women who were suddenly compelled by the ethos of feminism to enter the workforce did not feel liberated once they faced the hard truth that working outside the home did not mean work in the home would be equally shared with male partners. No-fault divorce proved to be more economically beneficial to men than women. As many black women/women of colour saw privileged white women benefiting economically more than other groups from reformist feminist gains, from gender being tacked on to racial affirmative action, it simply reaffirmed their fear that feminism was really about increasing white power. The most profound betrayal of feminist issues has been the lack of mass-based feminist protest challenging the government's assault on single mothers and the dismantling of the welfare system. Privileged women, many of whom call themselves feminists, have simply turned away from the 'feminisation of poverty'.

The voices of 'power feminism' tend to be highlighted in the mass media far more than the voices of individual feminist women who have gained class power without betraying their solidarity towards those groups without class privilege. Being true to feminist politics, their goals were and are to become economically self-sufficient and to find ways to assist other women in their efforts to better themselves economically. Their experiences counter the assumption that women can only gain economically by acting in collusion with the existing capitalist patriarchy. Individual American feminists with class power who support a revolutionary vision of social change share resources and use their power to aid reforms that will improve the lives of women irrespective of class.

The only genuine hope of feminist liberation lies with a vision of social change which challenges class elitism. Western women have gained class power and greater gender inequality because a global white supremacist patriarchy enslaves and/or subordinates masses of third-world women. In the USA the combined forces of a booming prison industry and workfare-oriented welfare in conjunction with a conservative immigration policy create and condone the conditions for indentured slavery. Ending welfare will create a new underclass of women and children to be abused and exploited by the existing structures of domination.

Given the changing realities of class in the USA, widening gaps between the rich and poor, and the continued feminisation of poverty, we desperately need a mass-based radical feminist movement that can build on the strength of the past, including the positive gains generated by reforms, while offering meaningful interrogation of existing feminist theory that was simply wrongminded while offering us new strategies. Significantly, a visionary movement would ground its work in the concrete conditions of working-class and poor women. That means creating a movement that begins education for critical consciousness where women, feminist women with class power, need to put in place low-income housing women can own. The creation of housing co-ops with feminist principles would show the ways feminist struggle is relevant to all women's lives.

When women with class power opportunistically use a feminist platform while undermining feminist politics, keeping in place a patriarchal system that will ultimately re-subordinate them, they do not just betray feminism; they betray themselves. Returning to a discussion of class, feminist women and men will restore the conditions needed for solidarity. We will then be better able to envision a world where resources are shared and opportunities for personal growth abound for everyone irrespective of their class.

Source: hooks, b. (2000) 'Feminist class struggle', *Feminism is for Everybody: Passionate politics*, South End Press. Copyright (c) 2000 by Gloria Watkins

Chapter 21

Valuing young people in community settings

Linda Milbourne

Introduction

Over some twenty years, the UK government has increasingly turned to third-sector and community providers to deliver a range of welfare services (Kendall, 2000). Community-based organisations are now providers of services from early years to old age, and have taken a growing role in children and young people's provision, particularly in socially deprived neighbourhoods.

Changing relationships with the state have drawn community-based organisations into partnerships and new arrangements, altering roles and the emphasis of their work (Harris and others, 2001), and bringing public and non-profit agencies together in new initiatives. It is often their flexible approaches which underlie community organisations' successful practice, but recent studies point to the challenges involved in maintaining user-focused services against the tide of organisational demands (Lewis, 2005; Milbourne, 2009).

Amidst these transitions, community organisations have been charged with building more engaged communities (Home Office, 2004; OTS, 2007); and reflecting trends in a number of other countries (Anheier and Kendall, 2002), there has been renewed emphasis on community-based solutions to social problems. This includes building community capacity for front-line work with young people, especially those alienated from schools and other services, using strategies such as volunteering and youth-led projects (DCSF, 2008).

This chapter explores young people's involvement in urban community settings within the frame of recent changes in UK youth policy and practice [...] including growing reliance on community organisations (Taylor, 2011), especially in reaching socially excluded young people (DfES, 2008). The chapter reflects on debates associated with citizenship, democratic participation and social inclusion, questioning motivations for increasing opportunities for young people's voice and participation in shaping services and in voluntary action. [...]

Study of community-based youth projects

This chapter draws on two discrete studies of youth projects in community settings. The first involved a short, intensive study of non-profit organisations providing services for children and young people, commissioned by a large authority (area A), undertaken in 2006-2007. The second study (2007-2008) considered changes in young people's services in a separate local authority (area B), focusing on youth-led projects and participation initiatives. Both studies were located in deprived inner-city areas with diverse populations, including significant numbers of recent refugees. Each area has benefited from recent community participation initiatives, with new agencies and cross-sector partnerships emerging, alongside long-standing community organisations with successful records of working with young people.

Both studies employed qualitative methods to examine the participatory space open to young people and community providers to influence services and to determine new projects, questioning young people's experiences of inclusion and exclusion. [...]

The studies use qualitative coding methods (Glaser, 1992), employing perspectives of critical social research (Harvey, 1990) to examine the data and question the consequences of policies in specific localities. [...]

Involving young people in community settings

Statutory- and community-based workers in my studies identified tensions and difficulties emerging from recent developments, alongside positive outcomes. Andrea, co-ordinating youth initiatives for the local authority in area B, pointed to mounting dependence on community providers, identifying her role as increasingly 'managing and monitoring project funding, much less about using my professional skills'. She highlighted projects including peer research; a drop-in centre; a multimedia bus and the Youth Council's work as 'really positive steps forward' enabled by recent Youth Funds. However, she also identified other valuable projects which had closed through lack of funding.

In area A, I have focused on examples from youth education and advice projects, including two working with young people out of school, a mediation project and a youth centre. Workers in these community organisations commonly included a mix of different professional backgrounds, including youth work, special needs teaching, youth justice and arts.

In area B, examples are mainly from three youth-led projects. The Youth Council (YC) involves twenty to thirty young people (aged 14-19). Some members meet several evenings a week, with varied tasks and roles, including resolving criteria and decisions for allocating Youth Funds; disseminating information on their work and other youth activities; developing strategy for the Children and Young People's Trust (C&YPT); providing peer training, mentoring and counselling; and organising events to attract new members. The formal Youth Council meets monthly but membership is not elected. YC members are supported by a Youth Participation worker and use community centre space, with limited facilities. Among aspirations, the YC strategy includes attracting 'hard to reach' young people and making participation fun (not just hard work).

A second project involved young people as researchers on a large housing estate, investigating young Asians' knowledge of, and participation in, local facilities. They took part in training to undertake research with peers. The third was a youth-led project to plan and establish MediaBus, supported by a consortium of four community organisations. The successful £80,000 bid from Youth Funds resulted in a bus equipped with a music studio, IT suite, coffee bar and spaces for advisory services and training. It travels to different locations most evenings, with late weekend opening hours. The project now has four workers and twenty young volunteers and trainee counsellors.

Examples of other recent projects in area B include a drop-in education project with a young people's forum; joint youth centre events to address territorial conflicts; a cross-generational arts project and a young refugees' project.

Opportunities and incentives: some positive outcomes

Many young people expressed the benefits from involvement in projects more broadly than gaining individual accreditation or skills. Daniella, with a positive identity as a learner, described both individual and wider gains. After a year's YC membership in area B, Daniella sometimes spent four evenings a week in YC task groups, including deciding criteria for allocating the Youth Funds, training youth groups for bids, arranging presentations and feedback to applicants:

What we do's good, it's helped me with speaking out and presentations, CV writing, how to research and we get training. But most, I think I've grown, I'm confident from working with the others ... (Daniella, 14)

Gemma (area A), aged 16, who was excluded from school for disruptive behaviour, also emphasised less tangible outcomes from flexible, community-based education: 'It took time, but it give me a better sense of myself ... It was all aggravation before...'.

Ferekher (area B), a YC member for nearly two years, described his motivation for involvement:

Why I got involved? Good vibes really ... before I didn't have much to do. ... There are incentives, I come through a friend and we had a induction, then straightaway I was lucky, there was a residential, you know, building a team but it was cool too ... (Ferekher, 17)

Ebo, involved in the YC for three years, discussed status as a motivator, contrasting this with how young people often used negative reputations. However, he recognised that status also required resources to offer real decision-making power:

As YC we have status. We get views from area youth forums, different clubs, we make decisions. Funding's important, gives you ways to make changes ... instead of getting into bad stuff because you got no status otherwise. (Ebo, 18)

Support from organisational workers was also important in maintaining motivation, as Akeisha, on the youth-led steering group for MediaBus outlined, describing time-consuming processes of meeting, project planning and developing funding bids:

I mean, first out we didn't know how hard it'd be, there's a lot of persuading, and we needed help how to present things, feel confident when mostly people don't listen to young people. (Akeisha, 17)

This support was crucial in overcoming barriers, especially when many young people lacked self-esteem and often had erratic social and educational histories. One worker stressed the importance of 'establishing relationships with young people first ... before you can help in more concrete ways'.

Sometimes key individuals or specific activities made a difference in young people's willingness to commit, when they had previously rejected schooling or other institutions. Donna (area A), working with school refusers, stressed, 'it has a lot to do with the individuals ... negotiating activities that young people see make sense for them'. Most community-based workers emphasised the importance of maintaining a culture responsive to young people, which meant shedding predescribed professional roles. While language differed, this view of flexible, cross-disciplinary work was shared by long-standing community workers and recently appointed youth participation workers.

Trust and respect: mixed outcomes

Trust emerged as a significant theme in young people's willingness to participate in a variety of projects: young people trusting adults; adult power-holders trusting young people and the need to promote wider trust in young people's abilities.

Raj (area A), out of school for over a year, explained that having his views respected was vital to his responding more positively when referred to a community project:

Like school or social workers never trusted me like I could achieve something ... so that's a first, them asking what do I think... (Raj, 16)

Many young people identified an organisational culture in which they were respected and listened to as key reasons for engaging in different projects.

However, trusting adult institutions, when many prior experiences involved rejection, was difficult and took time. Kwame, involved in MediaBus, explained young people's lack of trust in schemes which potentially replicated experiences of meaningless activities:

You need to see what can happen to believe it'd be different. ... It's hard to trust it's not just a con, making sure we're busy so we can't cause trouble. (Kwame, 17)

Temi, a YC member for five years, attending a university youth work programme, illustrated the mistrust with which some C&YPT members viewed the YC:

Some of them are on board with it but some ... not at all. ... They think we're too young, can't see why we have this role. Like we bring an idea, they'll listen but it's discounted. ... You can see they're thinking like ... why have them here? Has it put us off? No, but it's demotivating. (Temi, 19)

Amara, a MediaBus steering group member, contributed insights into why some young people withhold commitment, highlighting issues of differential power:

We went to meetings where it felt they [adults] weren't listening or ... some people could put their ideas across better – so that's what people heard, what they chose, it sounded good. ... But we still had to deal with outcomes they set down. (Amara, 17)

Amara's description of how ideas are heard and of preset limitations reflects criticisms made in area A of local authority consultations with young people on future services. Area A's plans identified young people as collaborators in determining plans for their services, but community organisations argued that less articulate and less accessible young people had not been reached or involved.

Tensions of participating

The examples above demonstrate the importance of building a culture which respects young people's ideas for maintaining their involvement. Kim (area A), running an education project for disaffected young people, underlined the value of 'carrots rather than sticks' in encouraging participation. 'Young people have all sorts of pressures to attend ... but if they see nothing to connect with, they won't be here'.

The Youth Participation worker (area B) contrasted the 'amazing amounts of time young people contributed' with the limited funds available for events regarded as social, ironically pointing to 'enjoyment' as one of five key goals in the Every Child Matters agenda (DfES, 2004). Michael, a YC member, working as a peer counsellor across several different youth clubs, stressed difficulties in balancing external demands and fun events to attract 'hard to reach' young people:

We gotta produce the goods or they [C&YPT] gonna put us down ... same time we need somet'ing you'd notice with music or talent shows like we done before to reach lots of people. We had different foods, advice too, but fun stuff between. Now funding for social, even a bit, is hard going, even though it's about achieving our strategy. (Michael, 18)

Temi expanded on this view:

When it comes to events, they want more work-based, training and skills. Sometimes it seems more about ticking their boxes. To attract new people and for YC members to stay involved even, there has to be a social side too. (Temi)

Employment-related priorities and individual skills meet short-term targets, but obscure understanding of how longer-term cultural changes, which will engage marginal young people, might be achieved. As Temi stated earlier, the reticence and limited comprehension of adult bodies could be demotivating.

Research carried out by young people on a large, predominantly Asian, housing estate in area B, involving some 150 responses, found that existing facilities were limited and unattractive to many young people. Their study reports that neither they nor existing community organisations 'are in a strong enough position' to pursue their recommendations but no action has otherwise resulted. Young researchers appreciated their learning from undertaking the study, but aspirations identified at the beginning, such as to 'make a difference' and 'to create change' in their area (Hajera and Sabia, 17) have not been met. Together with earlier examples, experiences from this project raise questions about definitions of 'positive activities' and the values, rewards and expectations implied when young people participate.

Exclusion and inclusion: the language of volunteering

With increasing emphasis on young people's participation in voluntary activities as routes to social inclusion, my studies, like Brooks' (2007), suggest that more able and articulate young people are more likely to volunteer, recognising the advantages of such activities for their future careers. However, the language of volunteering and associated perceptions may well deter others, adding to examples of ways in which recent participation schemes potentially exclude less advantaged young people.

Krisann, a YC member, distinguished her YC activities from volunteering. She saw schools encouraging pupils to volunteer but felt this rarely involved a choice to participate or collaborate with other young people:

I don't think we see ourselves as 'volunteers'. It's more we got involved when we saw ... what we could do ... it's like what you've chosen to do – not what's good for you. (Krisann, 19)

Chaz, an ex-gang member, was introduced by another MediaBus member, as 'rude boy turned volunteer champion' because of his presentations to large national audiences. Despite the label, Chaz reflected Krisann's view, stressing the unlikelihood of more marginal young people being attracted to volunteer:

Volunteering, no way they're gonna be interested 'less it's something they really wanna be into, but what we're doing, we don't see it like that, 'volunteering'. (Chaz, 19)

The negative connotations associated with 'volunteering' highlight failures to adopt more youth-friendly perspectives and discourse which could avoid perpetuating some young people's exclusion.

Power, influence and constraints

Area A had elected a Youth Mayor and Youth Council representatives through Schools Councils, youth forums and clubs. However, in several small youth projects, young people were either unaware of these structures or felt that these elected young people were distanced from their views. Young people in area B argued for a more fluid Youth Council membership, identifying elections as encouraging the most self-assured to take up positions, while discouraging others who lacked confidence or were not members of recognised youth forums. Josh, a YC member, aged 19, outlined what he described as a 'vexed question' around representation, with the C&YPT members periodically advocating elections in line with other areas:

It's been a big discussion all my time here. Other areas are different ... and this new proposal now with representatives – from each school, the organised clubs, area forums ... four from hard to reach groups. ... Way we see it, that excludes people, they don't all come from clubs, and there's more chance to reach people not involved, than if we limit numbers, have elections. What we do is concentrate on letting people know what we're doing ... and most will say they prefer our way, it's more about inclusion. (Josh)

In the same discussion, others questioned how 'hard to reach' groups could form an electorate and which groups would be defined or represented. Using conventional representative models may be inappropriate for such contexts, whereas openness to alternative approaches may avoid further marginalising those least likely to participate. The processes of elections and related structures may provide contexts for increasing the skills of more able or articulate young people, and even where purposes and actions aim for inclusivity, power embedded in such processes may result in diverse issues and voices being unintentionally inhibited or excluded.

Hasan, aged 19, involved in a youth centre and later the YC, questioned the limits of young people's decision-making power, highlighting insecurities for funded projects:

News is, there's more money, but we see more for one thing, maybe new, but it's taken from something else. So there's two problems, we have to rethink criteria for funding. ... Then for people leading projects, they're anxious for next year. ... And it kind of undercuts our influence, so who's really deciding like? (Hasan)

In earlier comments, Temi, Amara and Michael underlined constraints on young people's broader aspirations in youth-led projects because of the emphasis on meeting targets related to training and employment skills. A youth-centre worker illustrated how the imposition of nationally-driven performance targets restricted flexibility in developmental community work with young people:

New gangs – if you like – appear, so regular attenders get uncomfortable ... the gang moves on. But what we're faced with is competing for funding, that's the bottom line ... so we monitor membership, attendance, activities, when what's needed is more flexibility but we ... make the pretence of meeting targets and that to survive. (Paul, St Jude's Youth Centre, Area A)

Funding for community delivery of young people's services (as other services) is heavily underwritten by short-term performance targets, which are rarely negotiable but undermine providers' flexibility to negotiate with young people. Paul identifies how possible funding loss generates a cultural conspiracy to mask failures in achieving attendance and accreditation targets, when higher risk activities could offer ways to tackle more challenging youth work. Pressures on performance mean that centres focus on low-risk young people (target-achievers) rather than those outside the reach of most services.

In several projects, accommodating funders' requirements for prescribed activities and outcomes was coupled with resistance to relinquishing flexible activities and shared decision-making, which community-based workers saw as crucial negotiation space for engaging young people. Such external demands presented countervailing pressures to more responsive, participatory approaches to their work.

Discussion

Empowering young people in community-based activities?
My findings offer mixed messages on outcomes from recent youth initiatives. Developments in youth-led projects and activities are enabling perceptive and capable young people from diverse backgrounds to gain valuable skills. They are researching and running projects, managing decision-making processes, sharing skills and experience with others. Some projects have involved young people with quite negative histories of institutional engagement. Young people are also educating peers, supporting and advising others in different localities and taking on roles as youth activists, including speaking at local, regional and national events. These examples demonstrate valuable advances in space and possibilities available to young people individually and through co-operative, educative processes. Such achievements are encouraging, following a lengthy period of attrition of broader youth provision in many inner-city areas, with residual and functional activities targeted towards specific groups.

Nevertheless, the conflicting strategies evident in youth policy – those advancing active participation and greater autonomy, and those restricting actions or promoting hegemonic forms of inclusion – are visible from my findings. Considered through local experiences, the rhetoric of empowering young people and young people's experiences of how their views and actions are valued are at variance. Despite responsiveness in community projects, young people continue to be treated as 'others' in the dominant settings of adult institutions. They remain outsiders while powerful agencies determine the 'contextual rules' (Clegg, 1989:200), generating disillusionment at community level and among young people about the goals of participation.

Young people and small community projects are asked to trust powerful institutions which may discount their ideas and generate insecurity through continually changing funding and performance regimes. Raising hopes without commitment to action or change, as illustrated by the young people's research project and limited trust extended to Youth Council endeavours, produces demotivation and undercuts young people's influence and aspirations for development. Community-based, youth-led development work is fragile, and the risks for individual young people high, in a discontinuous funding environment over which they have little control.

My research, like Hutin's (2008), suggests that young people's voluntary actions are undervalued and considerably underestimated, and the language of volunteering, a strong component of government youth strategies, carries negative connotations for many. While youth action and activism offer more positive associations for young people, they convey challenging messages for dominant institutions.

Changing the culture of participation: whose reality counts?

Pressures to meet short-term, nationally-driven targets narrow the field of vision for local co-ordinating bodies. In contrast, young people hold a more expansive vision of longer-term development towards a culture of participation, drawing on direct knowledge and experience. What counts as legitimate knowledge is at issue here: that informed by the everyday lived experiences of young people or community workers, or that embedded in dominant forms of professional management. The more activities are specified, the less they are open to diversity and influence from young people. Bodies can be formally responsive to different groups, while more creative approaches to changing the culture of services, which might attract those currently excluded, are constrained by dominant managerial culture.

Top-down planning, funding and monitoring processes conflict with the bottom-up participatory model implied in youth-led approaches, curbing young people's influence in community-based developments. Local and regional bodies risk 'ticking the boxes' as Temi describes, through short-lived, high-profile schemes but missing the point of young people participating. Defining the terms on which young people can participate has detrimental implications for reaching and sustaining the participation of disengaged young people.

Shifts in professional and organisational cultures are not short-term enterprises, and successfully reaching disengaged young people may require recognition and adoption of alternative models. The community organisations illustrated here have struggled for some time with sustaining practice cultures which engage young people in negotiating services and activities. The emphasis on quantifiable targets and structured volunteer activities restricts participatory practices of this kind. Study of such initiatives suggests little evidence that an impoverished curriculum of youth activities, focused on individualised, work-related skills, will successfully attract disengaged young people.

Compliance, constructive participation or critical social engagement?
Young people's aspirations in reaching disengaged groups and improving local services and facilities for others are not fundamentally distinct from government rhetoric. However, the methods by which these goals might be achieved and their potential as broader educative processes for developing critical social engagement, as well as 'something for the CV' (Brooks, 2007), pose challenges to normative concepts of young people's roles and adult-led institutions. By finding ways of negotiating alternatives within limited autonomies, community organisations and youth-led projects engage with the tensions and possibilities of participatory education, with its related value for wider social participation and change. While such possibilities may offer greater empowerment for young people than their previous institutional experiences, the power of funders, embodied in regulatory targets, activities and performance outcomes, shapes and limits this space.

If young people gain greater skills and political power, and present their own – different – ideas, this demands changes in adult institutions, not a simple process of assimilating young people. My findings suggest potential for change in surrounding conditions, through young people gaining an understanding of using their collective participation to construct projects which improve their own and others' worlds. However, such processes generate tensions as they challenge models and space in existing institutions, problematising professional and managerial powers and practices.

Community and youth-led projects have simultaneously marginal and radical status as agents of change, but young people also recognise the necessity of endorsement from key adult bodies. However, these frameworks generate requirements for greater formalisation and pressures to distort what the groups are. Increased cross-sector work and dependence on community agencies have intensified isomorphic pressures so that powerful institutional arrangements and accountability mechanisms exert pervasive forces – inducing integration and adaption – constraining different ideas and models of action. The continuance of negotiable space within which young people can take greater control of their lives and access alternatives will depend on youth-led projects and their community workers pursuing models which resist, as well as accommodate, unproblematised youth strategies.

Participatory work with young people, by opening new youth spaces, suggests possibilities for a radical habitus, an ethos through which young people can develop projects which promote changes and less powerful groups can gain influence, as well as remedy institutional failures. However, if the space is colonised by young people with the most advantages, new strategies will do little to redress the barriers to participation of those currently excluded.

Recent policy goals concerned with young people's empowerment have been encompassed in wider citizenship, cohesion and participation strategies. However, without the flexibility and willingness to risk adopting new approaches and extending trust to young people, adult institutions and policy-makers alike are guilty of institutional bad faith (Bourdieu, 1999). The claim of youth-led, community-based projects transforming previous failures to engage alienated young people remains hollow, if the influence of new youth activities is safely circumscribed: approaches which secure compliance will prevail. Young people seen as threats will continue to be pressured into unproblematised structures and activities; poorly resourced community organisations will still grapple with intractable problems; and young people seeking changes will remain (albeit more articulate) outsiders.

Source: Milbourne, L. (2009) 'Valuing difference or securing compliance? Working to involve young people in community settings', *Children and Society* 2009, vol. 23, no. 5. Copyright (c) 2009 National Children's Bureau

References

Anheier, H., Kendall, J. (2002) *Third Sector Policy at the Crossroads*. London: Routledge

Bourdieu, P. (Ferguson, P. trans.) (1999) *The Weight of the World: Social Suffering in Contemporary Society.* Cambridge: Polity Press

Brooks, R. (2007) Young people's extra-curricular activities: critical social engagement – or something for the CV? *Journal of Social Policy* 36: 417-34

Clegg, S. (1989) *Frameworks of Power*. London: Sage

DCSF (2008) *Aiming High for Young People: A Ten Year Strategy for Positive Activities.* London: Department for Children Schools and Families

DfES (2004) *Every Child Matters: Change for Children*. London: Department for Education and Skills

Etzioni, A. (1995) *Rights and the Common Good: The Communitarian Perspective*. New York: St Martin's Press

Glaser, B. (1992) *Basics of Grounded Theory Analysis: Emergence Versus Forcing*. Mill Valley, CA: Sociology Press

Harris, M., Rochester, C., Halfpenny, P. (2001) Twenty years of change. In *Voluntary Organisations and Social Policy in Britain*. M. Harris, C, Rochester (eds). Basingstoke: Palgrave.1-20

Harvey, L. (1990) *Critical Social Research*. London: Unwin

Home Office (2004) *ChangeUp: Capacity Building and Infrastructure Framework for the Voluntary and Community Sector*. London: Active Communities

Hutin, M. (2008) *'Young People Help Out', Analysis From Helping Out: A Survey of Volunteering and Charitable Giving*. London: Institute of Volunteering Research

Kendall, J. (2000) The mainstreaming of the third sector into public policy in England in the late 1990s: whys and wherefores. *Policy and Politics* 28(4): 541-62

Lewis, J. (2005) New Labour's approach to the voluntary sector: independence and the meaning of partnership. *Social Policy and Society* 4: 121-25

Milbourne, L. (2009) Remodelling the Third Sector: advancing collaboration or competition in community based initiatives? *Journal of Social Policy* 38: 277-97

Office of the Third Sector (OTS) (2007) *The Future Role of the Third Sector in Social and Economic Regeneration.* London: Cabinet Office

Taylor, M. (2011) *Public Policy in the Community* (2nd ed.) Basingstoke: Palgrave Macmillan

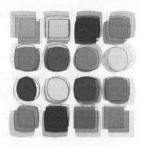

Chapter 22

From equality to diversity?
Ideas that keep us quiet

Jonathan Rix

It is not what you give to the poor that makes all the difference; it is what you have taken from them, and continue to take from them. (Hart, 2011:399)

Introduction

Our understanding of what constitutes, creates and perpetuates social inequality is interwoven with a complex web of personal, historical and cultural assumptions. The language we use in thinking about issues of social change and social control is a key part of society's 'hidden curriculum'. It not only gives rise to our ways of learning but also to our relationship with our systems and institutions.

Consideration of language as power struggle is particularly relevant to a book which in its title links equality and diversity with education. As Illich (1970) exhorts us to recognise, our schooling system adds prejudice to the discrimination endemic within our social networks, compounding our involvement and reaffirming the privilege of a minority over the majority; it 'serves as a ritual of initiation into a growth-oriented consumer society for rich and poor alike' (Illich, 1970:21).

This chapter ranges across a broad spectrum of issues from the individual to the global, aiming to highlight the complex web of historical and cultural assumptions which influence us and the communities in which we live and work. We examine how concepts of advancement frequently associated with education, and which seem fundamentally linked to the betterment of the human condition, are themselves a consequence and cause of inequitable policies and practices. We consider in particular key terms associated with overcoming social injustice, in the context of the neo-liberal agenda.[1]

We frame our discussion around equality and diversity but, given the manner in which the neo-liberal agenda has taken ownership of these terms, we also consider our understanding of globalisation, growth, participation and inclusion. In so doing we face a similar challenge to that laid down by Judith Butler (2004), a need to recognise that 'our most treasured values are under contestation and that they will remain contested zones of politics' (p175).

Equality
Whose equal?

The concept of equality takes many forms and has been used over many centuries by philosophers, theorists, campaigners, politicians and writers. Pojman (1995), for example, identifies sixteen varieties of use of the concept equality, categorising its wide range of application. Despite this slipperiness, the term appears in national and international legislation and policy with remarkable regularity, appearing for example over 180 times in eight of the United Nation conventions associated with the alleviation of oppression (Owen, 2011). It does so, though without clearly defining what it actually means. From the outset the fundamental nature of what is 'equal' has been open to interpretation and negotiation.[2] As a consequence the concept of equality which arose out of an era of civil rights and desegregation campaigns, with its focus upon universal rights and redistribution of material goods, has come to be interpreted differently in the context of globalised capitalism, with its focus upon individuality, competition and choice within a purported meritocracy.

Consider for example the notion of equal opportunities which has emerged in policy since the 1970s. It presupposes that everyone has the right to equal treatment and access to rights and goods, but as a consequence (and perhaps ironically) this suppresses our recognition of difference (Baltodano, 2006). Young (1990) suggests that this suppression leads to cultural imperialism. This 'universalisation of a dominant group's experience and culture, and its establishment as the norm' (p59, cited in Baltodano, 2006) leads to a more subtle and naturalised impression of social division than the one that came before.

The rhetoric of a multicultural melting pot also frames our understanding of delivering equality through universal services (including education). Within this rhetoric, cultural equality, pride and rights are endorsed and encouraged (Hale, 2005). However, there is an ongoing oppression of marginalised social groups. The dominant social groups are able to maintain the status quo whilst appearing to support those they marginalise. The notion of equality becomes a screen behind which the replication of inequality is hidden.

Equality, development and the individual

Within many policy and legislative documents, equality has become associated with development. For example within the Millennium Declaration (UN, 2000) under the heading of equality, it is stated that 'no individual and no nation must be denied the opportunity to benefit from development'. This not only begs the question as towards what is one supposed to develop, but also what is supposed to drive this development? The document makes it clear that development is meant to be *moving out of poverty*, and that the key is developing national resources to finance this. The development must also be sustainable.

Equality it would seem is only achievable via economic growth; and as Leal (2010) points out, no discussion seems to be required about what the underlying cause of poverty might be in the first place. Equality is withdrawn from the political arena and becomes about ensuring the conditions for survival (Dagnino, 2010). Either it becomes a place for charity or achieving it becomes the individual's responsibility.

As a consequence of this shift, influential international reports, such as those produced by the World Bank on youth development, are able to frame the development of young people's lives and learning by reference to work, capital and productivity (Sukarieh and Tannock, 2008). The individual and their skills and capacities seem to provide an answer to overcoming their poverty. The contradictions and conflicts between the nature of opportunities available to them and their capacity to develop economically valuable skills can be put to one side. The economically correct mantra that growth will alleviate suffering means there need be no discussion about the real value of those 'economically valuable' skills to the individual and to the general well-being of their communities.

The well established pattern of inequality via growth

From its outset as a political and economic driver, growth has created enormous social and geographical dislocations, leading to ever larger populations of underemployed adults and young people, either living in or migrating to expanding urban settings, and who become attached to identities and ways of life that are at odds with goals and values of the system (Sukarieh and Tannock, 2008).

As Hart (2011) details, these processes emerged from the 1600s onwards within the United Kingdom. These dislocations came out of the enclosing of land and clearances of agricultural communities, with the shift to a coin-based and then paper-based economy, where a healthy subsistence diet was replaced by payment for labour. Wages were increasingly driven down alongside rising prices by the use of short-term employment and travelling labour. The national debt was established to fund military campaigns and deepened to fund standing armies because of a purported danger from overseas and poverty-inspired revolutionaries. Corrupt politicians paid sinecures to friends and allies, protecting investors in the national debt and the burgeoning banking system, and funding huge building projects. Payments to the poor under the Poor Laws were repeatedly cut on grounds that they damaged the economy and rewarded the undeserving, and were replaced with institutions into which those on the margins were locked away. Empire building and emigration opened up new horizons of resources, markets and labour, and the most lauded writers and thinkers of their day, such as Malthus, Smith and More, provided the propaganda and intellectual arguments to justify the demonising of the poor[3] and the imposition of strategies to maximise the profit of a few.

When placed in this context we can look upon the development of our world not as a history of progress, but 'as *eine Verlustsgeschichte*, a history of successive losses' to our environment, 'social bonds and conviviality' (Rist, 2010:25). Rather than being a journey towards equality, growth is more akin to the metaphor of the Great Wen [a sebaceous cyst] which the 19th century activist William Cobbett applied to London.

Is equality achieved by involving ever more people in growth?

The same displacement processes described by Hart are currently evident in many communities across the world. These communities are generally labelled as developing or emerging, but if those heavily politicised terms are laid aside they can be described more honestly as the majority of humanity. The labels 'developing' and 'emerging' were applied within the Millennium Declaration (UN, 2000), alongside the notion of 'globalisation'. Globalisation is a key conceptual partner for growth and one that has a much longer history than is frequently suggested (Rix, 2010). Without globalisation you lose the capacity to grow new markets and new sources of labour and resources. Turning globalisation into a positive force for all has therefore been posed as a central challenge, but one that offers great opportunities – one which global organisations insist can be 'made fully inclusive and equitable' (UN, 2000, I,5. p2).

The opportunities for the positive force within globalisation would not appear to rest within the economic sphere however. Capital and goods move across boundaries, but relatively few workers can do so; technological developments mean many changes have produced no new jobs or have resulted in jobs moving to other locations. Employment changes have tended to benefit those who have the social and economic capacity to take advantage of the situation, with many traditional job roles disappearing. Market and currency dealings and freedom to shift production have compromised small producers and insecure workers. In addition, large national and transnational businesses have acquired resources and assets cheaply within much of the majority world.

The contradictions are evident in documents around youth policy. The World Bank, for example, wants young people to embrace responsibility and entrepreneurship and to develop their employability. But, in striking echoes of 18th and 19th century

Britain[4], the World Bank calls for the global extension of migration programmes for temporary and seasonal labour (Sukarieh and Tannock, 2008).

Controlling global movements for equality

The ongoing development of communication systems is frequently presented as the social justice success story of globalisation. Globalised communications have certainly resulted in brief flowerings of movements and activism which aim to disrupt the power structures that support the global market place (Guttal, 2010). However, the new communication technologies which have facilitated these global activists are increasingly run within a corporate framework, interwoven with the power structures that might be a threat.

It is perhaps unsurprising to see the new technologies so clearly in evidence in discussions about new curricula and around the need for an opening up of a global market in education. These corporate players fund and advise many such ventures. As a result a key part of any curriculum now focuses upon the kinds of products these organisations need to sell and, despite calls for the development of critical thinking, reflection and lateral thinking within the curricula documents they help write[5], it is evident that the mechanisms to encourage these outcomes are lacking (Rix, 2010).

Ironically, in embracing new technologies within education, the one aspect of globalisation which has created a platform for transformation may increasingly constrain our options to challenge the directions in which these technologies take us. These new channels for seeking equality will be marshalled by those who benefit from the world as it is. Once again, we will 'reproduce the culture as it has been'. (Bruner, 1996:83).

Diversity
Diversity as a restriction

The recognition of the diverse contexts out of which each of us emerge is a fundamental underpinning tenet of our rights as individuals and members of collective groups, both across and within those cultures (Sen, 1998). It has been the failure to provide this recognition that has led to so many of the human rights movements over the centuries. As a consequence it is possible to find issues of diversity at the heart of many reform agendas.

Consider for example the development of multicultural education in the United States. Since 1977 the National Council for Accreditation of Teacher Education (NCATE) has included multicultural education as an essential item within its accreditation criteria. From 2000 it had a specific standard on diversity. However, guidance for teacher-trainers focuses upon issues related to gender and minority groups; and their courses offer little encouragement to critically engage with the systems and processes in which students will work – systems and processes which palpably continue to discriminate against so many of these individuals (Baltadano, 2006):

Without a strong anti-hegemonic philosophy to guide its direction, multicultural education's initial social concerns with racial integration, gender equality, and linguistic difference have gradually degenerated into a checklist of diversity attributes and features, which reified and essentialised notions of difference, ultimately fossilising the movement. (p124)

The implication is that what began as a transformative response was appropriated within the status quo; by becoming one more mainstream policy, multiculturalism has been increasingly defined by the priorities of the dominant culture.

Similarly, within the United Kingdom, national policies for raising school standards appear to contradict policies encouraging diversity and inclusion, enhancing instead marginalisation and exclusion (Dyson *et al*, 2003). It is more common for the diversity of students to be seen as a 'problem' which needs to be minimised rather than as a resource for learning and inclusion (Booth *et al*, 1997). Underpinning this response is a sense of tolerance for difference, something which indicates that the school is part of a respectful, civil society, but which is enduring rather embracing diversity (Nieto, 2010).

The notion of diversity has become the dominant culture making space for something it has identified as 'other'. As has been identified within the Finnish and Norwegian context, there is a tendency amongst teachers, sometimes subtle but at other times open, to homogenise the majority and set up a division between them and the special minority (Arnesen *et al*, 2007). Such a response is unlikely to be confined to this one profession within the dominant culture.

Diversity has become a notion for managing inequality, a management strategy, a political stance and an economic imperative. As Benn puts it:

If we compare the obligations related to diversity (everyone must be nice to everyone) with those required by equality (some people must give up their wealth), it is easy to understand how commitment to diversity has transformed … into a programme that aims to make rich people with different skin colours or sexual orientations feel 'comfortable' without touching the one thing that makes them feel most 'comfortable' – money. (Benn, 2009)

Policy and practice dressed as diversity has opened the doors for a few. Its subsequent apparent openness to these groupings has disguised – and enabled denial of – the underlying inequalities that keep so many others out.

Diversity as selective participation

This capacity of the dominant culture to allow access to a relatively select few outsiders is not just a characteristic of neo-liberal governance; it is a central characteristic of power politics over the ages. Equally, the capacity to widen participation has long been a conception for social transformation. Within the emancipatory pedagogy of Paulo Freire, the participation of the teacher and learner in uncovering the reality of their situation was a fundamental tool for the transformation of social structures which oppress those living in poverty:

Attempting to liberate the oppressed without their reflective participation in the act of liberation is to treat them as objects which must be saved from a burning building; it is to lead them into the populist pitfall and transform them into masses which can be manipulated. (Freire, 1970:47)

The notion of participation is evident across many conventions, policy and legislative documents. However, it has frequently become the pseudo-participation which Freire highlighted as a risk (p51). Young people's experience in the UK, for example, is that when they do participate not that much changes (Taylor, 2008). Participation is in evidence across health, education and social care, but it is very rare to see that involvement at a strategic level (Oldfield and Fowler, 2004; Franklin and Sloper, 2006). The capacity to create meaningful change is therefore curtailed.

The response for some young people being involved in pseudo-participation will be further disengagement from the processes they were supposed to be participating in. For others however, involvement in relatively surface activities, such as opinion-gathering exercises and peer-training events, will have the effect of producing 'Plato's conformist citizen, content to consume and comment, to be led and represented' rather than 'Aristotle's dissenting citizen, for whom all things are open to question, capable both of governing and being governed' (Taylor, 2008:256).

At an international level, participation has had its negative impact too, becoming a cover for institutions such as the World Bank to encourage the removal of state control over resources and their placement within the 'free' market (Leal, 2010)[6]. It has become a tool not just for maintaining the status quo but also for deepening and widening the control of those economic forces which lead to the marginalisation and impoverishment of so many. This has been largely achieved through shifting the focus of participation away from its political goals and towards its techniques, so that the concern becomes which of the diversity groupings have been included, as opposed to the nature of their participation and its transformational outcomes (White, 1996).

Diversity leading to exclusion

It is evident that the inclusion of marginalised individuals is under the terms of those with the power to define the nature of their participation. Experiences in Sweden and the US, for example, suggest that the extension of choice within a marketplace, unless very tightly controlled, further excludes the disadvantaged (Bunar, 2010; Söderström and Uusitalo, 2010; Howe and Welner, 2002).

Within education, inclusion has been compromised by its association with those with a vested interest in maintaining the status quo. Rather than focusing upon how to achieve 'inclusion for all', policies have identified who should be the focus of inclusion, based around those groupings and issues associated with diversity (Black-Hawkins *et al,* 2007).

Policies on inclusion have also been compromised by the range of marketisation policy initiatives. In England, for example, this has included the traditionalist national curriculum, standardised testing, league tables and the investment in and development of a range of independent and alternative provision (Slee, 2006; Rix, 2011), resulting in increasing segregated and selective provision (Rix, 2006; Barron *et al*, 2007). This has coincided with ongoing and disproportionate referral of certain ethnic groupings and social classes to categories for intervention and treatment (Slee, 2008).

Intended as an 'assault on oppressive vestiges of the past as a way of contributing to alternative futures' (Slee and Allan, 2001:176), the term 'inclusion' and its underpinning lexicon have become subsumed by those within 'special' education (Rix, 2011). It has shifted from being a transformative process to being an option within the overall system. For many, therefore, the freedom to participate and to be included has simply changed the lexicon which leads to their separation.

Conclusions
Are schools part of an underlying contradiction?

Our systems and ways of working can be seen to be part of the problem and this is a major challenge for educationalists. Do we need to recognise (as Illich did) that our schools and universities are in many ways a barrier to transformation and a key driver of inequality? There can be little doubt that the rationale of education is inextricably linked with vested interests. It is fundamentally associated with governance and economically correct notions of advancement:

Greater production is the key to prosperity and peace. And the key to greater production is a wider and more vigorous application of modern scientific and technical knowledge. (President Harry Truman, 1949 cited in Hart, p383)

Education is a key player in delivering 'new knowledge', in establishing a techno-rationalist worldview, in which measurable, standardised practices dominate (Lankshear, 1997). However, one of the paradoxes associated with such a New Work Order (Gee, Hull and Lankshear, 1996), is that newly 'critical thinking' workers cannot really question the goals, visions, and values of the education system in which they operate. Teachers in England for example are supposed to help children become self-managers, creative thinkers, independent enquirers, reflective learners, team workers, and effective participators and yet the capacity to achieve these things – for themselves as teachers – is not evident in their training (Rix and Paige-Smith, 2011) nor their ways of working. Can the system allow practitioners genuine freedom in how they support learning and identify the foci of that learning? Is this possible when the system is driven by competitive market forces, and is focused upon economic prosperity and social control (Brown, 1990)?

This inability of established social systems to critically evaluate themselves puts a fundamental break on the transformation of our society. Illich (1970) considered how myths associated with growth restrict the transformative capability of schooling. These myths lead to a belief that development and investment inevitably lead to something of value, producing superior resources and outcomes. He cited the growth of curricula, materials and qualifications (Illich, 1970). Others have identified growth in different areas, for example the growth of special education budgets and categories of disability (Slee, 2008). Yet in perpetuating these myths our schooling system fails to recognise that 'growth conceived as open-ended consumption-eternal progress can never lead to maturity' (Illich, p40).

Ironically, too, we risk our notions of our globalised world becoming increasingly insular:

Once people have the idea schooled into them that values can be produced and measured, they tend to accept all kinds of rankings. There is a scale for the development of nations, another for the intelligence of babies, and even progress toward peace can be calculated according to body count. In a schooled world the road to happiness is paved with a consumer's index. (Illich, 1970:29)

As the universal principles of equality are increasingly applied to ever more specific categories of diversity, national policies acknowledge an ever wider range of differences between young people (Boyask *et al*, 2009). This increasing categorisation is part of the process of which Young (1990) warned, leading to an increasingly subtle impression that there is something natural about our divided society.

The final result

The dominant political and economic model of neo-liberalism depends on representing the world in what appears to be new ways, using new discourses and creating new identities, so as to legitimise the market economy, disciplinarian policies and a culture framed around a positive notion of enterprise and choice (Jessop, 2002). In so doing the neo-liberal agenda has taken control of all the key conceptual tools developed by the previous generations of activists who were eager to transform the social structures which drive inequality, marginalisation and poverty. These neo-liberal policies – including those around Education – have further entrenched the disenfranchisement of the majority of the world whilst claiming to empower us as individuals, free to benefit on an equal basis with everyone else.

The subsuming of these conceptual tools and the language associated with them should not hide from us the nature of the arguments being made, however. These arguments have an extended history, evident from the first justification of rural clearance over 400 years ago. The aim is to separate the yearning for wealth, comfort and power from the plight and desperate actions of the disenfranchised; and to do so despite the two lines of argument being contradictory. The intention is to persuade the populace that it is both natural for the disenfranchised to be in the condition they are in and that it is something for which the disenfranchised or their communities have ultimate responsibility. These are the arguments which envelope us from our earliest days, wrapping us within the hidden curriculum of our upbringing and everyday lives, shielding us from recognising our complicity and ensuring we resist only slightly the dominance of the minority. The critical issues for the 21st century, therefore are not much different to the critical issues for the last few centuries; they are around how we can genuinely transform an inequitable society against the odds.

Source: *newly commissioned for this volume.*

Notes

1   The neo-liberal agenda has been dominant within global politics since the 1980s. It is underpinned by the notion of the individual purportedly free to manage their own personal and economic growth within a growth economy, involving the manipulation of interest rates and the development of 'free-trade' and flexible labour supply (Peck and Tickell, 2002).

2   Within the Universal Declaration of Human Rights (UN, 1948) ten equalities are identified: equal in dignity and rights; equal before the law; equal protection of the law; equal protection against any discrimination; equal entitlement to a fair and public hearing; equal rights as to marriage; equal access to public service; equal suffrage; equal pay for equal work.; equal access based on merit to technical and professional education.

3   For example: 'If every poor man....would try to trace the evils which have befallen him to their proper source ... he would perhaps find that more of the hardships he now suffers are owing to his own fault than he would imagine. ... Either want of industry when he was young, or want of economy when he was a little older, and might easily have laid up money; want of temperance, chastity, sobriety, want of character for strict truth and exact integrity; want of prudence in some of the important steps of his life and above all want of religion, which is the root indeed of all the other sins I have named'. (Hannah More, *Hints to All Ranks of People*, p29 cited in Hart, 2011:158).

4   Impoverished Irish labour was used for the harvest in England and Scotland. The result was a halving of wages and a lowering in quality of diet for local labour, and increased profits for Anglo-Irish landlords, resulting in widespread rioting in the 1830s.

5   For example *The Intellectual and Policy Foundations of the 21st Century Skills Framework* (2007) published by Partnership for 21st Century Skills. Six of the eight founders of the Partnership work for DELL, Apple, Cisco systems, Aol Time Warner, Cable in the Classroom and Microsoft, as does one of the key partners, the Appalachian Technology in Education consortium; whilst the other key partner is the US Department of Education. In the list of authors for the 21st Century Skills Framework nearly all are from the Media and ICT business community. (Rix, 2010)

6   For example, funding is presented as creating individual choice and community engagement, but is made dependent upon the 'opening up' of markets in 'everything' (Sukarieh and Tannock, 2008) which includes all key resources such as public health, energy, water etc.

References

Arnesen, A., Mietola, R. and Lahelma, E. (2007) 'Language of inclusion and diversity: policy discourses and social practices in Finnish and Norwegian schools', *International Journal of Inclusive Education,* vol.11, no.1, p97-110

Baltodano, M. (2006) 'The accreditation of Schools of Education and the appropriation of diversity', *Cultural Studies <=> Critical Methodologies*, vol.6, no.1, p123-42

Barron, I., Holmes, R., MacLure, M., and Runswick-Cole, K. (2007) *Primary schools and other agencies* (Primary Review Research Survey 8/2), Cambridge, University of Cambridge

Benn Michaels, W. (2009) Neoliberalism: diversity and Inequality, Le Monde Diplomatique, Released: 25 Mar 2009 accessed from http://www.agenceglobal.com/article.asp?id=1950 5th August 2011

Black-Hawkins, K., Florian, L. and Rouse, M. (2007) *Achievement and inclusion in schools*, London: Routledge.

Booth, T., Ainscow, M. and Dyson, A. (1997) 'Understanding inclusion and exclusion in the English competitive education system', *International Journal of Inclusive Education,* vol.1, no.4, p337-55

Boyask, R., Carter, R., Waite, S. and Lawson, H. (2009) 'Changing concepts of diversity: relationships between policy and identity in English schools', in K. Quinlivan, R. Boyask and B. Kaur (eds) *Educational Enactments in a Globalised World: Intercultural Conversations*, Rotterdam: Sense, p115-28

Brown, P. (1990) 'The third wave: education and the ideology of parentocracy'. *British Journal of Sociology of Education,* vol.11, no.1, p65-85

Bruner, J. (1996) *The Culture of Education, the Complexity of Education Aims*, Massachusetts: Harvard University Press

Bunar, N. (2010) 'Choosing for quality or inequality: current perspectives on the implementation of school choice policy in Sweden', *Journal of Education Policy,* vol.25, no.1, p1-18

Butler, J. (2004) *Undoing Gender,* New York and London: Routledge

Dagnino, E. (2010) 'Citizenship: a perverse confluence', in Cornwall, A. and Eade, D. (eds) *Deconstructing Development Discourse* (p101-110) Rugby: Practical Action Publishing in association with Oxfam

Dyson, A., Gallannaugh, F. and Millward, A. (2003) 'Making spaces in the standards agenda: developing inclusive practices in schools', *European Educational Research Journal*, vol.2, no.2, p228-44

Franklin, A. and Sloper, P. (2006) 'Participation of disabled children and young people in decision making within social services departments: a survey of current and recent activities in England', *British Journal of Social Work*, vol.36, no.5, p723-41

Gee, J., Hull, G. and Lankshear, C. (1996) *The New Work Order, Behind the Language of the New Capitalism*, London: Allen and Unwin

Guttal, S. (2010) 'Globalisation', in Cornwall, A. and Eade, D. (eds) *Deconstructing Development Discourse*, Rugby: Practical Action Publishing in association with Oxfam

Hale, C. (2005) 'Neoliberal multiculturalism: the remaking of cultural rights and racial dominance in Central America', *PoLAR*, vol.28, no.1, p10-28

Hart, C. (2011) *Poverty and History: The Age of the Sentimental Mercenary,* Milton Keynes: AuthorHouse

Howe, K. and Welner, K. (2002) 'School choice and the pressure to perform – Déjà vu for children with disabilities?', *Remedial and Special Education*, vol.23, no.24, p212-21

Illich, I. (1970) *Deschooling Society*, accessed from http://www.davidtinapple.com/illich/1970_deschooling.html (on 5th August 2011)

Jessop, B. (2002) 'Liberalism, Neoliberalism and urban governance: a state-theoretical perspective', *Antipode,* vol.34, no.3, p452-72

Lankshear, C. (1997) 'Language and the new capitalism', *International Journal of Inclusive Education*, vol.1, no.4, p309-21

Leal, P. (2010) 'Participation: the ascendancy of a buzzword in the neo-liberal era', in Cornwall, A. and Eade, D. (eds) *Deconstructing Development Discourse*, Rugby: Practical Action Publishing in association with Oxfam

Nieto, S. (2004) *Affirming Diversity: The sociopolitical context of multicultural education* (4th ed.). Boston: Pearson

Oldfield, C. and Fowler, C. (2004) *Mapping Children and Young People's Participation in England,* London: DFES

Owen, S. (2011) *Unit 5, Perspectives on equality and diversity, E214, Equality, Participation and Inclusion: Learning from Each Other*, Milton Keynes: The Open University

Peck, J. and Tickell, A. (2002) 'Neoliberalizing space', *Antipode*, vol.34, no.3, p380-404

Pojman, L. (1995), 'Theories of equality: a critical analysis', *Behavior and Philosophy,* vol.23, no.2, at www.lrainc.com/swtaboo/taboos/lp_equal.html, accessed 21 December 2009

Rist, G. (2010) 'Development as a buzzword', in Cornwall, A. and Eade, D. (eds) *Deconstructing Development Discourse*, Rugby: Practical Action Publishing in association with Oxfam

Rix, J. (2006) 'From one professional to another', in Rix, B. (ed.) *All About Us,* London: MENCAP, p351-61

Rix, J. (2010) '21st Century Skills ... All dressed up in the technology of the Knowledge Age', in Sheehy, K., Ferguson, R. and Clough, G. (eds) *Controversies at the Frontier of Education* (Education in a Competitive and Globalizing World), New York: Nova Science

Rix, J. (2011) 'Repositioning of special schools within a specialist, personalised educational marketplace – the need for a representative principle', *International Journal of Inclusive Education*, vol.15, no.2, p263-79

Rix, J. and Paige-Smith, A. (2011) 'Exploring barriers to reflection and learning – developing a perspective lens', *Journal of Research in Special Educational Needs*, vol.11, no.1, p30-41

Sen, A. (1998) 'Universal truths: Human Rights and the Westernizing Illusion', *Harvard International Review,* vol.20, no.3, p 40-3

Slee, R. (2006) 'Limits to and possibilities for educational reform', *International Journal of Inclusive Education*, 10, 2-3, p109-19.

Slee, R. (2008) 'Beyond special and regular schooling? An inclusive education reform agenda', *International Studies in Sociology of Education*, 18: 2, p99-116

Slee, R. and Allan, J. (2001) 'Excluding the Included: a reconsideration of inclusive education', *International Studies in Sociology of Education*, vol.11, no.2, p173-91

Söderström, M. and Uusitalo, R. (2010) 'School choice and segregation: evidence from an admission reform', *Scandinavian Journal of Economics*, vol.112, no.1, p55-76

Sukarieh, M. and Tannock, S. (2008) 'In the best interests of youth or neoliberalism? The World Bank and the New Global Youth Empowerment Project', *Journal of Youth Studies*, vol.11, no.3, p301-12

Taylor, T. (2008) 'Young people, politics and participation: a youth work perspective', in *Youth and Policy,* vol.100, Summer/Autumn, p253-64

United Nations (1948) *Universal Declaration of Human Rights* accessed from http://www.ohchr.org/EN/UDHR/Documents/UDHR_Translations/eng.pdf on 10th August 2011

United Nations (2000) *United Nations Millennium Declaration: Resolution* adopted by the General Assembly, accessed from www.un.org/ millennium/declaration/ares552e.pdf. on 11 August 2011

White, Sarah C. (1996) 'Depoliticising development: the uses and abuses of participation', *Development in Practice*, vol.6, no.1, p6-15

Young, I.M. (1990) *Justice and the Politics of Difference*, Princeton, NJ: Princeton University Press

Index

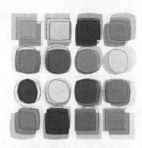